Christmas Plays and Programs

A collection of royalty-free plays, playlets, choral readings, poems, songs, and games for young people

By

AILEEN FISHER

Publishers   **PLAYS, INC.**   *Boston*

Library of Congress Catalog Card Number: 60-6053
ISBN: 0-8238-0017-2

Acknowledgments

Grateful acknowledgment is made to the following publications in which some of the material in this book first appeared: *Children's Activities* for "Before Christmas," "Christmas Bells," "In December," "On Christmas Eve," and "Sing a Song of Shopping"; *Child Life* for "Benjamin's Christmas Candy," "How to Get What You Want for Christmas," and "Tree Lights"; *The Instructor* for "The Heart Is an Inn," and "Signs of Christmas"; *My Weekly Reader* for "At Christmas," "Christmas," "Christmas Spelldown," "Christmas Lights," "Christmas-Tree Angel," "Riddle for December," and "Where Is Christmas"; *Plays, The Drama Magazine for Young People,* for "Nine Cheers for Christmas," "On Such a Night," "Setting Santa Straight," "Sing the Songs of Christmas," and "The Week Before Christmas"; *Story Parade* for "Holly Fairies," "The Christmas Pig," and "Legends of Christmas."

Plays

A TREE TO TRIM	3
THE INN AT BETHLEHEM	25
MR. SCROOGE FINDS CHRISTMAS	42
WHAT HAPPENED IN TOYLAND	61
CHRISTMAS IN COURT	77
CALLING ALL CHRISTMASES	88
ON SUCH A NIGHT	101
NINE CHEERS FOR CHRISTMAS	108
SING THE SONGS OF CHRISTMAS	116
SETTING SANTA STRAIGHT	135
MOTHER GOOSE'S PARTY	147
THE CHRISTMAS TABLECLOTH	156

Playlets and Spelldowns

STANDING UP FOR SANTA	165
WHAT'S FOR CHRISTMAS	171
CHRISTMAS IN QUARANTINE	175
SHOES AND STOCKINGS AND SOLOMON	180
SAY IT WITH RHYMES	184
THE WEEK BEFORE CHRISTMAS	186
STABLE AT MIDNIGHT	188
A GIFT FOR OLD ST. NICK	192
SOMETHING IN THE AIR	194
UP A CHRISTMAS TREE	196
CHRISTMAS SPELLDOWN	200
TRIMMING THE TREE	201

Group and Choral Readings

SONGS OF CHRISTMAS	205
AND ON EARTH PEACE	207
THE CHRISTMAS PIG	209

CONTENTS

THE NATIVITY   216
SIGNS OF CHRISTMAS   221
THE FALCONER'S CHRISTMAS   222
LITTLE LOST JESUS   228
NOW IS THE TIME   230
LONG AGO ON CHRISTMAS MORNING   231
GETTING READY FOR CHRISTMAS   232
STAR OF HOPE   233
WHERE IS CHRISTMAS?   237
THE WELL OF THE MAGI   238
CHRISTMAS ALL AROUND   240

Recitations

SANTA'S CHRISTMAS TREE   243
THE CHRISTMAS PROMISE   247
THE FINCH IN THE STABLE   252
INVESTMENT IN CHRISTMAS   258
NOT TAKING ANY CHANCES   263
SPEAKING OF PRESENTS   264

Poems

MERRY CHRISTMAS, EVERYONE   269
CHRISTMAS TREE   270
WHEN A STAR SHONE DOWN   271
RED AND GREEN   272
AROUND THE CORNER   273
WHAT CHRISTMAS IS   274
THE HEART IS AN INN   275
CHRISTMAS   276
LEGENDS OF CHRISTMAS   277
TREE LIGHTS   278
A JOLLY TIME   279
CHRISTMAS DREAMS   280

BEFORE CHRISTMAS 281
HOW TO GET WHAT YOU WANT FOR CHRISTMAS 282
CHRISTMAS-TREE ANGEL 283
CANDLE IN THE WINDOW 284
HOLLY FAIRIES 285
IN DECEMBER 286
CHRISTMAS SONG 287
CHRISTMAS LIGHTS 288
ON THE ROAD TO BETHLEHEM 289
OF COURSE THERE IS A SANTA CLAUS 290
AT CHRISTMAS 291
BENJAMIN'S CHRISTMAS CANDY 292
A CHRISTMAS TREE 293
CHRISTMAS GOOSE 294
WAITING FOR CHRISTMAS 295
THE SHORTEST DAYS 296
THE SMALLEST STAR 297
RIDDLE FOR DECEMBER 299

Songs

CHRISTMAS TIME 303
THERE IN THE STABLE 304
CHRISTMAS SPIRIT 305
WHEN CHRISTMAS IS ALMOST HERE 306
CHRISTMAS COLORS 307
CHRISTMAS BELLS 308
ON CHRISTMAS EVE 309
SING A SONG OF SHOPPING 310
CAROLING 311
SIGNS OF CHRISTMAS 312
SO SLOW 313
I HAD A LITTLE FIR TREE 314
CHRISTMAS BAKING 315
THE ANIMALS' CHRISTMAS 316
WATCHING THE CLOCK 317

CHRISTMAS PRESENTS   318
WAITING FOR CHRISTMAS   319
LIGHTS OF CHRISTMAS   320
THE CHRISTMAS STAR   321

Games

JINGLE BELLS   325
CHRISTMAS STAR AND CHRISTMAS TREE   326
CHRISTMAS DINNER   327
WHAT I WANT FOR CHRISTMAS   328
WHAT'S ON THE TREE?   329
READY FOR CHRISTMAS   330
SPELLDOWN GAME   331
SANTA'S INITIALS   332
FILLING SANTA'S PACK   333
THE HIDDEN ORNAMENT   334
SANTA'S FISH POND   335
THE LOST SHEEP   336
SING A SONG OF CHRISTMAS   337
THE RED AND THE GREEN   338
UNSCRAMBLING CHRISTMAS   339
SANTA'S REINDEER   340

PRODUCTION NOTES   341

PLAYS

A Tree to Trim

Characters

MR. ARCHIBALD, *an author*
MISS ROSE, *his secretary*
SAM, *his handyman*
LARRY ⎱
LINDA ⎬ *the children next door*
LOU ⎰

SETTING: *Mr. Archibald's study.*
AT RISE: MR. ARCHIBALD *is pacing up and down, dictating to his secretary,* MISS ROSE, *who is seated at the desk, holding a shorthand pad.*

MR. ARCHIBALD (*Stopping his pacing for a moment*): "It is important for all students of twelfth-century history to remember that in Lancashire . . ." do you have that. Miss Rose?

MISS ROSE: Yes, Mr. Archibald.

MR. ARCHIBALD: Very good. Now, where was I?

MISS ROSE: "It is important for all students of twelfth-century history to remember that in Lancashire . . ."

MR. ARCHIBALD: Oh, yes. In Lancashire. . . . or was it in Cheshire?

MISS ROSE: I'm sure I don't know, Mr. Archibald.

MR. ARCHIBALD (*Puzzled*): Was it in Lancashire or was it

in Cheshire? Dear me, how could I ever forget such an important point?

MISS ROSE: Perhaps you could look it up in one of your books.

MR. ARCHIBALD: Of course I can, Miss Rose. Just what I was about to suggest myself. I'll look it up. (*Calls off right.*) Sam! Sam! Oh, where *is* that lazy handyman of mine? Sam!

(SAM, *a slow and silent but good-natured fellow, appears in the doorway, at right.*)

MR. ARCHIBALD: Ah, there you are, Sam. I want you to take these files back to my library, and bring me a copy of the *Encyclopedia of Mediaeval England*. (SAM *picks up some cardboard file boxes, precariously balanced one on top of another, and gingerly begins to carry them to the doorway. Halfway, he stumbles and drops the files, spilling the contents all over the floor.*)

MISS ROSE (*Alarmed*): Oh, Sam, did you hurt yourself? (SAM *looks sheepish.*)

MR. ARCHIBALD (*Growling*): Never mind whether he hurt *himself*, Miss Rose! What's important is whether he hurt *my notes!* Look at them: my precious files all over the floor! I see I can't trust *you*, Sam, to bring me the book I need. I'll have to get it myself! While I'm gone, I want you to pick up all the cards you dropped—and see that you put them back in the right files. (MR. ARCHIBALD *goes out.*)

SAM: What a grouch!

MISS ROSE (*Going over to* SAM, *who is still on the floor*): Never mind Mr. Archibald, Sam. He didn't mean to be cross with you. Here, let me help you. (*Together they begin to pick up the notes.*)

SAM: You're a real friend, Miss Rose, but I don't know how you put up with him.

MISS ROSE: I know Mr. Archibald *sounds* grumpy, but

that's because he has his mind on the book he's writing. He is a very serious historian, you know, and that's why he gets annoyed sometimes. You mustn't mind him, though.

SAM (*Smiling at* MISS ROSE): I guess if you can stand him, I can.

MISS ROSE: There! All the notes are back where they belong. (*There is a knock at the door.*) I wonder who that can be. Sam, you take the files into the library—and be careful! I'll see who's at the door.

SAM: Thanks a lot for your help, Miss Rose. (SAM *picks up files and goes off right.* MISS ROSE *opens door at left, and admits* LARRY, LINDA *and* LOU, *three children dressed in winter clothes. They look around tentatively.*)

MISS ROSE: Why, good afternoon, children! What a pleasant surprise!

LARRY: Good afternoon, Miss Rose.

MISS ROSE: What can I do for you?

LINDA: We're sorry to trouble you like this, but it's awfully important! (*Looks around*) Is Mr. Archibald in?

MISS ROSE: Well—yes, he is. But I'm afraid that Mr. Archibald is very busy right now, and can't be disturbed.

LARRY (*Crestfallen*): Aw—

MISS ROSE: Perhaps it's something that I can help you with?

LINDA: Thank you, Miss Rose, but— I guess we really need Mr. Archibald.

LOU: Yes. You see, we need the help of a writer. A real author!

MISS ROSE: What is it? You all seem so mysterious!

LARRY (*Eagerly*): Well—we thought that since Christmas is coming soon, this would be a good time for us to try to do something for somebody who wouldn't have much of a Christmas.

LINDA: There are lots of children in the orphanage who won't have much fun.

LOU: So Larry, Linda and I decided to do something about it.

MISS ROSE: What a wonderful idea! But I don't see why you need Mr. Archibald's help.

LINDA: We thought that perhaps—if he wanted to, of course—Mr. Archibald could write a Christmas play for us to put on at the orphanage on Christmas Eve.

LARRY: We'd write the play ourselves, but Christmas is only a few days away, and it would take *us* months and months to write one.

LINDA: Since Mr. Archibald is an experienced, *professional* writer—why, it wouldn't take *him* much time at all!

LARRY (*Glumly*): But I guess if he's busy . . .

MISS ROSE: I'll tell you what I'll do: I'll tell Mr. Archibald what you want, and though I can't promise a thing, I'm quite sure that when he hears your good idea, he'll want to do everything he can to help.

LINDA: Oh, would you, Miss Rose? That would be wonderful!

LARRY: Just think: a Christmas play by the famous writer, Mr. Archibald!

MISS ROSE (*As the children move to the door.*): Of course, it isn't exactly in his line; but I'll tell him.

LOU (*Going out*): Thank you so much, Miss Rose.

MISS ROSE (*Talking to the children who are now outside the room*): It was nice of you to think of him. (*Pause*) I'll certainly tell him. (MR. ARCHIBALD *enters, carrying a book, from right.*)

MISS ROSE (*Without seeing him*): Yes, I'll let you know. Goodbye.

MR. ARCHIBALD: Please close the door, Miss Rose. You're letting in enough of a draft to freeze my brain!

MISS ROSE (*Closing the door, hurriedly*): I'm sorry, Mr. Archibald. Did you find the information you wanted?

MR. ARCHIBALD (*Grumpily*): Yes. It was Lancashire all the time. I *knew* it was Lancashire! But all your chatter out here didn't help me any! You know I insist on perfect silence while I work!

MISS ROSE: I'm sorry, sir.

MR. ARCHIBALD: Whom were you talking to anyway, Miss Rose, at this time of day?

MISS ROSE: It was the children next door, Mr. Archibald. You know, Larry, Linda and Lou.

MR. ARCHIBALD: Oh. (*He looks at pages, scratches his head, then looks up.*) The children next door? What did they want? I've told their mother time and time again that they're not to bother me.

MISS ROSE (*Hesitating*): Well, it's—it's a rather unusual thing, sir. They—they want you to write a play for them.

MR. ARCHIBALD (*Exploding*): A play! Why on earth do they think I would write a play for them? I happen to be a historian, *not* a playwright. Did you tell them that?

MISS ROSE: Yes, I did mention it.

MR. ARCHIBALD: Here I am, in the midst of a new book about the twelfth century, and they think I should write a play! I hope you told them I could not waste my time writing plays.

MISS ROSE: I told them you were very busy.

MR. ARCHIBALD: I am indeed. (*He returns to his notes for a moment, then looks up.*) And what, may I ask, was this play to be about?

MISS ROSE: It's a play for Christmas.

MR. ARCHIBALD: Christmas! Why should an historian write a play about Christmas? If you ask me, there's altogether too much fuss made about Christmas these days, anyhow.

MISS ROSE (*Timidly*): Well, you see, sir, the children want to put on a little play for the orphans over at the Children's Home on Christmas Eve. I—I think it's a very nice idea, sir. A thoughtful idea. Well, a *Christmasy* idea.

MR. ARCHIBALD (*Sharply*): Oh, you do?

MISS ROSE (*Bravely*): Yes, sir, I do!

MR. ARCHIBALD (*Suspiciously*): And what did you tell the children, Miss Rose?

MISS ROSE (*Timidly*): I said I thought you might possibly —perhaps—*maybe* write a play for them.

MR. ARCHIBALD (*Jumping up, and letting the manuscript pages fall*): Oh, you did, did you? You ought to know better than that! (*Looks at pages*) *Now* see what's happened to my manuscript! And all on account of Christmas! (*He and* MISS ROSE *scramble about picking up pages.*)

MISS ROSE: Oh, dear! If we get these pages mixed up, we'll *never* be able to sort them out again!

MR. ARCHIBALD: Why not? Aren't the pages numbered?

MISS ROSE: Yes, sir, but you keep changing the order! Let me think: did page 16 come after page 4, this time—or after page 24?

MR. ARCHIBALD: Authors are entitled to change their minds, Miss Rose.

MISS ROSE: Yes, I suppose everyone should be able to change his mind.

MR. ARCHIBALD (*Handing papers to* MISS ROSE): That's good enough for now. I'll look them over again in the morning.

MISS ROSE (*Taking the sheets to her desk*): Yes, sir. (*She sighs*) You've certainly done a lot of writing lately. (*Shakes her head, then looks at* MR. ARCHIBALD *admiringly*) You know, I think you could write a wonderful play for Christmas, after all that practice.

MR. ARCHIBALD (*Pleased in spite of himself*): You do?

MISS ROSE: My, yes! A man with your imagination . . .

MR. ARCHIBALD: Well, maybe I could. Maybe I could. But why should I? It's all stuff and nonsense. Why should I waste my time on a little Christmas play, an important, famous, *professional* writer like me?

MISS ROSE: Why, Mr. Archibald! Those are the very words the children used!

MR. ARCHIBALD (*Lighting up*): They did?

MISS ROSE: That was why they wanted *you* to write the play for them—because they knew you would do such a fine job. I think it was Larry who said they came to you because you were an experienced, professional writer. No, I'm wrong. That was Linda! It was Larry who called you famous.

MR. ARCHIBALD (*Pleased*): They said those things about me, did they? How perceptive. Of course, I always *said* they were intelligent children! Larry called me a famous writer, eh?

MISS ROSE: That's right, Mr. Archibald. And I agree with them. I think you're the perfect person to write the Christmas play.

MR. ARCHIBALD: Well, maybe I could at that. I've always wanted to write a play, you know. Maybe—(*Stops suddenly*) No, it's ridiculous. I don't have the time.

MISS ROSE: But it wouldn't take long. Why, I'll bet you could write a whole play in an hour. After all, you did all of this difficult writing—(*Holds up paper*)—in a week.

MR. ARCHIBALD: I suppose you're right. It wouldn't take me too long. (*Thinks, then shakes his head.*) But I don't have a Christmas thought in my head.

MISS ROSE (*Picking up her stenographer's pad*): Let's see. The play could be about the Star of Bethlehem—or Santa Claus—or—

MR. ARCHIBALD (*Warming up*): Or what about a historical Christmas play? That's it! I'll do a historical Christmas play! (*Stops, shakes his head*) No. I need a change
from history.

MISS ROSE: Well—what about a Christmas tree?

MR. ARCHIBALD: A Christmas tree, eh? Hmm. A Christmas
tree! Miss Rose, that's it! A Christmas tree! A nice little
fir tree, smelling like a balsam pillow. Or a nice little
blue spruce with silvered needles. Ah! (*He calls out
loudly*) Sam! I say, Sam! (SAM *enters from right.*) Sam,
because of your carelessness as a handyman, I've decided
to take that job away from you. (SAM *clasps his hands in
a pleading manner.*)

MISS ROSE: Oh, Mr. Archibald . . .

MR. ARCHIBALD: Don't worry. Come here, Sam. You're
going to be a stagehand instead. (SAM *does a spritely
little skip over to* MR. ARCHIBALD.) Now, look. I'm
going to write a play—a play for Christmas. This is the
stage. (*He makes a sweeping gesture around room.*)
Out there is the audience. (*Points at audience.*) All you
have to do is use your imagination. (SAM *thinks a moment, then bows grandly to audience.*) No, no, Sam.
You aren't going to be an actor. You're going to be a
stagehand. A stagehand! (SAM *looks blank.*)

MISS ROSE (*Patiently*): What Mr. Archibald means, Sam,
is that you will bring in the things we need for the play.

MR. ARCHIBALD: Right! For instance, if I say "Stagehand!
I shall need an elephant!" all you will have to do is
bring in an elephant. (SAM *looks panicky, his mouth
open.*) But I'm sure I shan't need an elephant! (SAM
gives deep sigh of relief.) Now let's see. Where were we,
Miss Rose?

MISS ROSE: We got as far as the Christmas tree.

MR. ARCHIBALD: Oh yes, the Christmas tree. (*He bows to
SAM.*) Stagehand, I shall need a Christmas tree. A nice,

green Christmas tree—not too big, not too small, but just right. (SAM *nods slowly.* MR. ARCHIBALD *turns him around, heads him to the door, gives him a gentle push.* SAM *marches out.*) Now, Miss Rose, when we get the Christmas tree, what shall we do with it?

MISS ROSE: Put it right in the middle of the stage.

MR. ARCHIBALD (*Impatiently*): Of *course* we'll put it right in the middle of the stage! But that isn't enough, you know. We can't just say to the audience, "Here is a Christmas tree. Isn't it a pretty one? THE END!" Now can we?

MISS ROSE: Oh, no! The Christmas tree will have to *mean* something.

MR. ARCHIBALD: That's it, Miss Rose. What we need is a plan. A plot!

MISS ROSE (*Thinking hard*): A plan—a plot—I know! Let's have the tree be a *magic* Christmas tree, Mr. Archibald.

MR. ARCHIBALD (*Annoyed*): Now, see here, Miss Rose. I cannot write a play about magic. If the children want magic, they'll have to ask someone else. According to my history books, the existence of magic has been disproved in the 2nd, 4th, 6th, 8th, 14th, 16th, 18th and 20th centuries inclusive!

MISS ROSE (*Wistfully*): But there *is* a kind of magic about Christmas. (*Brightly*) And the way you find out things about the 12th century—that seems like magic to me.

MR. ARCHIBALD (*Happily*): It does? Very well then: Let the children have a magic Christmas tree.

MISS ROSE: What about a magic Christmas tree that will be very hard to trim?

MR. ARCHIBALD: Of *course* it will be very hard to trim.

MISS ROSE: And the whole idea of the play will be to get the tree trimmed somehow!

MR. ARCHIBALD (*Excitedly*): A tree to trim! A tree to

trim! Put that down, Miss Rose. The perfect title! "A Tree to Trim," by Archibald Archibald. (MISS ROSE *writes.*) Ah. . . . (*He rubs his hands as* SAM *enters with a Christmas tree on a standard.*) Set the tree right in the middle of the floor, stagehand. (SAM *goes to a great deal of trouble getting the tree in the middle. He paces the floor, measures with a yardstick, finally gets it right. Admiring the tree, he goes out right.*)

MISS ROSE: That's just perfect!

MR. ARCHIBALD: In just what respect would you say this was a magic tree, Miss Rose? (*Walking around it, examining it closely.*) It looks very much like an ordinary Christmas tree to me.

MISS ROSE: The magic doesn't show, sir. You see, it has a spirit hidden inside.

MR. ARCHIBALD: A spirit?

MISS ROSE: Why, yes. You know—the spirit of Christmas.

MR. ARCHIBALD: Of course! Just what I was going to say. You took the words right out of my mouth. The spirit of Christmas! Did you get that down, Miss Rose? (MISS ROSE *begins to write quickly, then begins to talk as she writes.*)

MISS ROSE (*Reading from her notebook*): ". . . and since this tree contains the spirit of Christmas, it is a very difficult tree to trim."

MR. ARCHIBALD: Just a minute, there! In writing a play, the author must be logical; he must be reasonable! Just because this is a magic tree with the spirit of Christmas, why would *that* make it hard to trim?

MISS ROSE (*Looking at* MR. ARCHIBALD *in surprise*): Don't you know? (*She laughs.*) You're only trying to fool me by making believe you don't know!

MR. ARCHIBALD (*A little embarrassed, but trying to put up a bold front*): Er—well, write it down, Miss Rose. Write it down.

MISS ROSE (*Talking as she writes*): "The magic tree is hard to trim because it can be decorated only with wishes."

MR. ARCHIBALD: With wishes!

MISS ROSE (*Continuing*): "It can be decorated only with wishes that contain the spirit of Christmas."

MR. ARCHIBALD (*Slowly*): I don't think I make myself quite clear, Miss Rose.

MISS ROSE (*Still writing*): "Wishes that have the spirit of Christmas in them will turn into big golden stars on the tree."

MR. ARCHIBALD: Ah! Precisely! And wishes without the spirit of Christmas, Miss Rose?

MISS ROSE (*Looking up and flicking her hand*): Whiff! They won't be anything at all.

MR. ARCHIBALD: "Whiff!" A very suggestive word. Did you get all that down, Miss Rose?

MISS ROSE (*Writing*): Yes. I think you are doing very well, sir.

MR. ARCHIBALD: Don't mention it. Writing is my business, you know. Of course, play writing isn't quite my line, but since you promised the children. . . . (*Thinking*) Well, now, let's see. . . . We must get someone to trim the tree, mustn't we?

MISS ROSE: Yes.

MR. ARCHIBALD (*Thinking hard*): Hmm. Someone to trim the tree . . .

MISS ROSE: And you must give them a reward if they succeed.

MR. ARCHIBALD: To be sure. A reward. (*Rubs his hands.*) Why, I do believe it's more fun to write a play than to write about the history of the twelfth century!

MISS ROSE: Oh, isn't it! (*Suddenly*) You know, I think I have an idea.

MR. ARCHIBALD: Not really!

MISS ROSE: Why don't you get the children next door to trim the tree?

MR. ARCHIBALD (*Excited at the idea*): The obvious solution! The perfect solution. (*Calls out loudly.*) Stagehand! Stagehand! (SAM *comes in.*) We shall need the children next door—all three of them. Bring them in, stagehand. (SAM *nods and exits.*)

MISS ROSE: They'll be so pleased, sir.

MR. ARCHIBALD (*Turning his pockets inside out*): I suppose I shall have to hunt up a reward. They will probably get the tree trimmed in no time. Let's see (*Examines contents of pockets*) . . . some paper clips, keys, rubber bands, matches . . .

MISS ROSE (*Laughing*): You're trying to fool me again, sir. Looking in your pockets for a reward!

MR. ARCHIBALD (*Trying to laugh*): Of course, you mean . . .

MISS ROSE: That the reward isn't finished yet.

MR. ARCHIBALD (*Stops laughing, and repeats slowly*): Not finished yet . . .

MISS ROSE: Don't you like to tease, though! Of course, the best reward you could give the children is the play . . . and it isn't finished yet. (*Turns to notebook*) Look, we're not very far along.

MR. ARCHIBALD (*Sighing*): I do have a hard time keeping up with myself.

MISS ROSE: Of course, I don't know how you plan to end your play, sir; but I think that as soon as all the children think of a Christmas wish that turns into a big gold star, you should reward them by giving them the play.

MR. ARCHIBALD: Remarkable, Miss Rose . . . remarkable how you can read my thoughts!

MISS ROSE: Thank you, sir. (SAM *comes in with* LINDA,

LARRY, *and* LOU. *The children look around wonderingly.* MR. ARCHIBALD *paces up and down in deep thought.*)

LINDA (*In a loud whisper as she passes* MISS ROSE's *desk.*): Is he going to write us one?

MISS ROSE (*Nodding, indicating the notebook*): It's half done already.

LINDA: That's great!

LARRY (*Clearing his throat loudly*): Did you want us, Mr. Archibald?

MR. ARCHIBALD (*Stopping short*): Oh, hello there! Come in. Come in. (*As the children move up toward the tree,* SAM *goes out.*) Now, my dear children, I have hatched a little plot for you. Haven't I, Miss Rose?

MISS ROSE: Yes, indeed, sir. You certainly have.

MR. ARCHIBALD: Do you see this Christmas tree?

CHILDREN (*Looking at it carefully*): Yes.

MR. ARCHIBALD: I was wondering if I could get you to trim it for me.

CHILDREN (*Variously*): Sure! You bet! When do we start?

LARRY: We're good at trimming Christmas trees, Mr. Archibald. Where are the ornaments?

LINDA: Do you have some red balls, and blue ones, and yellow ones?

LOU: And a bright gold star for the top?

MR. ARCHIBALD: Ah, that's just it.

LARRY: What's just it, sir?

MISS ROSE: Mr. Archibald means he doesn't have any ornaments. You see, for many years he has been so full of the twelfth century, he hasn't had time to think of Christmas trees.

LARRY: But . . . what shall we trim it with, then?

LINDA: We could string cranberries.

LOU: And make popcorn balls.

Mr. Archibald: No, no. That would never do. You see (*He speaks very impressively and mysteriously.*) this is a special kind of Christmas tree.

Linda: Oh! Is it really? (*They peer at the tree.*)

Larry: It doesn't look different, does it?

Miss Rose: It is a magic tree!

Children (*Amazed*): Magic? Honest-to-goodness magic?

Mr. Archibald: This magic tree can be trimmed only with . . . ah . . . ah . . . How would you put it, Miss Rose?

Miss Rose: Only with certain kinds of Christmas wishes.

Larry: With wishes! Christmas wishes! We never heard of doing that.

Mr. Archibald (*Very much pleased with himself*): Just so, my dear children. You are taking part in something very unusual. You shall each take turns at wishing.

Miss Rose: The right kind of wishes will turn into big gold stars.

Children (*Looking at each other in surprise*): Into stars!

Mr. Archibald: And as soon as all of you make wishes that turn into stars, I shall give you a reward. I shall give you the play you wanted! (*He puffs out his chest.*)

Linda (*Eagerly*): Oh, how wonderful! Our play!

Mr. Archibald (*To* Miss Rose): Are you getting this all down, Miss Rose?

Miss Rose: I haven't missed a word, sir.

Mr. Archibald: All right, then, let's begin. Linda, what is your biggest wish for Christmas?

Linda (*Quickly, very eager*): Oh, I wish for lots and lots of presents.

Mr. Archibald (*Calling*): Stagehand! (Sam *appears.*) Will you please bring us a wish for lots and lots of presents? (Sam *scratches his head, moves his tongue up and down inside his cheek, and goes over to* Miss Rose, *who whispers something to him.*)

LINDA: Do you mean he can *bring* a wish?

LARRY: I didn't know a wish was anything you could carry.

LOU: Can he hang a wish on the magic tree?

MR. ARCHIBALD (*Looking rather baffled, raises his eyebrows at* MISS ROSE, *who confidently nods her head*): Well . . . ah . . . er . . . it will probably work out all right. Sam is a very good stagehand! (SAM *comes in with a soap-bubble pipe. He walks up to the tree, and blows some beautiful big soap bubbles on it, but of course they all burst and vanish. When the pipe will blow no more bubbles,* SAM *shrugs and goes out.*)

MISS ROSE (*Softly*): Whiff! Your wish was just a whiff, Linda.

LINDA: What did you say?

MISS ROSE: Don't mind me. (*She begins to write.*) I was just trying to write it all down.

MR. ARCHIBALD: H'mm. Linda, you didn't make the kind of wish that turns into a golden star on a magic Christmas tree. Now, why do you think that was? (*Scratches his head.*) Well, Larry, you try next. What's your biggest wish for Christmas?

LARRY (*Quickly, as if he had it all figured out.*): I don't wish for lots and lots of presents like Linda. All I want is a bicycle!

MR. ARCHIBALD: Stagehand! (SAM *appears.*) Will you please bring in a wish for a bicycle? (SAM *looks at* LARRY, *opens his mouth as if to say something, then saunters out.*)

LINDA: I wonder if your wish will work, Larry.

LARRY: Will it, Mr. Archibald?

MR. ARCHIBALD: Well, I . . . I'd rather not say. It would spoil the plot, you know. Nobody should ever know what's going to happen before it happens. Isn't that right, Miss Rose?

MISS ROSE (*Writing*): By all means. (SAM *comes in with a big cardboard box. He sets it down near the Christmas tree and takes off the cover. The children lean over to look, then turn to each other in surprise.* MR. ARCHIBALD *tiptoes over to look, too.* MISS ROSE *stays at her desk and nods, as if she knew what was in the box without looking. Carefully* SAM *makes believe he is taking things out and hanging them on the tree. But there is nothing in the box. When* SAM *finishes, he turns the carton upside down, shakes it, and carries it out.*) Another whiff!

LARRY (*Walking around the tree and looking*): My wish doesn't show for anything, does it?

LINDA: Just like mine.

LARRY: Are you sure, Mr. Archibald, that some wishes will really turn into stars?

MR. ARCHIBALD: Certainly, certainly. They have to. It's the plot, you see. Miss Rose has it all down on paper; haven't you, Miss Rose?

MISS ROSE: Oh, yes, indeed.

MR. ARCHIBALD: It's Lou's turn now. Come, Lou, what is *your* biggest wish for Christmas?

LOU (*Slowly, as if she is thinking it out while she speaks*): Linda wished for lots and lots of presents for herself. Larry wished for a bicycle. And I wish . . . well, I wish everybody would get presents.

MR. ARCHIBALD: Ah! Stagehand! (SAM *appears.*) Stagehand, will you kindly bring us a wish for everyone to get presents? (SAM, *baffled as usual, goes out.*)

LINDA: I bet it won't work.

LARRY: I think it has to be a wish for something besides presents in order to turn into a star. Doesn't it, Mr. Archibald?

MR. ARCHIBALD: That would be telling! (*He walks over to see what* MISS ROSE *has been writing.* SAM *comes in with a stool and a bright red Christmas stocking. He stands on the stool with his back to the audience and hangs the stocking near the top of the tree. As he climbs down, the red stocking—which has a string attached to it that* SAM *can pull—comes off; and there, at the top of the tree, is a bright gold star. It had been hidden behind the stocking.*)

CHILDREN (*Greatly excited*): Oh, a star! A golden star!

MR. ARCHIBALD (*To* MISS ROSE): By jove, it *is* a magic tree, isn't it?

MISS ROSE (*Coming around to see the star*): What a beautiful star!

LINDA (*Thoughtfully*): I wished for something for myself. Larry wished for something for himself. But Lou wished for something for other people. That's the magic, isn't it, Mr. Archibald?

MR. ARCHIBALD: Well, now . . . do you think we should answer that question, Miss Rose?

MISS ROSE: My, no. You mustn't give away your plot.

LINDA: Could I have another wish?

MR. ARCHIBALD: By all means, by all means. We must get this tree trimmed right away. What shall it be, Linda?

LINDA (*Laughing*): You know . . . now that I have another turn, I don't know what to wish!

MR. ARCHIBALD: Dear me.

MISS ROSE (*Helpfully*): Did you ever read the story of Tiny Tim, Linda?

LINDA: Oh, yes. That's in *A Christmas Carol*.

MR. ARCHIBALD (*Under his breath*): I didn't happen to write it, but it's a good story anyway.

MISS ROSE: And Mr. Scrooge? Did you like him?

LINDA: Goodness, no! Not until he stopped being mean and selfish. (*She suddenly jumps up and down excitedly.*) I know! I know what I'm going to wish. I'm going to wish that all the mean and selfish people in the world would turn out to be nice like Mr. Scrooge on Christmas Day.

MR. ARCHIBALD (*Approvingly*): I couldn't have done better myself. (*Calls out loudly*) Stagehand! We need another wish here! (SAM *enters.*) We need a wish for—how shall I put it?

MISS ROSE: A wish that all the mean "Mr. Scrooges" will turn out to be kind. (SAM's *jaw drops as he looks from one to another. He rubs his chin, pulls his ear, and goes out.*)

MISS ROSE (*Writing*): ". . . will turn out to be nice like Mr. Scrooge on Christmas Day."

LARRY: I wonder if it will work.

LOU: The magic tree will know.

MR. ARCHIBALD (*To* MISS ROSE): I'm doing pretty well, don't you think?

MISS ROSE: Yes. Yes. (SAM *comes in carrying a big, red Christmas bell. He goes to the tree and begins to hang it. He decides to put it on the right side of the tree. But, as he turns to leave, the bell—which, like the stocking, had a string on it—falls off, and there, shining and bright, is a gold star. It had been hidden behind the bell.* SAM *looks as surprised as the others. He picks up the bell, and goes out backwards.*)

LINDA: Another star!

MR. ARCHIBALD: I never thought I could do it.

LARRY: Do what?

MR. ARCHIBALD: Why, write a Christmas play . . . after all my work on the twelfth century.

MISS ROSE: Only one more star, and the children will get their reward!

MR. ARCHIBALD: That's right. Larry, how would you like another turn?

LARRY (*Scratching his head.*): Well, I can't think of anything fancy like Linda. All I can think of is something common. But I think it's a good wish.

LOU: What is it, Larry?

MR. ARCHIBALD: Come on, Larry, don't keep us in suspense.

LARRY: Well, it's just that I want to wish everyone a Merry Christmas! That's all.

MR. ARCHIBALD: Not bad. (*Calls out.*) Stagehand! (SAM *sticks his head in.*) What about bringing us a good old-fashioned wish for a Merry Christmas for everybody? (SAM *pulls his ear, scratches his nose, blinks, and disappears.*)

LINDA: Where in the world did you get this magic Christmas tree anyway, Mr. Archibald?

MR. ARCHIBALD (*Importantly*): I didn't get it anywhere in the world, Linda. I got it out of my head—didn't we, Miss Rose?

MISS ROSE: Of course. You made it all up. It's a play, you see, Linda.

MR. ARCHIBALD: You can always have magic in a play. (SAM *comes in with a holly wreath. He goes to the tree, left side, and attempts to tie on the wreath; but as he turns away, the wreath drops, just the way the stocking and the bell did. And there is a star—the third bright star.*)

CHILDREN (*Variously*): Another star! Three stars! Three golden stars!

MISS ROSE: How beautiful they are!

MR. ARCHIBALD (*Very pleased with himself*): Well, what do you think of that!

LINDA: It's the most wonderful thing I've ever seen.

LOU: The children at the orphanage will love a play about magic stars.

LARRY: Mr. Archibald, you said that if we succeeded in

decorating the tree, you'd give us the play for a reward. Have we earned our reward?

MR. ARCHIBALD: Let me see. Is the reward ready, Miss Rose?

MISS ROSE: All we have left to write is the ending. And the tree should have a few more decorations, don't you think?

MR. ARCHIBALD: Yes, yes, of course. . . . About the ending, Miss Rose. What do you think the ending should have in it? I mean . . .

MISS ROSE: Oh, Mr. Archibald, you're teasing again. Everyone knows what the ending of a Christmas play should have in it.

MR. ARCHIBALD (*Puzzled*): Everyone? (*Regaining his composure*) Why, yes, of course——everyone.

LARRY: Tell us, Miss Rose!

MR. ARCHIBALD (*Nodding*): An excellent idea, Larry.

MISS ROSE: Why, the ending of the play should remind everybody that the true meaning of Christmas is a warm feeling inside your heart . . . (SAM *comes in, unnoticed, and hangs a gold star on tree.*) a feeling of peace and good will.

LOU: And shouldn't it tell about the star in Bethlehem, too? (SAM *hangs another star.*)

LARRY: And the angels singing out the news of the newborn King? (SAM *hangs another star on tree.*)

LINDA: And the Wisemen bringing gifts? (SAM *hangs another star on tree.*)

MISS ROSE: It tells about all those things between the lines by showing that Christmas means peace . . . and brotherhood . . . and the joy of giving. (SAM *hangs another star on tree, then tiptoes out.*)

MR. ARCHIBALD: Exactly.

MISS ROSE (*Tearing out the pages*): Here you are, children. There's nothing more to write.

LARRY: Do you mean it's finished? The play is finished?

MR. ARCHIBALD: Your reward. The play you wanted me to write. (*Notices tree*) Why . . . look at that, would you!

CHILDREN: More stars!

MR. ARCHIBALD: Where in the world . . .

MISS ROSE: The play isn't *quite* finished, the tree isn't *quite* trimmed. And we ought to sing a Christmas carol before you go.

MR. ARCHIBALD (*Suddenly*): One moment, please. Sam! I say, Sam . . . (*Goes to door and calls*) Where is that stagehand, anyway? (*Exits*)

LARRY (*Looking at script*): "A Tree to Trim." That's a good title, Miss Rose. (*Reads*) "Characters: Mr. Archibald, an author. Miss Rose, his secretary. Sam, his handyman. Larry, Linda, Lou, the children next door." (*Looks up*) Why, the play is about *us!*

LINDA (*Eagerly*): Let's start to rehearse right away.

MR. ARCHIBALD (*Hurrying in*): Just a moment. Just a moment. Don't do anything rash. I've just thought of the perfect ending. What's Christmas without a carol? (MISS ROSE *hides a smile.*) Answer me that, children. Answer me that, Miss Rose. And, if I may quote a well-known motto of the twelfth century . . . there's nothing like killing two birds with one stone. So I suggest we finish the play with a carol while we hang the rest of our good wishes on the tree.

MISS ROSE: Why, Mr. Archibald! You're not only famous . . . you're a genius! (*Gaily they begin to sing a carol and hang the stars which* MR. ARCHIBALD *distributes.*)

MR. ARCHIBALD (*Thoughtfully, when tree is trimmed*): A tree to trim! How in the world did this all happen, Miss Rose?

MISS ROSE (*Laughing*): It didn't happen "in the world," Mr. Archibald.

MR. ARCHIBALD: It didn't? You mean it all happened in my head?

MISS ROSE (*Smiling*): Not in your head, either. It happened where the true spirit of Christmas lives . . . and where it will live forever. It happened . . . in your heart!

THE END

The Inn at Bethlehem

Characters

MIRIAM THE WISE, *a prophetess*
BENJAMIN
SUSANNA, *his sister*
ELI, *their brother*
JONAH, *yardman at the inn*
INNKEEPER
INNKEEPER'S WIFE
BARUCH⎫
AMOZ ⎬ *guests at the inn*
STRANGER
SERVANT
AARON, *a traveler*
LEAH, *his wife*
MARY
JOSEPH
LEMUEL, *a shepherd*
CHILDREN

SCENE 1

TIME: *The eve of the first Christmas.*
SETTING: *A street in Bethlehem.*
BEFORE RISE: MIRIAM *enters, in front of curtain.*

25

MIRIAM: Seven hundred years since Isaiah foretold the coming of a Saviour! Seven hundred years of waiting—wondering—hoping, in Israel! "The Lord Himself shall give you a sign," said Isaiah. (*Stops, looks around*) All my life I have been looking for the sign. (*After a pause walks again, slowly*) Almost seven hundred years since Micah foretold the coming of a Ruler out of Bethlehem, who would be great unto the ends of the earth. And still we are waiting. (*Stands, as if listening*) Now something tells me that the long watch is drawing to a close. Yet, what sign shall we look for? Where will it be given? When will this come to pass? (BENJAMIN *comes running in, sees* MIRIAM, *stops and bows respectfully.*)

BENJAMIN: Good afternoon, Miriam the Wise.

MIRIAM: Where are you going in such a hurry?

BENJAMIN: To the inn yard.

MIRIAM: Why to the inn yard, Benjamin?

BENJAMIN: Because (*Hesitates*)—you yourself have taught the children of Bethlehem—

MIRIAM: What have I taught you?

BENJAMIN: That out of Bethlehem, though it is little among the towns of Judah, there shall come forth a Ruler who shall be great unto the ends of the earth. What better time for a Ruler to come than now, when Bethlehem is crowded with people who must register for the census? And what better place than the inn yard where strangers will be gathered?

MIRIAM: Well spoken, Benjamin. Whom will you look for in the inn yard?

BENJAMIN: A rich man dressed like a king.

MIRIAM: Why a king?

BENJAMIN: Did you not teach us the prophecy of Jeremiah—that the days would come when the Lord would raise unto David a King who would reign and prosper and execute judgment and justice in the earth? Bethlehem is the city of David. And might not this King be among the strangers who come to register?

MIRIAM: You have not remembered everything I taught you.

BENJAMIN: What have I not remembered?

MIRIAM: That Isaiah said: "He shall feed his flock like a shepherd; he shall gather the lambs with his arm, and carry them in his bosom, and shall gently lead those that are with young." Does that sound like any rich king you ever heard of?

BENJAMIN: No. (*Looks around furtively*) Surely not like King Herod in Jerusalem. That sounds like a shepherd. Shall I look for a strange shepherd, then, who has come to the town of his ancestors to register?

MIRIAM: Again you have forgotten. I am afraid I am not a very good teacher.

BENJAMIN: There are so many prophecies! They do not always say the same thing. (*Thinks hard*) Do you mean the one about the Prophet who shall rise up from the midst of us? King—Shepherd—Prophet. Why are these things so hard to understand?

MIRIAM: Because we must practice patience and humility, and not weaken in our reverence for the Lord. For seven hundred years we have been strong in our faith that a Saviour would come. Now, Benjamin, something tells me that the long wait is almost over.

BENJAMIN: The best place to look for the Saviour is at the inn, isn't it? If I see a sign I will hurry to tell you. (*Pauses thoughtfully*) But how will I know the sign if I see it?

MIRIAM: You will know. The sign, when it comes, will leave no doubt.

BENJAMIN: I just hope it will come soon. I have to take a pouch of food to my brother Eli who is watching the flocks in the hills. What kind of sign do you think it will

be? Like lightning? Or thunder? Or wind? Or the sound
of rushing water?

MIRIAM: That is one of the mysteries no one can foretell,
not even the wisest man in Israel. You must hurry to
me, Benjamin, if you see anything unusual. (*She exits
one side, he the other.*)

CURTAIN

*   *   *

SCENE 2

TIME: *A little later, the same evening.*

SETTING: *The yard of the inn. Part of the inn may show
at one side. There is a well near center of stage, with a
bench nearby. Toward the wings, front, is a gate.*

AT RISE: JONAH *is at the well, getting water.* BARUCH *and*
AMOZ *walk up and down, talking.* BENJAMIN *comes in
at back, sees* JONAH, *hurries to well.*

BENJAMIN: Have many come, Jonah?

JONAH: Have many come! You should see! And still several hours before dark! The master has had to go in
search of more mats for travelers to lie on, but where
he will put more mats in the already crowded inn, I
can't imagine. (*Looks at sky*) If the sky clears, I suppose some of the latecomers can sleep in the inn yard.

BENJAMIN: Do you think it will clear?

JONAH (*Shrugging*) : We could stand it after three days of
winter rain.

BENJAMIN: Have any kings come, Jonah?

JONAH: Kings? Not that I've seen. There's one rich man
and his wife and servant from Jericho. The master gave
them the best rooms.

BENJAMIN: Any shepherds?

JONAH: Shepherds! Would shepherds pay to stay at an inn when they're used to sleeping in the fields?

BENJAMIN: What about a prophet?

JONAH: I know nothing about prophets, but I can tell you there are children! (*Several* CHILDREN, *chasing each other, rush out of the inn, almost tip over* JONAH's *water jar, circle the inn yard and run screaming into the inn again.*) You see? I will be glad when this enrollment is over and we have some peace again.

INNKEEPER'S WIFE (*At door, calling out*): What are you doing, Jonah? *Digging* the well? Hurry!

JONAH: I'm coming.

INNKEEPER'S WIFE: They keep asking for water. They never get enough. (JONAH *hurries in with water.* BENJA-MIN *sits on bench near well.* BARUCH *and* AMOZ *walk near front of stage, talking.*)

BARUCH: Of course, it's obvious why Caesar Augustus has decreed that a census of the whole world be taken.

AMOZ: The whole world meaning the *Roman* world! As if India and other countries to the southeast didn't exist.

BARUCH: For the Romans, nothing exists that doesn't be-long to Rome. As I say, the reason for the census is obvious—to make sure everybody is on the tax rolls. As if we weren't already taxed out of all reason.

AMOZ (*Counting on fingers*): Soil tax, poll tax, personal property tax, Temple tax, export tax, import tax, taxes on practically everything we sell or buy. I already pay out a third of my earnings in taxes!

BARUCH: Don't we all?

AMOZ: *Ridiculous* that we should have to go back to our ancestral homes to be registered at the very worst season of the year—when traveling is hard and accommoda-tions miserable. What we need is that long-promised Messiah to save us from our oppressors. Certainly we can't expect anything from King Herod. He is under the thumb of our Roman masters.

BARUCH: He doesn't want to lose his luxurious palace in Jerusalem!

AMOZ: Centuries ago, it was written that the Lord would raise up a Prophet from the midst of us, and that we should hearken unto Him. We are ready to hearken, but the Prophet does not appear. (*Knocking at gate interrupts conversation.*)

BARUCH: Here come some more people, and the inn already full! (JONAH *hurries from inn to open the gate.*)

INNKEEPER'S WIFE (*Calling after him*): Tell them they will have to lie on mats in the common room. (*When* JONAH *opens the gate,* SUSANNA *slips in, and hurries to* BENJAMIN *with leather bag and cloak.* JONAH *stands talking at gate with* STRANGER *and his* SERVANT.)

JONAH: No, we have nothing better.

SERVANT: My master will pay well.

SUSANNA (*To* BENJAMIN): Benjamin, here is the food for Eli. Mama says you'll have to hurry. It's a long way there and back, and afternoons are so short now. Here's a warm cloak in case it rains again.

BENJAMIN: I can't go yet, Susanna. I'll run all the way, so I won't have to start so soon.

SERVANT (*At gate*): My master insists on speaking to the innkeeper.

JONAH: Then you will have to wait. No, here he comes now— (*Points offstage*) that man leading the donkey. I see he has found some mats. (JONAH *goes out gate.*)

SUSANNA: Why are you so eager to hang around the inn yard, Benjamin? You always liked being in the hills with the shepherds.

BENJAMIN: Today there are many people to watch here, and I'm looking for someone.

SUSANNA: Who?

BENJAMIN: I don't know, but I hope to find out.

SUSANNA: You're teasing me.

INNKEEPER (*Coming in with* STRANGER *and* SERVANT): I tell you the only space we have left is on the floor of the common room. (*Calls back over shoulder*) Hurry with those mats, Jonah, and put the donkey out to pasture.

SERVANT: My master is a man of means. We have come all the way from Capernaum on the Sea of Galilee for the enrollment. Had my master known that Bethlehem would be so crowded, he would have spent the night in Jerusalem and ridden over in the morning. As it is, he is too weary to ride the five miles back to the Holy City. (*Clinks coins*) Ten pieces of Tyrian silver for a room, my good innkeeper.

INNKEEPER: Ten pieces? But I have told you the situation.

SERVANT: Surely there must be some way to free a room. (JONAH *comes in with several mats, hurries into inn.* BENJAMIN *and* SUSANNA, BARUCH *and* AMOZ *listen as* SERVANT *tempts* INNKEEPER *with money.*)

INNKEEPER: There is the small room my wife and I use. We could put our mats in the kitchen. I would not like to turn away such a worthy man as your master. (JONAH *comes out*) Take care of the horses of these guests, Jonah.

JONAH: Only one empty stall remains in the stable, master, and that is the place where I sleep.

SERVANT: Tie the horses in the yard, then. See that they are well fed and watered. First help me take the luggage off their backs. (SERVANT *and* JONAH *exit, returning in a few minutes with blankets, baskets, etc.* INNKEEPER *takes* STRANGER *into inn.*)

JONAH (*As he comes back with luggage*): What is your master's business, may I ask?

SERVANT: That, may I answer, is no business of yours. (*They go into inn.*)

BARUCH: So the innkeeper will sleep in the kitchen.

AMOZ: I wonder what the stranger does for a living. His servant doesn't seem to want to tell. Why? The man obviously has money.

BARUCH: He may be a tax collector. That would be something to hide! An Israelite who has sold himself to the Romans, and gets rich squeezing tax money out of us!

AMOZ: Yes, the man must be a tax collector! (*They go into inn.*)

BENJAMIN: There is certainly no sign that the one I am looking for has come yet. (*Sighs*)

SUSANNA: You must go, Benjamin. Mama says you mustn't wait too long.

BENJAMIN: If the prophecy isn't fulfilled this time, Susanna— They say the next census will not come for fourteen years. I will be a grown man by then.

SUSANNA: Have you been talking to Miriam the Wise, again, brother?

BENJAMIN: Yes. She thinks the long watch is drawing to a close. (*Shrugs*) But I can't help remembering that she taught us a thousand years in the Lord's sight is but a watch in the night. So perhaps we have to wait still longer. (*Knock at gate*) Someone else is coming. (*Calls*) Jonah! (JONAH *hurries out of inn, starts for gate, complaining as he goes.* CHILDREN *chase each other through yard again.*)

JONAH: No rest, no peace! A curse on Caesar Augustus for decreeing the census! (*At gate, to* AARON *and* LEAH) The inn is full.

AARON: We don't need much. Just a little shelter in case it should rain again.

LEAH: Surely there is a corner somewhere.

JONAH: Even the innkeeper and his wife are sleeping in

the kitchen tonight. Bethlehem is not a large town. This is not a large inn. It is already full.

AARON (*Giving* JONAH *a coin*): May I have a word with your master? (JONAH *shrugs and goes for* INNKEEPER. SUSANNA *looks inquiringly at* BENJAMIN. *He shakes his head.*)

INNKEEPER (*Coming out*): A young man and his wife? Why didn't you tell them we are full?

JONAH: I did. But he wants a word with you. Perhaps it is about something else.

INNKEEPER: What else? Everybody wants shelter tonight. There is nothing else!

AARON (*Stepping up*): We have walked from Joppa, sir, for the enrollment. We are young and strong and we did not mind the journey—but our feet!

LEAH: Our feet are not used to so much walking.

AARON: We can pay a reasonable rate for shelter.

INNKEEPER: Every place is taken.

LEAH: Every square inch?

INNKEEPER: I can think of only one possibility. In one room are two women and three children, in another room three men. If you can persuade them to take one more in each room—

AARON: No, no, that would never do. (*Looks around*) We could stay here in the inn yard. It isn't going to rain again, is it?

INNKEEPER (*Looking at sky*): In the rainy season, who can say? But the clouds seem to be breaking.

AARON: Do you have a piece of tent cloth, by any chance?

INNKEEPER: I think there is a piece in the stable, left by a camel train several years ago. Am I right, Jonah?

JONAH: Yes, master.

AARON: If your man could put a few poles in the corner there and stretch the tent cloth over, we would be quite content. (*Offers coins*)

INNKEEPER (*Taking coins*): See to it, Jonah. (*To* AARON *and* LEAH) There is water in the well. You have your own bread?

LEAH: Yes, bread and cheese. We will be no trouble. (JONAH *goes out for poles,* INNKEEPER *returns to inn.*)

SUSANNA (*Nudging* BENJAMIN): Now, Benjamin, you really must go.

BENJAMIN (*Rising, taking food pouch and cloak*): Yes, I guess I might as well. Perhaps the inn yard wasn't the best place to look, after all. It might have been better to sit by the roadside. Some travelers must certainly stay with relatives and friends. No kings, or shepherds, or prophets have come here. Are you staying, Susanna?

SUSANNA: A little while. I want to see the tent cloth. (BENJAMIN *goes out the gate.* JONAH *returns with poles. He is not very handy with them.* AARON *tries to help.* LEAH *and* SUSANNA *unfold the cloth.*) The cloth is so thick. What is it made of?

LEAH: It is woven from the hair of black goats. A tent of this cloth holds out both rain and the heat of the sun. You are the innkeeper's daughter?

SUSANNA: No. I came to find my brother. He likes to linger here. He is fascinated by strangers.

LEAH (*Laughing*): Yes, I suppose we are a queer lot!

SUSANNA: He is always hoping to find someone.

LEAH: Today, with the inn so crowded, he has many to choose from.

SUSANNA: The right one hasn't come.

LEAH: The right one? (BENJAMIN *comes hurrying back into inn yard, excited and out of breath.*)

BENJAMIN: Jonah! Come, help!

JONAH (*Looking around, dropping poles*): What now? I thought you had gone.

BENJAMIN: I met two travelers, a man, and a young

woman on a donkey, coming along the road. The man asked where the inn was.

JONAH: You told them we were full, Benjamin, didn't you?

BENJAMIN: The woman looks so pale and weary, I'm afraid she will fall off the donkey. Come, help them to the inn, Jonah.

JONAH: You know we have no room.

BENJAMIN: Where can they go? You must at least let them rest in the inn yard a while.

LEAH (*To* JONAH): I'll go with you, my good man. We can't let the poor woman fall from the donkey.

JONAH: Her husband can hold her on.

BENJAMIN: He can't lead the donkey at the same time.

AARON: I'll go, too. (JONAH, LEAH *and* AARON *go out.* BENJAMIN *starts to follow, but* SUSANNA *holds him back.*)

SUSANNA: Benjamin, it's so late now—how can you take the food to Eli and be back before dark? You'll get lost in the hills.

BENJAMIN: I couldn't just leave those people there in the road. (*Gets an idea*) I know. I'll stay with the shepherds and come home in the morning. Tell Mama, so she won't worry.

SUSANNA: You'll be cold, Benjamin.

BENJAMIN: They will have a little fire, and I can wrap the cloak around me. (*Sighs*) I've given up expecting the King, Susanna. I should have known He wouldn't come today.

SUSANNA: Why?

BENJAMIN: If a king were coming, he would have sent a servant or a soldier well ahead of time to reserve rooms. No king would come this late, without preparation.

SUSANNA: Of course. Neither of us thought of that. (Jo-

SEPH *and* JONAH *come in, supporting* MARY *between them. She has a cloak around her.* AARON *and* LEAH *follow*.)

JOSEPH: We are Joseph and Mary, from Nazareth in Galilee. My wife's cousin Elizabeth lives not far away from here. I had expected to take my wife there and come back to Bethlehem to register, but we can go no farther tonight.

JONAH: There is no room here. I am sorry, sir.

INNKEEPER (*Coming out*): More travelers, Jonah? You know we are full.

JONAH: The young woman is too ill to go on, master. They have come all the way from Nazareth in Galilee.

INNKEEPER: That is too long a journey for one in her condition.

JOSEPH: We have a little donkey. We did not think the trip would be so difficult.

INNKEEPER: There is no room indoors, but you are welcome to rest here in the inn yard. (*He goes back to inn. Others make* MARY *comfortable on bench*.)

MARY: Thank you kindly.

AARON: We are to sleep under this shelter here in the yard tonight, if we can get the poles to hold together.

JOSEPH: Let me help! I am a carpenter. What you need is a brace, a diagonal brace. That will have the strength of three uprights. Where is another pole? (JONAH *picks up pole and hands it to* JOSEPH. *Deftly,* JOSEPH *braces frame and ties it together*.) There! Now for the tent cloth.

JONAH (*Impressed*): Thank you, sir.

LEAH: What a nice little corner for us, Aaron. Look, now that we have a shelter, the sky is clearing.

JONAH: It will be a cold, clear night, with a sky full of stars.

BENJAMIN (*To* SUSANNA): Too cold for the woman from Nazareth to stay in the inn yard. My pallet will be empty at home tonight, Susanna, if I stay with the shepherds.

SUSANNA: Your pallet! On the stone ledge, in a room where others are sleeping! It would do for a single man, but not for the woman, Benjamin. Besides, her husband would not leave her.

BENJAMIN (*Suddenly*): Jonah! (*Takes him to one side*) There is the empty stall where you sleep in the stable. Let these strangers use it! You can have my pallet to-night when I am in the hills. You can have my share of hot lamb stew for supper.

SUSANNA: Benjamin, if you don't go right away, you won't even *get* there before dark! You have to hurry. (*Curtain*)

*　　*　　*

SCENE 3

TIME: *Before dawn, the next morning.*

SETTING: *Same as Scene 1. The stage is darkened except for one bright light above.*

BEFORE RISE: MIRIAM *enters, in front of curtain.*

MIRIAM: "The people that walked in darkness have seen a great light." And what a light, filling the sky at the height of the rainy season! What a star hanging over our little town of Bethlehem! It seems to stand above the inn. I must hurry. Something tells me I am needed there, in the stable. (*Stops thoughtfully*) In the stable! Why in the stable, I wonder? (*Walks on*) My heart is strangely full of joy this night. What is that refrain that rings in my ears over and over again? (*Listens*) "The grass withereth, the flower fadeth: but the word of our God shall stand forever." (*Goes out. For a moment all is silence, then* ELI *and* LEMUEL *walk before curtain. They are half-frightened, half-expectant.*)

ELI: Benjamin said to wait for him here.

LEMUEL: He said he promised to tell old Miriam about the sign.

ELI: She herself must have seen the star. How could she miss it? Still, she would not have heard the voices we heard in the hills.

LEMUEL: Perhaps she heard different voices. I tell you, Eli, my knees were shaking when those strange words came out of nowhere. "Fear not, for behold, I bring you tidings of great joy, which shall be to all people."

ELI: "For unto you is born this day in the city of David a Saviour, which is Christ, the Lord." (BENJAMIN *comes running in.*)

BENJAMIN: Miriam the Wise, has gone. I can't find her. Her house is dark and empty.

ELI: Then she, too, must have seen the star and heard the voices. Perhaps she, too, was told about the sign.

BENJAMIN (*Recalling slowly*): "And this shall be a sign unto you; ye shall find the babe wrapped in swaddling clothes, lying in a manger." But what manger? There are many mangers in Bethlehem.

ELI (*Looking around*): The town is asleep. We saw no light in any of the stables we passed.

LEMUEL: The inn lies ahead. Let's see if there is a light there, in the stable.

BENJAMIN: If Jonah slept on my pallet, who will open the gate?

ELI: Why would Jonah sleep on your pallet? He sleeps in the stable. Come along. (*They go out.*)

CURTAIN

*   *   *

SCENE 4

SETTING: *Same as Scene 2.*

AT RISE: *Curtain opens on the darkened inn yard. Another crude shelter has been built near the gate. Everything is quiet. There is a soft knock on the gate.* JONAH, *sleepy, emerges from the shelter, stretches, listens. Knock comes again.* JONAH *goes to gate.*

JONAH: Quiet there! The inn is full. Do not waken the guests!

BENJAMIN: It's Benjamin, Jonah.

JONAH (*Opening gate*): Benjamin? What are you doing here at this hour, before the break of dawn? (BENJAMIN, ELI *and* LEMUEL *enter.*)

BENJAMIN: You know my brother, Eli, and this is another shepherd, Lemuel. We are seeking the sign.

JONAH: What sign?

BENJAMIN: A babe wrapped in swaddling clothes, lying in a manger.

JONAH: Are you dreaming? What babe? What manger?

BENJAMIN: Where have you been sleeping, Jonah?

JONAH: Here on a bed of hay under this shelter near the gate. The carpenter from Nazareth built it, and I must say it made answering the gate easier. The carpenter and his wife have my place in the stable.

BENJAMIN: Has someone else come?

JONAH: Old Miriam, about an hour ago.

BENJAMIN: Miriam the Wise! Then this is the place! Let us see the child in the manger, Jonah.

JONAH: What are you talking about? I know of no child in the manger. (MIRIAM *comes from back.*)

MIRIAM: "The people that walked in darkness have seen a great light." The light centers upon a child wrapped in swaddling clothes, lying in the manger.

BENJAMIN: The sign! The sign we have been waiting for!

MIRIAM: The first to recognize the sign shall be the first to see. Come, Benjamin, and your brother, and the other shepherd. And Jonah. Come, see Mary's child, born in the stable this night.

BENJAMIN: I will give him my cloak for a gift.

ELI: I will give my leather pouch.

LEMUEL: I will give my shepherd's flute.

JONAH: I have nothing.

BENJAMIN: You have already given your bed, Jonah. (*They go into the stable.* MIRIAM *stands in inn yard, looking at the sky.* INNKEEPER *comes out of inn.*)

INNKEEPER: What's happening here? Is anything the matter? Is it you, old Miriam? Where did you come from?

MIRIAM: I was needed. A child has been born.

INNKEEPER: Here?

MIRIAM: In your stable.

INNKEEPER: The woman from Nazareth? (*Looks around*) Where does all the light come from? Where did they get the lanterns? (*Looks up*) What great star is that?

MIRIAM: The star of Bethlehem.

INNKEEPER: Strange! I must tell my wife. (*Goes out*)

LEAH (*Sticking head out of shelter*): Is anything wrong?

MIRIAM: Everything is more right than it has been in seven hundred years. (BENJAMIN *and others come from stable.*)

BENJAMIN: I was looking for a King—a Shepherd—a Prophet—and it turns out to be a new-born Child!

MIRIAM: In the Child you will find a King to rule with judgment and justice. In the Child you will find a Shepherd who will feed His flock and gather the lambs with His arm. In the Child you will find the Prophet to whom you shall hearken. You see, Benjamin, you did not remember everything I taught you. But this was not a matter of the mind. Your heart understood more than your head. "For unto us . . ."

BENJAMIN (*Eagerly*): "For unto us a child is born, unto us a son is given, and the government shall be upon his shoulder; and His name shall be called Wonderful, Counsellor, The mighty God, The everlasting Father, The Prince of Peace." Now is the prophecy come true! (*Strains of "Adeste Fidelis" as the curtain closes*)

THE END

Mr. Scrooge Finds Christmas

(Adapted from "A Christmas Carol," by Charles Dickens)

Characters

MARLEY'S GHOST
GHOST OF CHRISTMAS PAST
GHOST OF CHRISTMAS PRESENT   } *three spirits*
GHOST OF CHRISTMAS YET TO COME
EBENEZER SCROOGE
BOB CRATCHIT, *his clerk*
FRED, *Scrooge's nephew*
A SOLICITOR
BOY CAROLERS
BELINDA
PETER
BOY
GIRL   } *the Cratchit family*
MRS. CRATCHIT
MARTHA
TINY TIM
TWO MEN, *from the Stock Exchange*
POULTRYMAN
(*A number of parts may be doubled up.*)

SCENE 1

TIME: *Afternoon of Christmas Eve.*
SETTING: *A darkened stage, with spotlight on one side;*

42

or the meeting between MARLEY'S GHOST *and the* THREE SPIRITS *may be acted in front of the curtain. Behind the curtain the stage is set for the office of "Scrooge and Marley."*

AT RISE: MARLEY'S GHOST *and* THREE SPIRITS *are in spotlight (or walk in front of the curtain).*

MARLEY: Thank you for coming, friends. I am in dire need of your help. There is a soul to be saved! My name is Marley—Jacob Marley. Rather, I should say, that was my name on earth. And you . . . which is which?

1ST SPIRIT (*Stepping forward*): I am the Ghost of Christmas Past.

2ND SPIRIT (*Stepping forward*): I am the Ghost of Christmas Present.

3RD SPIRIT (*Stepping forward*): I am the Ghost of Christmas Yet to Come.

1ST SPIRIT: We hurried right off to this London street, as soon as your message came, Mr. Marley. We hope we can help you. Have you been over on our side of the world long, sir?

MARLEY: Seven years, this very night. (*Points toward wings*) And, look, my partner never had my name painted out! See, there above the warehouse door— SCROOGE AND MARLEY.

1ST SPIRIT: Brokers?

MARLEY: Connected with the London Exchange. You see, he's not entirely bad, my friends. Just blind, so to speak. Going around with his eyes closed to the things that really matter . . . the way I used to. Thinking that money is everything. (*Rattles chain*) He's forging himself a chain as heavy as mine.

2ND SPIRIT: Who, sir?

MARLEY: Ebenezer Scrooge. Poor fellow.

3RD SPIRIT: And what do you want us to do?

MARLEY: Help me get him to see the light. It's just a case of reaching through to him. And what better time than Christmas Eve?

1ST SPIRIT: Scrooge, you say?

MARLEY (*Nodding*): My former partner, executor, and heir—Ebenezer Scrooge. (*Sighs*) He has the reputation of being a squeezing, wrenching, grasping, scraping, clutching, covetous old sinner. But don't take my word for it. Come along, step inside the countinghouse with me for a few minutes and see for yourselves what kind of man he is—to outward appearances, at least. This way, my friends. No one will see us. (*They go out. If the scene has been acted in front of the curtain, curtain rises; if on stage, lights go on.*)

*   *   *

SCENE 2

SETTING: *The office of Scrooge and Marley.*

AT RISE: *On a stool, hunched over a high bookkeeper's desk, sits* BOB CRATCHIT. *He has a long white muffler around his neck.* SCROOGE *sits at his desk at the other side of the room. There is a meager fire in the grate on each side of the room.* BOB *shivers, rubs his hands. Then, with a furtive glance at* SCROOGE, *gets off his stool, takes the coal shovel and carefully approaches the coal-box.*

SCROOGE (*Looking up, angrily*): At three o'clock in the afternoon, Cratchit? Wasting coal, so close to closing time?

BOB: It's cold and foggy, sir. Penetrating . . .

SCROOGE: Cold, nonsense! Haven't you a candle there on your desk?

BOB: Yes, sir. But the figures suffer when my hand shakes.

SCROOGE: Warm your hands over the candle, then. How many times do I have to tell you? If you persist in being so extravagant with the coal, we shall have to part company, you and I. I can get another clerk, you know. More easily than you can get another position, I warrant.

BOB (*Going back to stool*): Yes, sir. (*Rubs hands over candle. Huddles in muffler. After a moment of silence,* FRED *bursts into the room.*)

FRED (*Cheerfully*): A Merry Christmas, uncle! God save you!

SCROOGE (*Without looking up*): Bah! Humbug!

FRED: Christmas a humbug, uncle? You don't mean that, I am sure!

SCROOGE: I do. Merry Christmas! What reason have you to be merry? You're poor enough.

FRED: Come, then, what reason have you to be dismal? You're rich enough.

SCROOGE (*Banging down ruler*): Bah! Humbug!

FRED: Don't be cross, uncle.

SCROOGE: What else can I be when I live in such a world of fools as this? What's Christmas-time to you but a time for paying bills without money; a time for finding yourself a year older, and not an hour richer? If I could work my will, every idiot who goes about with "Merry Christmas" on his lips should be boiled with his own pudding, and buried with a stake of holly through his heart.

FRED: Uncle!

SCROOGE: Keep Christmas in your own way, and let me keep it in mine. Much good it has ever done you!

FRED: I have always thought of Christmas-time as a good time . . . a kind, forgiving, charitable, pleasant time; the only time I know of when men and women seem by

one consent to open their shut-up hearts freely . . . I
say, God bless it! (Bob *claps his hands, then, embarrassed at his impulse, huddles over his work.*)

SCROOGE (*To* Bob): Let me hear another sound from *you,*
and you'll keep your Christmas by losing your position.

FRED: Don't be angry, uncle. Come, dine with us tomorrow.

SCROOGE: Good afternoon!

FRED: I want nothing from you. I ask nothing of you. Why
cannot we be friends?

SCROOGE: Good afternoon!

FRED (*Shrugging, cheerfully*): Well, Merry Christmas,
uncle! And a happy New Year!

SCROOGE: Good *afternoon!* (FRED *stops at* Bob's *desk, and
they exchange smiles and greetings.* Bob *goes with him
to the door. As* FRED *exits, a* SOLICITOR *comes in with
books and papers.* Bob *gestures him toward* SCROOGE,
then goes back to his work.)

SOLICITOR: Scrooge and Marley's, I believe? Have I the
pleasure of addressing Mr. Scrooge or Mr. Marley?

SCROOGE: Mr. Marley has been dead these seven years

SOLICITOR (*Presenting credentials*): At this festive season
of the year, Mr. Scrooge, it is more than usually desira-
ble that we should make some slight provision for the
poor and destitute . . .

SCROOGE: Are there no prisons? No workhouses?

SOLICITOR: There are. But, under the impression that they
scarcely furnish Christian cheer, a few of us are en-
deavoring to raise a fund to buy the poor some meat
and drink, and means of warmth. What shall I put you
down for?

SCROOGE: Nothing!

SOLICITOR: You wish to be anonymous—is that it?

SCROOGE: I wish to be left alone. I don't make merry myself at Christmas, and I can't afford to make idle people

merry. Good afternoon, sir.

SOLICITOR: *Good afternoon!* (SOLICITOR *goes out, shaking his head.* BOB *opens door for him, then hurries back to his stool.*)

SCROOGE (*Glaring at* BOB): *You'll* want all day tomorrow, I suppose?

BOB: If quite convenient, sir.

SCROOGE: It's not convenient, and it's not fair.

BOB: It's only once a year, sir.

SCROOGE (*Bangs down ruler*): A poor excuse for picking a man's pocket every twenty-fifth of December!

Curtain

*   *   *

SCENE 3

BEFORE RISE: MARLEY'S GHOST *and* THREE SPIRITS *appear in spotlight on darkened stage* (*or enter before curtain*).

MARLEY: There!

1ST SPIRIT: I see what you mean, Mr. Marley. Ebenezer Scrooge is a bad case.

2ND SPIRIT: No wonder you need help, if you want to try to reform *him.*

3RD SPIRIT: He's been this way so long, I'm afraid it's a bad habit.

MARLEY: Surely we must try to save him, my friends. We can at least warn him, at least give him a chance to escape my fate. (*Clanks chain*) Poor man, he has no idea what lies ahead of him if he doesn't change his ways.

1ST SPIRIT: What is your plan? How can we warn him? When?

MARLEY: This very night of Christmas Eve! After closing the office, he will take his dinner in the usual tavern, read the papers, go over his accounts, and then home to bed. I know his lodgings well. Fact is, they used to be-

long to me. He will be quite alone in the house. I will
appear before him as he gets drowsy.

2ND SPIRIT: Won't it be rather a shock to him—to see you?

MARLEY: He needs a shock to open his eyes, poor fellow.

3RD SPIRIT: And what about us? Where do we come in?

MARLEY: You wait in the shadows until I call you. First
I must lay the groundwork. When I stand before Ebenezer in my usual waistcoat, tights, and boots, I will clank
this infernal chain about my middle—this chain made of
cash-boxes, keys, padlocks, ledgers, deeds, and heavy
purses wrought in steel!

1ST SPIRIT: He will be scared out of his wits!

MARLEY: He needs to be. I will tell him that he is forging
a chain just like mine, that I have no rest, no peace,
because in life my spirit never roved beyond the narrow
limits of our countinghouse. It is no way to live.

2ND SPIRIT: Can a man of business understand such talk,
Mr. Marley?

MARLEY: We must *make* him understand, my friends. We
must get him to see that mankind, not money, is his
business. That common welfare is his business. Charity,
mercy, forbearance, and benevolence are all his business! And you are to impress it upon him.

SPIRITS: How?

MARLEY: I will warn Ebenezer that he will be haunted by
three Spirits in his sleep tonight. (*Points to* 1ST SPIRIT)
As Ghost of Christmas Past, you will take him back to
his life as a schoolboy and as an apprentice, and show
him that Christmas meant something to him then. That
he shouted "Merry Christmas" with the rest of them, in
good spirit. (*Points to* 2ND SPIRIT) As Ghost of Christmas Present, you will show him how joyously his clerk
Bob Cratchit will celebrate Christmas with his family
tomorrow, for all Bob's meager salary. (*Points to* 3RD
SPIRIT) And you, as Ghost of Christmas Yet to Come,

will show him what will happen if he dies as he is—if he does not change.

1ST SPIRIT: And all this to be done tonight?

MARLEY: Tonight, while Ebenezer Scrooge lies abed. Otherwise, we shall be too late for Christmas tomorrow.

SPIRITS: Lead on! We're with you! (*In a moment* BOY CAROLERS *come in singing,* "God Rest You Merry, Gentlemen." *After a stanza or two, they move on. A brief pause . . . then* SCROOGE *and* GHOST OF CHRISTMAS PAST *enter before curtain.*)

SCROOGE: Where now, Spirit?

1ST SPIRIT: You'll see.

SCROOGE: You've whisked me back to Christmas of my childhood and my school days. I'd forgotten how my heart used to beat with the excitement of the occasion. (*Hardens*) But what's Christmas to me now? Out with it! What good is it?

1ST SPIRIT: One more place, Mr. Scrooge. Do you recognize the thoroughfares of this city? (*Stops, points toward wings*) Do you know that warehouse door?

SCROOGE: Know it? I served my apprenticeship here.

1ST SPIRIT: Look in the window. (*They step closer, peering toward wings.*)

SCROOGE (*Pleased*): Why, it's old Fezziwig! Bless his heart! It's Fezziwig alive again.

1ST SPIRIT: He's laying down his pen, looking at the clock, laughing all over himself as he calls out, "Ebenezer! Dick!"

SCROOGE: He's calling me and Dick Wilkins, his two apprentices.

1ST SPIRIT: He's saying, "No more work tonight. Christmas Eve, Dick. Christmas, Ebenezer! Hilli-ho! Clear away, my lads, and let's have lots of room here for the party."

SCROOGE (*Excited, as he watches*): The floor swept . . .

the lamps trimmed . . . fuel heaped upon the fire. There comes the fiddler with his music book. Here comes Mrs. Fezziwig, with her substantial smile. And the three Miss Fezziwigs . . . and all the young men and women employed in the business, one after another . . .

1ST SPIRIT (*As if calling out a dance*): Hands half round and back again the other way . . . down the middle and up again . . . round and round . . .

SCROOGE: Look, cold roast beef and cold boiled beef! And mince pies. And ale. Dear old Fezziwig, giving us a Christmas party like that!

1ST SPIRIT (*Imitating the unregenerate* SCROOGE): A small matter, to make these silly folks so full of gratitude.

SCROOGE (*Turning on him*): Small!

1ST SPIRIT: Is it not? He has spent but a few pounds of your mortal money.

SCROOGE (*With heat*): It isn't that. The happiness he gives is quite as great as if it cost a fortune. (*Hesitates*) I . . .

1ST SPIRIT: What's the matter?

SCROOGE: Nothing particular.

1ST SPIRIT: Something, I think?

SCROOGE (*Meekly*): No. I should like to be able to say a word or two to my clerk Bob Cratchit just now. That's all. (*They go out.* CAROLERS *come in again, sing another stanza or two of "God Rest You Merry, Gentlemen," then move on. Shortly* SCROOGE *comes in with* GHOST OF CHRISTMAS PRESENT.)

SCROOGE: As Ghost of Christmas Present, you are to show me Christmas as it is here and now, I take it. Conduct me where you will. If you have anything to teach me, let me profit by it.

2ND SPIRIT: Are you familiar with this section of the city, Mr. Scrooge?

SCROOGE: Can't say that I am.

2ND SPIRIT: Hard-working, respectable people live here, doing their best to make ends meet on meager salaries.

SCROOGE: I don't doubt it.

2ND SPIRIT (*Stopping, pointing*): In that four-room house lives a kind and honest man with a large family to support . . . on fifteen bob a week.

SCROOGE: Fifteen bob? Why, that's what I pay my clerk Bob Cratchit.

2ND SPIRIT: I know. And do you ever wonder how the family manages to live on it? I'll tell you. The oldest girl, though she's still young, goodness knows, has to work out, apprentice to a milliner. That's Martha. Bob's wife has to keep making over clothes. She's turned her best dress twice, investing sixpence in ribbons. Belinda, the second girl, also depends upon a few brave ribbons. Master Peter Cratchit swims in one of his father's shirt collars. Tiny Tim . . . they can't afford the proper care for him. One wonders where they got money for a crutch and iron braces for his thin little legs. Then there are the two young Cratchits . . . Stand back! Here they come now. . . . (2ND SPIRIT *pushes* SCROOGE *back to wings.*)

* * *

SCENE 4

SETTING: *Kitchen-dining room of* CRATCHIT *house.*

AT RISE: PETER *is trying to keep the fire burning.* BELINDA *is setting the table. The two young Cratchits dash in.*

BOY: We smelled the goose!

GIRL: We were outside the baker's and smelled the goose!

PETER (*Blowing on fire*): How do you know it was ours?

BOTH: Sage and onion, Peter!

PETER: The goose won't do much good if I can't keep the fire burning under the potatoes.

BELINDA: Did you see Martha coming? Or Father and Tiny Tim coming home from church?

BOY: We only smelled the goose.

GIRL: Maybe it isn't very big, Belinda. But it *smells* big. (MRS. CRATCHIT *comes from other room, and bustles around as she talks.*)

MRS. CRATCHIT: What has ever kept your precious father? And your brother, Tiny Tim? And Martha wasn't as late last Christmas Day.

MARTHA (*Opening door*): Here's Martha, Mother!

BOY: Here's Martha!

MRS. CRATCHIT (*Kissing* MARTHA): Why, bless your heart alive, my dear, how late you are!

MARTHA: We'd a deal of work to finish up last night, and had to clear away this morning. (*Sighs, takes off coat*) I'm tired.

MRS. CRATCHIT: Sit before the fire, my dear, and warm yourself, Lord bless you.

PETER: Sit here, Martha. (*Makes a place for her.*)

BOY (*At window*): Father's coming.

GIRL: Hide, Martha, hide! (MARTHA *hides behind the closet door.* BOB CRATCHIT, *his long muffler dangling, comes in with* TINY TIM. BOB *stoops to rub* TIM'S *hands to warm them; then he looks around.*)

BOB: Why, where's our Martha?

MRS. CRATCHIT: Not coming.

BOB: Not coming! Not coming upon Christmas Day!

MARTHA (*Running out from hiding place to her father's arms*): Not coming, because I'm *here*.

BOY and GIRL (*Jumping around*): Merry Christmas, Merry Christmas! (*They take* TINY TIM *with them into other room.*)

MRS. CRATCHIT: And how did little Tim behave?

BOB: As good as gold, and better. He told me, coming home, that he hoped the people saw him in church, because he was a cripple, and it might be pleasant for them to remember, upon Christmas Day, who made lame beggars walk and blind men see. (*Turns to BE-LINDA*) And now, where's the saucepan, Belinda? Time for me to mix up something hot for us to toast with on Christmas Day. And the lemons? (BOB *and* BELINDA *work merrily at kitchen table.* BOB *puts saucepan on hob.* PETER *continues to blow on the fire.*)

MRS. CRATCHIT: Peter, you mash the potatoes before going with the two young 'uns to fetch the goose. Belinda, you sweeten up the applesauce. Martha, can you find glassware for drinking the toast?

MARTHA (*At cupboard*): Two tumblers and a custard-cup without a handle.

BOB: They'll hold the hot stuff as well as golden goblets. Here we are! (*Takes pan from hob, pours into glasses. Hands a glass to* MRS. CRATCHIT *and* MARTHA *and takes one himself. Holds it high.*) A Merry Christmas to us all, my dears. God bless us!

OTHERS: A Merry Christmas to us all!

TINY TIM (*Standing with crutch at door*): God bless us, every one! (*The glasses make the rounds. When* BOB *gets his back, he raises it again.*)

BOB: To Mr. Scrooge! I'll give you Mr. Scrooge, the founder of the feast!

MRS. CRATCHIT: The founder of the feast, indeed! I wish I had him here. I'd give him a piece of my mind to feast upon, and hope he'd have a good appetite for it.

BOB: My dear, the children! Christmas Day.

MRS. CRATCHIT: I'll drink his health for your sake, and the Day's, not for his. (*Raises her glass*) Long life to him! A

Merry Christmas and a Happy New Year! (*Curtain falls, as* BOB *drains his glass.*)

*   *   *

SCENE 5

SETTING: *In front of curtain.*
BEFORE RISE: SCROOGE *and* GHOST OF CHRISTMAS PRESENT *come in.*

SCROOGE: Spirit, tell me, will Tiny Tim live?

2ND SPIRIT: I see a vacant seat in the poor chimney corner, and a crutch without an owner, carefully preserved. If these shadows remain unaltered by the Future, the child will die.

SCROOGE: No, no! Oh, no, kind Spirit! Say he will be spared.

2ND SPIRIT: If these shadows remain unaltered by the Future, he will die.

SCROOGE (*As they go out*): No . . . no. (BOY CAROLERS *come in again, sing another stanza or two of "God Rest You Merry, Gentlemen." They move on. After a slight pause,* SCROOGE *and* GHOST OF CHRISTMAS YET TO COME *appear before curtain or in spotlight on darkened stage.*) You are about to show me shadows of the things that will happen in the time before us. Is that so, Ghost of Christmas Yet to Come? (3RD SPIRIT *does not answer.*) I fear you more than any specter I have seen. But as I know your purpose is to do me good, and as I hope to live to be another man than what I was, I am prepared to bear you company. Oh, are you taking me to the Stock Exchange? I shall be among friends there. (3RD SPIRIT *draws him to one side as* TWO MEN *from the Exchange enter.*)

1ST MAN: I don't know much about it either way, and I don't care. I only know he's dead.

2ND MAN: When did he die? His partner went years ago. I thought he'd never die. What was the matter with him?

1ST MAN: God knows. (*Shrugs*) It's likely to be a very cheap funeral, for, upon my life, I don't know of anybody to go to it. That tight-fisted old sinner! (*They exit.*)

SCROOGE (*With a shiver*): They couldn't be talking about *me*, could they? Could they? (*Looks imploringly at* SPIRIT, *gets no answer.*) Where now, Spirit? (*They take a few steps back and forth;* SPIRIT *does not speak.*) Oh, Bob Cratchit's house again? This looks like the street. Yes, there's his little house. . . . (*They walk off.*)

* * *

SCENE 6

SETTING: *The same room in Cratchit's house.*

AT RISE: MRS. CRATCHIT *and* BELINDA *sit at table, sewing.* PETER *is near the grate, reading aloud from the Bible. The two* YOUNG CRATCHITS, *quiet and subdued, listen intently.*

PETER (*Reading*): "And he took a little child, and set him in the midst of them."

MRS. CRATCHIT (*With muffled sob, laying work on table, putting hand to eyes*): The color hurts my eyes. (*After a pause*) I wouldn't show red eyes to your father when he comes home, for the world. It must be nearly time for him.

PETER (*Closing book*): Past it, rather. But I think he has walked a little slower than he used to, these few last evenings, Mother.

MRS. CRATCHIT: I have known him walk with—I have known him walk with Tiny Tim upon his shoulder very fast indeed.

PETER: And so have I. Often.

BELINDA: And so have I.

MRS. CRATCHIT: But he was very light to carry, and his father loved him so that it was no trouble—no trouble. (*There is a noise at the door.*) And there is your father at the door! (BOB CRATCHIT *enters, quietly takes off his long muffler.*)

BOB: Good evening, my dears. (*Sits near the others*)

MRS. CRATCHIT: Let me pour you a cup of tea. (MRS. CRATCHIT *brings tea, the two* YOUNG CRATCHITS *kneel beside* BOB.)

BOY: Don't mind it, Father.

GIRL: Don't be so grieved.

BOB: No. No. (*Suddenly brightens*) You can't imagine the extraordinary kindness of Mr. Scrooge's nephew today. I'd scarcely seen him but once or twice before. He's the pleasantest-spoken gentleman you ever heard. Met me on the street today and said—said he thought I looked a little—just a little down, you know. So I told him about Tiny Tim.

MRS. CRATCHIT: I'm sure he's a good soul.

BOB: He gave me his card and said, "That's where I live. Pray come to me if I can be of service to you in any way." It really seemed as if he had known our Tiny Tim, and felt with us. (*Pause*) I shouldn't be at all surprised if he got Peter a better position.

MRS. CRATCHIT: Only hear that, Peter!

BOB (*After a pause*): I am sure we shall none of us forget our poor Tiny Tim—shall we?

OTHERS: Never! Never! (SCROOGE *and* 3RD SPIRIT *enter darkened stage in spotlight, or come before curtain.* SCROOGE *is much shaken.*)

SCROOGE (*Falling to his knees before* 3RD SPIRIT): Good Spirit, assure me that I may yet change these shadows you have shown me by living a different life! (3RD

SPIRIT *kindly helps him to his feet.*) I will honor Christmas in my heart, and try to keep it all the year. I will live in the past, present, and the future. The Spirits of all three shall strive within me. I will not shut out the lessons that they teach. Good Spirit, assure me . . . (3RD SPIRIT *takes his arm, and they go out.* BOY CAROLERS *come by again, singing; exit.*)

Curtain

*   *   *

SCENE 7

SETTING: *In front of curtain.*

BEFORE RISE: MARLEY'S GHOST *and the* THREE SPIRITS *enter.*

MARLEY: Well done, my friends.

1ST SPIRIT: How well done remains to be seen.

2ND SPIRIT: Do you think we have opened his eyes?

3RD SPIRIT: Will he *really* change, or was his repentance only a passing whim?

MARLEY: If I know Ebenezer Scrooge, what he has gone through will make a different man of him from now on.

1ST SPIRIT: It's Christmas morning. We shall soon see. (*Bells ring and* CAROLERS *enter.*)

2ND SPIRIT: Christmas morning in good old London.

3RD SPIRIT: Look, Mr. Scrooge is coming . . . (*They stand aside, watching.* SCROOGE *hurries in, calling . . .*)

SCROOGE: Boy, boy! You there, boy! (*One of* CAROLERS *comes forward.*) What's today, my fine fellow?

BOY: Today! Why, *Christmas Day.*

SCROOGE: Do you know the poulterer's in the next street, at the corner?

BOY: Of course, I do.

SCROOGE: Do you know whether they've sold the prize turkey that was hanging there?

BOY: The one as big as me? It's hanging there now.

SCROOGE: Is it? Go tell them I want to buy it. Come back with the man and I'll give you a shilling. (BOY *runs out.* SCROOGE *begins to cross stage. The* SOLICITOR *approaches.*) Wait . . . don't I know this gentleman? (*Stops* SOLICITOR) Merry Christmas, sir. I hope you succeeded in raising a big fund for the poor and needy. It was very kind of you.

SOLICITOR: Mr. Scrooge?

SCROOGE: Yes, that's my name, and I fear it may not be pleasant to you. Allow me to ask your pardon. And will you have the goodness . . . (*He whispers something in* SOLICITOR's *ear.*)

SOLICITOR: Lord bless me! My dear Mr. Scrooge, are you serious?

SCROOGE: If you please, not a farthing less. A great many back payments are included in it, I assure you. Will you do me that favor?

SOLICITOR: My dear sir, I don't know what to say to such munifi . . .

SCROOGE: Don't say anything, please. Bless you! (SOLICITOR, *still unbelieving, goes out.* POULTRYMAN *returns with* BOY. POULTRYMAN *carries large turkey in bundle under his arm.*) Ah, here we are. (*Gives* BOY *a coin*)

BOY: Thank you, sir. (*Merrily*) Merry Christmas!

SCROOGE: That *is* a turkey. Impossible to carry a bird as big as that to Camden Town where my clerk Bob Cratchit lives. You must take a cab, my dear fellow. Here . . . (*Scribbles address*) . . . this is the address. (*Gives him money*) And here's more than enough for the turkey and the cab and your trouble. Merry Christmas to you!

POULTRYMAN (*Much pleased*): And to you, sir. Thank

you, sir. (*Hurries out. Several passers-by cross stage.* Scrooge, *beaming, smiles "Merry Christmas" to them. Then* Fred *enters.*)

Scrooge: Fred!

Fred: Why, bless my soul, if it isn't my Uncle Scrooge! What are you doing out on Christmas morning, sir? Going to church? You don't mean . . .

Scrooge: What are *you* doing out on Christmas morning?

Fred (*Laughing*): Last minute errand for my wife. Forgot the lemons for the punch!

Scrooge: I was planning to go to your house for Christmas dinner, Fred. If you'll let me come . . .

Fred: If I'll let you! Why, uncle, we'll be delighted, my wife and I. Come along. I always said there was nothing like a family dinner on Christmas Day. (*They go out arm in arm.* Marley's Ghost *and* Three Spirits *come forward.* Marley's Ghost *no longer wears a heavy chain, but merely a large watchchain holding his waist-coat together.*)

Marley: He sees! He really sees. He won't slip back now. I'd bet my bottom dollar on it . . . if I had a dollar. Spirit of Christmas Yet to Come, tell us what you see *now* in the future.

1st *and* 2nd Spirits: Yes, tell us!

3rd Spirit: He will be better than his word. He will do more, infinitely more. He will raise Bob Cratchit's salary first of all. And Tiny Tim will *not* die, for Scrooge will get the best doctors in London for him. He'll be a second father to him. Scrooge will become as good a friend, as good a master, and as good a man as the good old City ever knew, or any other good old city, town, or borough in the good old world.

Marley: Thank you! Thank you again, my friends. If we lived in a world where toasts were in order, I would propose a toast to you. (*Raises hand in mock toast*) To Christmas—past, present, and future. (*Suddenly*) My chain! What has happened to my chain?

1ST SPIRIT: It's gone, Mr. Marley. Most of it is gone!

2ND SPIRIT: Only a few links left—just enough to hold your waistcoat in place!

3RD SPIRIT: It's because Christmas came to your heart, too, sir. (*Holds up hand in mock toast*) As Tiny Tim would say, "God Bless Us, Every One!"

ALL: Every one! Everywhere! (*Curtain*)

THE END

What Happened in Toyland

Characters

ANNOUNCER
PETE ⎱ *electricians*
JOE ⎰
MR. WINKLE, *owner of the Mammoth Department Store*
MISS SNELL, *a saleslady at the doll counter*
SHOPPERS
MR. BANKS, *advertising manager of the Mammoth Department Store*
RICKY RIGGS
RUTHY RIGGS
COS, *a mysterious visitor to Toyland*
CHORUS

SETTING: *A corner of the toy department in the Mammoth Department Store.*

AT RISE: *The stage is bustling with activity.* MISS SNELL *stands behind the doll display counter, busily tidying things. Center stage, the* ANNOUNCER *stands, holding a portable microphone, talking with two radio technicians. A number of shoppers, men and women, boys and girls, are crossing the stage from both sides, carrying packages. Some stop at* MISS SNELL'S *counter; others watch the* ANNOUNCER *with interest.*

PETE (*To the* ANNOUNCER): Only thirty more seconds, and we're on the air!

ANNOUNCER (*Taking control of the situation*): Fine! Ladies and gentlemen, would you clear this area, please? It's almost time for us to go on the air!

PETE: Fifteen seconds!

ANNOUNCER (*As the shoppers move toward the exits*): Just move a little out of the way, please. That's it! Thank you!

PETE: Ten seconds!

LITTLE GIRL (*To* ANNOUNCER): Are you going to talk on the radio, Mister?

ANNOUNCER: That's right. Now stand back, please. (LITTLE GIRL *moves down right. Shoppers remain down right and down left to watch the proceedings.*)

PETE: Five seconds more!

ANNOUNCER: Is my voice level all right?

JOE (*Nodding*): O.K.

PETE: Hold it! You're on the air! (*Points his finger at* ANNOUNCER.)

ANNOUNCER (*Facing front, speaking into mike*): Ladies and gentlemen, this is your Christmas reporter, broadcasting direct to you from the Toy Department of the Mammoth Department Store, and reminding you that there are only four more shopping days till Christmas. You just ought to see this toyland! Dolls, trucks, bicycles—and of course, Santa Claus, with every kind of toy and game imaginable. And what a mob of people, doing their last-minute shopping, gazing and gaping at all the wonderful toys! Ladies and gentlemen, it's certainly exciting. The air is filled to overflowing with Christmas cheer! Just listen to the activity around here! (*Swings mike around.* MR. WINKLE, *the store owner, enters. He is a blustery man and a bit foolish. He goes angrily to the* ANNOUNCER.)

MR. WINKLE: What are you just standing around for? Don't you think it's time you went on the air?

ANNOUNCER: But Mr. Winkle! We *are* on the air!

MR. WINKLE (*Taken aback*): We are? (*Apologetically*) Oh, I see. Well, in that case, go right on with the program by all means.

ANNOUNCER: Ladies and gentlemen out there in radioland, the voice you just heard was that of Mr. Winkle, the owner of Mammoth Department Store. Mr. Winkle, won't you say a few words to our listening audience?

MR. WINKLE (*Instantly befuddled*): Who, me? I can't talk on the radio!

ANNOUNCER (*Laughing*): But Mr. Winkle, you've already *been* talking on the radio!

MR. WINKLE: Well—well— Ladies and gentlemen . . . (*Clears his throat*) . . . on behalf of the Mammoth Department Store, I'd like to wish you all a very Merry Christmas. We have prepared a special holiday broadcast for you, and we hope you enjoy it. (PETE *ushers the* CHORUS *in.*) On with the show!

ANNOUNCER: Thank you very much, Mr. Winkle. Now I see the Chorus is about ready to sing, and so ladies and gentlemen, I present for your listening pleasure, the Mammoth Department Store's special Chorus singing . . . (ANNOUNCER *names a carol, and the* CHORUS *sings.* MR. WINKLE *exits.*)

ANNOUNCER (*After song*): Thank you very much. That was beautiful! (CHORUS *exits.*) Now, I'm going to interview one of the salesladies here in Toyland, the lady in charge of the doll counter. You should see it piled with a most unusual display of dolls. (*Going over to* MISS SNELL) Merry Christmas, Miss . . . Miss . . .

MISS SNELL (*Speaking into the mike*): Snell. Miss Snell.

ANNOUNCER: Miss Snell, can you tell us something about these dolls you have for sale here? They're rather different, aren't they?

MISS SNELL: Oh, I should say they are. They're the contest dolls, you know.

ANNOUNCER: The contest dolls?

MISS SNELL: Yes. Here's one of the contest leaflets. (*Hands him a paper*)

ANNOUNCER (*Reading*): "Boys and girls! Here is a chance for you to earn some Christmas money. Think up a snappy name for these unusual dolls. What shall it be? *Magic Maggie* and *Space-Age Sam?* Try your luck. Think up a name. A prize of fifty dollars will be given for the best name submitted by 3:30 o'clock this afternoon." Fifty dollars for a name! Well, what do you think of that? Who's going to judge the entries, Miss Snell?

MISS SNELL: Mr. Winkle and our advertising manager, Mr. Banks. He comes and collects the slips every half hour so he has all the entries right up to date. He will be able to announce the winner just five minutes after the contest closes.

ANNOUNCER: That's fine! Then I can announce the winner before the end of our broadcast!

MISS SNELL: Oh, that will be wonderful! Thousands of children have already suggested names for these very special dolls.

ANNOUNCER: Thank you, Miss Snell. Now ladies and gentlemen, we're going to move through the crowds here to eavesdrop on some of the holiday talk. Then we're going to interview Santa Claus himself! (*Moves off stage, followed by the crowds and technicians. Two of the children who have been watching the broadcast,* RUTHY *and* RICKY, *stay behind.* RICKY *goes over to* MISS SNELL *at her counter.*)

RICKY: Excuse me, ma'am.

MISS SNELL: Yes, young man? What can I do for you? Do you want to buy one of these dolls for a Christmas present?

RICKY: No, not exactly.

MISS SNELL: What is it, then?

RICKY: It's about that contest.

MISS SNELL: Yes?

RICKY: Are they really giving fifty dollars for the best name?

MISS SNELL: Indeed we are! Maybe you or your sister can win! Just think up a good name. . . .

RICKY: Gee, fifty dollars!

RUTHY: Just for a name!

RICKY: If we had fifty dollars, we could buy presents for everybody!

RUTHY: Maybe we could even get one of these dolls for Patsy.

RICKY: But I've got only fourteen cents, and you have sixteen.

RUTHY: Oh, wouldn't it be fun if we could buy presents for everybody? If only we could think of a name!

RICKY: We can try. Somebody's got to win.

RUTHY: The contest closes at 3:30.

RICKY: That gives us thirty minutes. We ought to be able to think of lots of names in half an hour.

RUTHY: If only we could think of fifty dollars' worth! But we have as much chance of winning that money as the man on the moon! I wonder if they have Christmas on the moon. Do you think they do?

RICKY: I think they have to have Christmas everywhere, because it wouldn't be December without Christmas. There wouldn't be anything to wait for all year.

RUTHY: That's right. I don't see how people could live without Christmas! (*There is a great commotion and stir of voices off left.*)

RICKY (*Looking off*): I wonder what all the noise is about? Everyone seems to be running!

Miss Snell: Children, can you see what's happening over there? Has someone been hurt?

Ricky: There are so many people, I can't see over their heads. Come on, Ruthy. (*They hurry towards left, as* Mr. Winkle *enters quickly.*)

Mr. Winkle (*Excitedly*): Did he come this way, Miss Snell?

Miss Snell (*Puzzled*): Who, Mr. Winkle?

Mr. Winkle: I was sure I saw him dart in here. But I don't see him anywhere!

Miss Snell: *Whom* don't you see, Mr. Winkle?

Mr. Winkle: Why, the little fellow in blue, of course!

Ruthy *and* Ricky (*Together*): A little fellow in blue?

Mr. Winkle: The one who just came rocketing through the ceiling of my toy department! He tore a hole in the ceiling.

Miss Snell: Mr. Winkle, are you sure you haven't been working too hard?

Mr. Winkle: I know it sounds queer, Miss Snell, but a little fellow in blue *did* come rocketing through the ceiling just a few minutes ago. And we've got to find him! It could be the biggest publicity stunt in years!

Miss Snell: Did you see anyone like that come in here, children?

Ruthy: No, we didn't.

Mr. Winkle: Well, you look that way, Miss Snell (*Points left*), and I'll look this way (*Points right*). We'll find him yet!

Miss Snell (*Shrugging her shoulders*): Very well, Mr. Winkle. (*She goes off left, and* Mr. Winkle *goes off right.*)

Ricky: What do you suppose *that* was all about? Do you think there really *was* a little fellow in blue?

Ruthy: There couldn't have been! We'd have seen him. (Ricky *and* Ruthy *are standing downstage of the*

*counter, with their backs to it. Cos pokes his head out
from behind the counter and listens to their conversation.*)

Cos (*Stepping out from behind the counter*): But you
didn't. I slipped in behind the counter when you were
looking the other way. I'm used to slipping and sliding.

Ruthy (*Holding on to Ricky, frightened*): Well, what
. . . who are you?

Ricky: Where did you come from?

Cos (*Proudly*): You heard what the man said. I came
whizzing right down through the ceiling of this place.

Ruthy: Didn't you hurt yourself?

Cos: Oh no, not me. I'm used to whizzing through space.
It's all I've been doing this past month.

Ricky: My name's Ricky. This is my sister, Ruthy. What's
your name?

Cos: Where I come from, we don't have names—just numbers. It's simpler that way. I'm Number 2376594867
dash X49!

Ruthy (*Laughing*): Oh dear, what a long number! We
could never call you that!

Cos: Well then, call me Cos, if you want, since I came out
of the cosmos.

Ricky: Cosmos? Cosmos! I never heard of it. Is it in
Illinois? (NOTE: *Use name of state in which play is
being performed.*)

Cos: I should say not! It's the universe! The cosmos
stretches billions and billions of miles out from here in
every direction. Do you mean to say you never heard of
the cosmos?

Ruthy: I saw it in the dictionary once, but it didn't have
a picture.

Cos: Why, this earth you live on is only a speck of dust,
compared to the cosmos.

Ricky: Honest?

Cos: The cosmos is a mammoth collection of stars and planets moving around in space and never getting out of line. Take me, for instance: I come from one of the smaller planets.

Ricky: You wouldn't kid us, would you?

Cos: I should say not. I'm a very serious fellow! We're all serious people where I come from. Maybe that's the trouble.

Ruthy: What trouble? That your planet is so far away?

Cos: No, no! That we're serious. You see, we realize that we lack something on our planet. We have life figured out from A to Z and from 1 to 100—yet we lack something. Our king realizes it, but he can't put his finger on it. Our wise men know it, but they don't like to admit it. We all know we lack something, but we don't know what it is.

Ricky: That sounds serious, all right— I mean, if we can take you seriously.

Cos: You *must* take me seriously. That's why I'm here.

Ruthy: Oh!

Cos: I have been sent on a mission. You'll have to forgive the sudden way I came, but I suppose it was meant to be like this.

Ricky: How did you get here anyway, Cos? Are there jets on your planet, too?

Cos: Jets? Humph! We gave up flying machines back in the dark ages on our planet. They're too slow. We've figured out a way to get comets to take us where we want to go. We hang on to their tails and steer by radio, and away we go! We carry an auxiliary rocket for making a landing.

Ruthy: That sounds like magic!

Cos: Sure, everything's magic. The whole cosmos! I know, because I come from a specially progressive part of it.

On our planet we spend most of our waking hours thinking about serious things.

RICKY: Say, with all that practice, do you suppose you could think of a name for a doll contest?

COS (*Scornfully*): Serious things, I said! Look—as a result of our thinking, we've solved all the problems of science, arithmetic and spelling. We have organized industry so that no one has to work more than two hours a day. No one on our planet ever goes hungry—or even needs to have his shoes resoled. We have figured things out so carefully that we no longer have unemployment, mosquitoes, sneezes, below-zero weather or weeds in our gardens. In short, we think we have everything except . . .

RICKY: Except?

RUTHY: Except?

COS: Except whatever it is that we lack. Something I haven't been able to find! Yet . . .

MR. WINKLE'S VOICE (*From off stage*): There he is by the contest display! (MR. WINKLE *and* MR. BANKS *enter from right;* MISS SNELL *and the* ANNOUNCER *enter from left.*)

MR. WINKLE (*Rushing up to* COS): So here you are!

MR. BANKS (*Grabbing* COS's *arm*): Better hold on to him, Mr. Winkle! He might try to slip away again!

ANNOUNCER (*Talking into microphone eagerly*): Ladies and gentlemen out there in radioland, this is the most amazing thing I've ever seen. Mr. Winkle, the owner of this store, and Mr. Banks, the advertising manager, have captured a little fellow in blue who came plummeting through the toy department roof out of nowhere. They're about to question him, ladies and gentlemen, and you'll be able to hear it all. This is a rare interview indeed, brought to you through the courtesy of the

Mammoth Department Store. (ANNOUNCER *holds microphone so that it can pick up the following.*)

COS: Let go of me.

RUTHY: You can let go of him, sir. He won't hurt anyone! He was sent here on a mission, and he *had* to land somewhere.

MR. WINKLE (*Releasing him*): What's your name?

COS: Cos. It stands for cosmos. That's where I come from!

MR. BANKS: From the Cosmos! Just think, Mr. Winkle, what publicity copy this will make. "Visitor from Cosmos comes to Toyland." *Our* Toyland!

MR. WINKLE: And how did you know about our Toyland here in the Mammoth Department Store?

COS: I'm looking for something, and I thought this might be the place to find it.

MR. WINKLE: Certainly this is the place to find it. Look around! Our slogan is: "We can fill your every need!" We have thousands of items—the largest stock of any store in the world.

MR. BANKS (*Happily*): Satisfaction guaranteed, or your money back!

MR. WINKLE: What is it that you need, Cos? Speak up. I'm sure we have it!

RUTHY: The trouble is, Cos doesn't know what he needs!

RICKY: He's looking for something he's never heard of before.

MR. WINKLE (*Patronizingly*): Take your time and look around, Cos. Nobody has ever been disappointed in our stock yet.

ANNOUNCER (*Into mike*): Ladies and gentlemen, while the little fellow from the cosmos is trying to collect his thoughts, let's listen to the Chorus sing another favorite song. (CHORUS *enters and sings "Jolly Old St. Nicholas." As they sing, COS listens, a look of curiosity on his face. After the song, the CHORUS exits.*)

COS: That was a nice tune, but what's it all about?

RUTHY: It's about jolly old St. Nicholas.

COS: Who's he? I've never heard of him anywhere in the cosmos.

RICKY: You haven't!

RUTHY: He's the same as Santa Claus. You've heard of Santa Claus, of course.

COS: No, I haven't. You see, where I come from, nobody has names—just numbers!

RICKY: You mean you've never heard of Santa Claus? What kind of Christmas do you have, anyway?

COS: Christmas? Christmas? Who's Christmas? (*Everyone is astounded and begins to talk at once.* SHOPPERS *begin to enter at both sides, and stand at the sides of the stage.*)

RUTHY *and* RICKY: Never heard of Christmas!

MISS SNELL: Why, that's amazing!

MR. WINKLE: It's preposterous!

COS (*Protesting*): But it's true!

ANNOUNCER (*Excitedly, into mike*): Ladies and gentlemen, this is positively the most amazing thing I've ever reported! I wish I had a television camera here so you could see the look of surprise on everyone's face! The little fellow has actually never heard of Christmas!

COS (*Plaintively*): Won't someone tell me what all the fuss is about? What *is* Christmas, anyway?

RUTHY: Why, it's the most important holiday in the world!

RICKY: It's the most fun . . .

RUTHY: *And* the most beautiful.

1ST CHILD SHOPPER: We hang red bells around the house, bright like the sound of Christmas music.

2ND CHILD SHOPPER: And on top of the tree we put a star, as gold as the star of Bethlehem.

RUTHY: And in the windows, we hang wreaths of green and red, the colors of Christmas.

RICKY: Everywhere there is music, bringing tidings of great joy: "Peace on earth, good will to men."

3RD CHILD SHOPPER: And in the crèche, the Christ Child lies in the manger near the sheep and cows.

4TH CHILD SHOPPER: There are presents wrapped in colored paper under the Christmas tree.

RUTHY: And in the window, we set a lighted candle to show the Christ Child the way.

RICKY: And everybody is happy, and the church bells ring.

COS (*Jumping up and down, joyfully*): That's it! That's the very thing!

MR. WINKLE: What very thing?

COS (*Excited*): It's what we lack on our planet. Christmas!

CHILDREN: Christmas! Christmas!

COS: We have figured out all the problems of science, arithmetic and spelling. We have done more thinking on our planet than people have done anywhere else. But —we don't have Christmas! We used only our minds; we forgot about our hearts.

RICKY: Without Christmas, you miss the best part of the year.

COS: That's just what I've been finding out.

RUTHY: You miss the magic of the year. Nothing else is like Christmas.

COS: Ah . . . my mission is over. I am going to take Christmas and all it means back to my planet!

MR. WINKLE: Did you hear that, Mr. Banks? He's going to take Christmas back to his planet! Isn't that wonderful? (*Suddenly getting a thought*) But does that mean he isn't going to buy anything?

MR. BANKS: That doesn't matter. The publicity alone is worth a fortune! Cos, come along with me, will you?

Since you got the idea for Christmas right here in Toyland, we'd like to have a picture of you and Mr. Winkle for the newspapers.

Cos: But I wouldn't show on a picture. I'd just be a blank. My wave lengths are different, you know. Here. Take a picture of Ruthy and Ricky instead. They're my friends, the best friends I have on Earth. I'm grateful to them and to all of you for this wonderful gift of Christmas. Merry Christmas, everybody! (*With a sudden dash,* Cos *exits. Shrill noise of slide whistle is heard off-stage.*)

Mr. Winkle (*Alarmed*): He's getting into his rocket. Stop him, somebody! (*Rushes out*)

Mr. Banks: I'm sure we could get a picture with our up-to-date equipment. (*Rushes out. Crowd hurries off,* Ricky *and* Ruthy *remain.*)

Ruthy: He's gone, and they won't catch him. I'll bet he's up through the roof already, heading for the cosmos. Oh, Ricky, did you ever see such excitement?

Ricky: Do you believe it, Ruthy?

Ruthy (*Slowly*): Yes, yes, I believe it. It's part of the magic of Christmas.

Ricky: Well, I don't. It was just an advertising stunt, that's all. Just a stunt to sell something. I'll bet my fourteen cents it isn't true.

Ruthy: Your fourteen cents! Ricky! We forgot all about the contest!

Ricky: That's right—the contest. We haven't thought of a name yet!

Ruthy: How could we? We were too busy thinking about Cos. Ricky, he must have come from another world. He looked so different.

Ricky: Yes, he looked different. (*Thoughtfully*) And yet, Ruthy, didn't he remind you of somebody we've seen before?

Ruthy (*Slowly*): Yes—he *did* remind me of someone.

RICKY: I can't think who, though. Can you?

RUTHY (*Suddenly*): The dolls! Ricky, he looked like the dolls. Not like people in this world. He looked—

RICKY: Cosmic! That's the way he looked!

RUTHY: Cosmic! I wonder . . .

RICKY: That's *it,* Ruthy!

RUTHY: That's what?

RICKY: Cosmic Wonder. That's the name for the dolls! It took both of us to think of it. It just fits those dolls, don't you think? "Cosmic Wonder" dolls!

RUTHY: Let's hurry and enter the contest. There are only a few minutes left.

RICKY: I hope nobody else thought of that name.

RUTHY: Miss Snell! Miss Snell! (MISS SNELL *comes hurrying in.*)

MISS SNELL: He's gone, disappeared. There's not a sign of him anywhere. (*Sees children*) What can I do for you?

RUTHY: We'd like an entry blank for the contest.

MISS SNELL (*Handing her a slip of paper*): Here you are. (*Dreamily*) The little fellow is gone. (*Back to earth*) You'd better hurry and fill in the blank. I have to turn all of the slips in to Mr. Banks in just a minute or two. (RUTHY *sits down, takes pencil out of her pocket, and begins to write.*)

RUTHY (*Continuing to write*): It's almost filled in.

RICKY: Hurry, Ruthy, hurry! (MR. BANKS *and* MR. WINKLE *enter.*)

MR. BANKS: Do you have the rest of the contest entries, Miss Snell? There's just time to judge the last batch before our program goes off the air. Whew! What an afternoon!

MISS SNELL: I'm just waiting for the last one.

RUTHY (*Getting up and handing entry to* MISS SNELL): There! It's finished. (MISS SNELL *takes* RUTHY'S *entry, puts it on pile on her desk.*)

MISS SNELL (*As she straightens pile, then picks up all of the entries and hands them to* MR. BANKS.): Here you are, Mr. Banks. (CHORUS *enters.*)

ANNOUNCER: And now, ladies and gentlemen, while the judges are deciding the winner of the doll contest, we shall hear another selection by the Mammoth Department Store's Carolers. (CHORUS *sings another Christmas carol. At the end of song,* CHORUS *exits.*) And now we come to the high point in this afternoon's program. Mr. Banks, the advertising manager of the Mammoth Department Store, will announce the winner of the doll-naming contest. Mr. Banks.

MR. BANKS: Ladies and gentlemen, before announcing the winner, I want to thank everyone here who participated in this contest, and particularly those who helped our visitor, Cos, discover what his planet lacked. Mr. Winkle and I have selected the winning name, and considering all that has happened here this afternoon, it's a very appropriate name indeed. The winners of the doll-naming contest are Ruthy and Ricky Riggs.

RUTHY *and* RICKY (*Jumping up and down excitedly*): We won, we won!

MR. BANKS: The winning name is "Cosmic Wonder." (*Turning to* RUTHY *and* RICKY) Congratulations, Ruthy and Ricky. I'm glad to give you this prize of fifty dollars. (*He takes envelope from his pocket and hands it to* RUTHY.)

RUTHY: Thanks a lot, Mr. Banks!

RICKY: That's great. Now we can buy presents for everybody!

MR. BANKS: And now everyone can have a memento of this eventful day by purchasing a Cosmic Wonder doll, made especially for the Mammoth Department Store.

MR. WINKLE (*Slightly aside*): Maybe 50,000 dolls won't be enough.

MR. BANKS (*To* RUTHY *and* RICKY): Your pictures will be in the paper tomorrow.

MR. WINKLE: Say, aren't you the ones Cos said should have their pictures taken?

MR. BANKS: Yes, they are. Do you suppose he knew ahead of time?

RUTHY: Oh, Ricky. *Now* will you believe there's a magic in Christmas?

RICKY: I can believe in *anything* now . . . even the Cosmos! (*As the curtains close, all join in singing "Jolly Old St. Nicholas."*)

THE END

Christmas in Court

Characters

POLICE OFFICER   BOYS AND GIRLS
HOLLY   JUDGE
IVY   JURY
MRS. STICKLE   CHRISTMAS TREE
MISTLETOE

SCENE 1

TIME: *A few days before Christmas.*
SETTING: *In front of the curtain.*
BEFORE RISE: HOLLY *and* IVY *come in from one side.*

HOLLY: Oh, aren't you glad it's almost Christmas, Ivy? Now we'll be in the spotlight again. (*She does a little dance.*)

IVY: I'm afraid I'm not in your class, though, Holly. You're so bright and shiny and red and green for Christmas. I'm only green. And people don't go in for ivy-decorated wassail bowls the way they used to in Merrie Old England. I tell you, I was much in favor in those days when Christmas came around.

HOLLY: You're still in favor, and don't let anyone say otherwise!

All songs in this script can be found in *A Treasury of Christmas Songs and Carols,* published by Houghton Mifflin Company, Boston, 1955.

Ivy: Of course, I'm still in the "Wassail Song," and everybody knows that.

HOLLY: Practically everybody.

Ivy (*Singing*): "Here we come a-wassailing
  Among the leaves so green . . ." That's *me*. The leaves so green. Green for Christmas when most leaves are dead and dry.

HOLLY: I like "The Holly and the Ivy" carol even better, because we're *both* in it. (OFFICER *comes in and stands near wings, listening. He takes a piece of paper from his pocket, consults it, puts it back in pocket.* HOLLY *sings.*)
  "The holly and the ivy
  When they are both full grown,
  Of all the trees that are in the wood,
  The holly bears the crown." (Ivy *joins in chorus.*
  HOLLY *and* Ivy *start out, see* OFFICER, *nod cheerily as they pass.*)

HOLLY *and* Ivy: Merry Christmas, Officer. Isn't it wonderful!

OFFICER: Same to you. Yes, it is. (*He begins to cross stage, looking up and around, baffled.* MRS. STICKLE *hurries in.*)

MRS. STICKLE: Officer! Officer! May I speak to you a moment? (*He turns and waits.*) You are prepared to do your duty this Christmas season, I trust? You have received the new instructions from headquarters?

OFFICER (*Taking out paper*): You mean *this?*

MRS. STICKLE (*Looking*): Yes, of course. The Campaign to Remove the Frills and Fripperies from Christmas. Those foolish displays that have nothing to do with the true meaning of the holiday! Our Ladies' Club is behind the campaign, and we mean to get action. Something should have been done about it ages ago.

OFFICER: Frills and fripperies? (*He pushes back his cap and scratches his head.*)

Mrs. Stickle: You have your instructions. The Ladies' Club is depending on the police force to get into this campaign with both feet, as it were, and sweep the Christmas scene clean, right down to the fundamentals.

Officer: If I only knew what you were talking about, madam . . .

Mrs. Stickle: What I am talking about? You realize why we celebrate Christmas, don't you?

Officer: Because it's the birthday of the Christ Child, you mean?

Mrs. Stickle: Exactly. That's what the word Christmas stands for—Christ-mass. And the Ladies' Club, of which I am president, takes the position that anything in the celebration not related to the birth of Christ ought to be done away with. No more frills and fripperies!

Officer (*Thinking hard*): Hmmm. Let's see, now. Santa Claus doesn't have anything to do with the birth of the Christ Child, does he? Do you mean I am to hail Santa Claus into court if I see him?

Mrs. Stickle (*Flustered*): Well, n-o-o-o. The Chamber of Commerce insists that we make an exception for Santa Claus. They say their plans for a Santa Claus celebration have gone too far to stop. But there are other fripperies, Officer. Plenty of them. And you have your instructions from headquarters.

Officer (*Glancing this way and that*): But, ma'am, I really don't know what to look for. (Holly *and* Ivy *return, arm in arm, singing* "What Sweeter Music." *They sing the fourth stanza and chorus:* "Which we will give Him, and bequeath/This holly and this ivy wreath," *etc.* Officer *and* Mrs. Stickle *stand back and watch as* Holly *and* Ivy *cross the stage.*)

Mrs. Stickle (*Excited*): There, Officer, is a frill, if I ever saw one. Two, in fact! Holly and Ivy.

OFFICER: Them? Why, they've been around for years and never caused a particle of trouble.

MRS. STICKLE: But what have Holly and Ivy to do with the Christ Child's birthday? Can you tell me that?

OFFICER: No—I'm afraid I can't.

MRS. STICKLE (*Giving him a little push*): Then do your duty. (*He reluctantly goes out after* HOLLY *and* IVY. MRS. STICKLE *calls after him.*) And do your duty with all the other frills and fripperies you come across, too! (MISTLETOE *comes jigging in, chanting.*)

MISTLETOE: "The mistletoe hung in the castle hall,
The holly branch shone on the old oak wall,
And the Baron's retainers were blithe and gay,
And keeping their Christmas holiday."

MRS. STICKLE (*Advancing on him sternly, shaking her finger*): Mistletoe! You—you little frippery you!

MISTLETOE (*Taken aback*): Me?

MRS. STICKLE: Yes, you. (*She starts to run after him, but* MISTLETOE *runs faster. They both exit. Just after they go out, a group of* BOYS *and* GIRLS *come from the other side of stage, singing the second stanza of a carol written by a group of high school students in 1902—"A Day of Joy and Feasting." They sing second stanza and chorus only.*)

BOYS *and* GIRLS: "All hail the shining holly,
All hail the mistletoe," etc. (*They exit.*)

* * *

SCENE 2

SETTING: *A courtroom, where a trial is already in progress.*

AT RISE: JUDGE *sits behind desk in middle of stage toward back.* JURY *sits at one side; chairs and table for the defendants are at the other side.* OFFICER *with* HOLLY *and* MRS. STICKLE *are standing before the* JUDGE. IVY,

MISTLETOE, *and* CHRISTMAS TREE *are seated at de-fendants' table.*

JUDGE (*Somewhat baffled*): Do you mean to say, Officer, that this defendant is a frill and a frippery?

OFFICER (*Nodding toward* MRS. STICKLE): That's what *she* says, Your Honor. She's behind all this, she and her Ladies' Club.

MRS. STICKLE: If it please the Court, our campaign has the approval of the City Council. The Mayor, as you may be aware, is my husband. I submit that the defendant, Holly, should have no place in our observance of Christmas. She has nothing to do with the true meaning of the holiday, which everyone knows is supposed to commemorate the birth of the Christ Child.

JUDGE (*To* HOLLY): What do you have to say for yourself, young lady?

HOLLY: All I can say is that I came first, Your Honor.

MRS. STICKLE: First? First? What do you mean?

JUDGE: Explain yourself, Holly.

HOLLY: Centuries before the birth of Christ, the Romans used me for decorations at their winter festival. That came just after the shortest day of the year. They liked me for my bright green leaves and red berries at a time when days were dark and dreary.

JUDGE: I can certainly understand that.

HOLLY: And in ancient Britain, Ireland, and France the Druid priests used to hang me indoors—so the spirits of the forests would have a place to go during bad weather.

OFFICER (*Much interested*): And this was *before* the birth of Christ? (*To* JUDGE) Your Honor, if Holly came first, I don't see that there is anything the Ladies' Club can do about it—if it please the Court.

HOLLY: I came first, and I came afterward, too. Oh, I was quite somebody in Merrie Old England. (*Looks around nervously*) I wish the carolers would come. They promised to be witnesses for me . . . (*There is commotion in the audience. Then* BOYS *and* GIRLS *come up gaily singing "Deck the Halls with Boughs of Holly". They do their song and dance on stage, others moving back to make room for them, then go back to their places in the audience.*)

JUDGE: Everyone loves that famous old Welsh carol. Do you mean to say, Mrs. Stickle, you'd like to do away with it?

MRS. STICKLE (*Stubbornly*): It hasn't anything to do with the true meaning of Christmas. And neither has Holly.

HOLLY: But I *do* have a connection with Christmas, Your Honor!

JUDGE: How's that, Miss?

HOLLY: The Christmas colors are my colors—red and green. And there's an old tradition in our family that the holly tree was once called the *holy* tree, because it sprang up beneath the footsteps of Christ. (OFFICER *gives* MRS. STICKLE *an I-told-you-so look.*)

HOLLY: And I am supposed to be the symbol of the crown of thorns which Christ wore—with my prickly leaves and bright berries.

JUDGE (*Nodding judiciously*): Pertinent evidence, I should say. (*To* MRS. STICKLE) Do you have any more evidence to bring against this defendant, Madam?

MRS. STICKLE (*Confused*): No, not right now, Your Honor.

JUDGE: Now or never! (*To* JURY) It won't be necessary for you to retire to the jury room in this case. Ladies and gentlemen of the jury, do you find Holly guilty or not guilty?

JURY (*Loudly*): Not guilty!

JUDGE: Charges dismissed. (*Nods at* OFFICER, *who takes*

HOLLY *to her seat at the table.*) Next? (OFFICER *brings* IVY.)

IVY (*Timidly*): Your Honor, I'm not important like Holly. Nowadays people make very little fuss over me. But I came first, too.

MRS. STICKLE: You did?

IVY: Yes. The Romans used me in their wintertime festival because they liked my green color. They thought I expressed joy—in the midst of winter.

OFFICER: And was that before the manger in Bethlehem, and the shepherds watching their flocks in the fields, and the bright star in the sky, and the Wise Men?

IVY: Oh, yes, long before. And later in Merrie England I was an important decoration around the wassail bowl, and . . .

MRS. STICKLE (*Hurriedly*): I consent to have the charges against Ivy dismissed, Your Honor. Ivy isn't much of a frill any more, anyway. But I intend to press the charges against Mistletoe, I can tell you!

JUDGE: Next, please. (OFFICER *takes* IVY *to seat and brings* MISTLETOE.)

MRS. STICKLE (*Gesturing toward* MISTLETOE): Your Honor, if anything can be more of a frippery as far as Christmas is concerned, I'd like to know what it is. This absurd habit of kissing under a sprig of mistletoe! I submit that the defendant is guilty on the face of things. And such a silly name, too—Mistletoe.

JUDGE: The defendant will state his case.

MISTLETOE: Your Honor, I too have a long and ancient history. I don't have a tree of my own, but I grow on other trees, and they don't seem to mind. And as for my name . . .

MRS. STICKLE: Mistle-toe! It hasn't a leg to stand on!

MISTLETOE: There is a perfectly good reason for it, really. The first mistletoe plant is supposed to have been

brought from heaven by a missel thrush, a messenger of
the gods. One day the thrush appeared with a berry
stuck to his toe. He rubbed the seed off on the bark of
a tree, and it took root and started to grow. That's how
I got my name. And I've been growing on trees ever
since.

MRS. STICKLE: This has nothing to do with the case,
Your Honor.

OFFICER: Except that Mistletoe was here first, too, madam.
Before that night when there wasn't any room in the
inn.

MISTLETOE: Oh, yes, long before. I was used in the celebration of the winter solstice, just like Holly and Ivy. Because of the enduring green of my foliage and the purity
of my berries, I was thought of as a symbol of peace and
hope. The Druids considered me very important.

MRS. STICKLE: Well, I don't.

MISTLETOE: As for the habit of kissing under a sprig of
mistletoe, there is a perfectly good reason for it.

MRS. STICKLE: Ridiculous!

MISTLETOE: It wasn't ridiculous at all, Your Honor. Back
in the old days, mistletoe was a symbol of peace, and so
the Druids gave sprigs to the people to hang up in their
houses. Whenever two people met under the mistletoe
they were expected to embrace and forget all their
disagreements and jealousies. That is how the custom of
kissing under the mistletoe began, and I don't think it's
such a bad custom, do you, Your Honor? It's certainly
better than quarreling.

JUDGE: It's a case for the Jury to decide. (*Turns to* JURY)
Do you find Mistletoe guilty or not guilty?

JURY: Not guilty!

JUDGE: Case dismissed. (*Consults paper*) And now we
come to the last defendant on today's docket—Christ-

mas Tree. (OFFICER *conducts* MISTLETOE *to his seat and brings* CHRISTMAS TREE *before* JUDGE.)

MRS. STICKLE: The biggest frippery of all, in size and shape and the absurdity of its ornaments! (*As* CHRISTMAS TREE *takes his place before the* JUDGE, *the* JURY *rises and begins to sing "O Tannenbaum.*")

JURY: "We stand before the Christmas tree,
A symbol for the faithful:
Its foliage green will always grow
Through summer sun and winter snow:
We stand before the Christmas tree,
A symbol for the faithful."

MRS. STICKLE: I object, Your Honor! The Jury is definitely prejudiced. How can we have a fair trial with a prejudiced jury?

JUDGE (*Waving* JURY *to be seated*): I am afraid it would be impossible to find an impartial jury, madam, where Christmas trees are concerned. But calm yourself. The Jury is under oath to judge the case solely on its merits. (*To* JURY) You will bear that in mind, each and all of you.

JURY: Yes, Your Honor.

JUDGE: Proceed with the testimony. Christmas Tree has the floor.

MRS. STICKLE: I suppose you'll say you came first, too.

CHRISTMAS TREE: I am probably the oldest of all symbols in the celebration of the winter festival, Mrs. Stickle. I was used even before history was written down, but of course just as an evergreen, not with lights and decorations. That came later.

MRS. STICKLE: Frills and fripperies!

CHRISTMAS TREE: I date back to the ancient Germans and Scandinavians. Their time of great festivity was the period from the shortest day to about Twelfth Night. That was when they celebrated the return of the sun and the lengthening of days. As a tree that stayed fresh and green in the coldest weather, I was the symbol of enduring life.

OFFICER: Fair enough.

CHRISTMAS TREE: In fact, many ancient people thought of me as the "tree of life."

MRS. STICKLE: All of which has absolutely nothing to do with Christmas.

CHRISTMAS TREE: Your Honor, I wish to make the point that it was a famous religious leader who first thought of making me into a Christmas tree.

MRS. STICKLE: It can't be true.

CHRISTMAS TREE: There is a tradition of long standing in my family that Martin Luther originated the Christmas Tree. That was more than 400 years ago. It happened like this. When Martin Luther was walking home along a forest road one Christmas Eve, he was struck by the beauty of the stars glinting in the branches of fir trees. So he cut down a little fir, took it home, and had his wife put on lighted candles to represent the stars. Then he woke up his children to see the lighted tree.

MRS. STICKLE: He did? Goodness, I don't believe the Ladies' Club ever heard of that!

OFFICER: Too many frills on their mind!

CHRISTMAS TREE: Martin Luther thought the lights on the tree would remind people not only of the beauty of the heavens but of "the Light that lighteth every man that cometh into the world."

MRS. STICKLE: Oh, then you *do* have something to do with Christmas!

CHRISTMAS TREE: To those with eyes to see, the shine of a Christmas tree represents the light of the Saviour's birth.

JURY (*Singing softly*): "We stand before the Christmas tree,
A symbol for the faithful."

MRS. STICKLE: Judge, if you'll excuse me, I want to call a special meeting of the Ladies' Club immediately. I am afraid there has been a great lack of understanding about the frills and fripperies of Christmas. I must set the ladies straight. Officer, would you mind handing me those instructions from headquarters? (OFFICER *hands her the slip of paper. She tears it to pieces, then turns and nods to* JURY, JUDGE, *and defendants.*) The campaign is definitely called off. (*Smiles cheerfully*) For all the many joyous, wonderful things Christmas stands for, I wish you a happy holiday on behalf of the Ladies' Club and myself. Merry Christmas, everyone!

OTHERS: Merry Christmas! (MRS. STICKLE *hurries out as* JURY *and others on stage join ranks to dance and sing* "*Deck the Halls.*" *Curtain.*)

THE END

Calling All Christmases

(A mock broadcast)

Characters

MASTER OF CEREMONIES (M.C.)
CHILDREN'S CHORUS, *any number of voices*
PEDRO OF MEXICO
EDWINA AND JONATHAN OF ENGLAND
ANDERS OF SWEDEN
HILDA OF HOLLAND
JEAN AND JEANNETTE OF FRANCE
DIEGO OF SPAIN
FRIEDA OF GERMANY
ANTONIO OF ITALY
GIRL, *from studio audience.*

SETTING: *Bare stage with a "microphone" (real or facsimile) near front of stage and another near rear of stage. There is a row of chairs near back of stage for chorus.*

AT RISE: MASTER OF CEREMONIES *stands in front of microphone at front of stage throughout the program. Members of* CHORUS *and children with speaking parts are seated near back of stage.*

MASTER OF CEREMONIES: Ladies and gentlemen of the radio audience, Merry Christmas! Buon Natale! (Ex-

88

cuse me if my tongue gets twisted up.) Fröeliche Weinachten! Glaedelig Jul! . . . depending on the country
you inhabit. In other words, whoever you are, wherever
you live, we of the Globeview Network, U. S. A., send
you our Christmas greetings!

Today it is our pleasure to present a special Christmas broadcast, something new, at least, not done before on such a scale. We have arranged to call in boys
and girls from many different lands, and get reports on
Christmas, here and there: what songs the people sing,
what legends they believe—in other words, what Christmas means throughout the Christian world.

But first let's have a song to set the stage. Our children in the studio will sing a famous song about a newborn King. (CHORUS *sings "O Come, All Ye Faithful."*)

M. C. (*Excitedly*): My friends, the strangest thing! I'm
mystified. While they were singing, something happened here: a sudden light engulfed the studio. I never
saw a glow like that before! The engineer, behind his
house of glass, was baffled too. I saw him looking out in
wonderment. The strangest light . . .

But now I see the engineer is giving me a sign. Stand
by, my friends, a schoolboy down in Mexico is waiting
to be interviewed. Hello! This is the Globeview Network, U. S. A., calling Pedro. Are you there? Hello!
And what is Christmas like in Mexico?

PEDRO: I wonder if you'd rather hear about "Posadas" or
"piñata," if you please?

M. C.: Why, both of them! I'm sure we'd like to know.

PEDRO: "Posada" is the Spanish for an inn, a lodging
house. And the Posadas is a celebration here when fami-
lies act a sort of pilgrim-play and ask for shelter, just as
Joseph did when he and Mary entered Bethlehem. It
lasts nine nights, and ends on Christmas Eve. The members of the family gather first the 16th of December,

after dark, and say the Rosary, and sing a while. And then, with children in the lead, they go from room to room throughout the house, by candlelight, to seek a lodging place. There's someone waiting in the living room to answer when they knock. . . .

M. C.: And are they given shelter?

PEDRO: Eight nights they go from room to room and seek, but shelter is denied; and then at last, the ninth request (which comes on Christmas Eve) is answered "yes." Then everybody sings, and says a prayer, and the Posadas . . . well, it's over then.

M. C.: And what's the prayer, Pedro, that they say?

PEDRO: It goes like this: "O grant that we, good Lord, may never close our hearts against Thy knock."

M. C. (*Excitedly*): That light again! That golden flash of light—

PEDRO: Do I have time to tell how we get sweets and nuts on Christmas Eve?

M. C.: Three minutes yet. Go right ahead, my boy.

PEDRO: We have no Santa Claus, no Christmas trees, down here, in Mexico. The Magi bring us gifts and toys each year on Twelfth Night, which is January 6th, instead of on Christmas Day. But Christmas Eve, a jar of pottery ("piñata" it is called), which may look like a bird or animal, is decked with streamers and with paper fringe and then suspended in the patio. We children all are blindfolded, and come with sticks, and try to break the jar. It's fun! And when the jar is finally hit and cracked, the nuts and fruits and candies tumble down, and we go after them!

M. C.: I'll bet you do. Well, thank you, Pedro. We must leave you now—a signal from abroad is coming in. We send a hearty greeting to you all in Mexico! Hello. . . . Oh, Liverpool. . . . How's Christmas over there?

EDWINA: This is Edwina.

JONATHAN: This is Jonathan.

EDWINA: We don't know where to start. There's such a *lot* to Christmas over here, with Dickens, and the Christmas carols and all.

JONATHAN: Since British carols are famous, shall we sing you one?

M. C.: A good idea.

EDWINA: This old one comes from Wales. (EDWINA *and* JONATHAN *sing "Deck the Halls with Boughs of Holly."*)

M. C.: That's very nice. Now tell us something of the customs there at Christmas time, across the English countryside.

EDWINA: Well, England has been famous many years for its plum pudding . . .

M. C.: So it has indeed.

EDWINA: But do you know plum pudding was an accident, according to the stories people tell?

M. C.: An accident! How's that?

JONATHAN: It came about because the king got lost one time, in olden days . . .

M. C.: Because the king got lost? What's that you're saying?

EDWINA: You see, in olden times our king went hunting at Christmas time. Once, a storm came up, and so the king, his cook, and followers got stranded in the forest far from home.

JONATHAN: They had to stay all night. And next day was Christmas, too!

EDWINA: Their food supplies were rather low by then, and so the cook put everything he had into the pot, for dinner Christmas day.

JONATHAN: He put in flour, and since they had killed a stag the day before, he chopped up venison and added it . . . and eggs and apples and some English ale . . .

EDWINA: And dry, sweet plums. He took the stones out

first, and cracked the nuts, and put the nutmeats in. And then he put in sugar—all they had—and then he tried to stir.

JONATHAN: But it was sticky, very hard to mix. And so he pressed it in a cotton bag, and boiled it well, and . . .

EDWINA: That's the way plum pudding got its start! It's much the same today.

M. C.: Quite a story! Quite an accident! And now what else have you to say about your Christmas holiday?

EDWINA: We go to pantomimes, and bring the Yule log in . . .

JONATHAN: And don't forget, we English were the first to send out cards at Christmas time. 1846, I think it was, that someone thought of it.

EDWINA: We like to go to church on Christmas Day to hear about the Christ Child and the star.

M. C.: The light! My friends, the light has flashed again!

JONATHAN: Is that a signal we should leave the air?

M. C.: Your time is almost up, but no one sent a light to signal you. It's very mystifying.

JONATHAN: Well, cheerio, and Merry Christmas from us over here.

EDWINA: And, in the words of somebody you know, "God bless us, every one."

M. C.: We go to Sweden next. Hello, out there! Calling Sweden. Anders, take the air. . . .

ANDERS (*Faintly*): This is Anders speaking.

M. C.: The signal's not too clear.

ANDERS (*Louder*): Anders . . . Sweden. . . .

M. C.: There, that's better now. And what's a Swedish Christmas like, my boy?

ANDERS: It's wonderful. It lasts a good long time: the women clean and bake for weeks ahead, and oh, the things to eat! There's special bread, and special fish, and cakes, at Christmas time. And it's traditional, on Christmas Eve, to eat rice pudding cooked with milk, with cinnamon on top, and one lone almond lost somewhere inside. . . . Everybody served must say a poem, and the one who finds the almond in his dish, will have good luck all year!

M. C.: Good luck all year! That almond's worth a lot.

ANDERS: It surely is. I got it once myself! And now about our gifts. We always open them on Christmas Eve, around the tree, and there are funny rhymes and poems to read attached to wrappings. And we sing, and sing. And Christmas morning, early, we get up. . . .

M. C.: But why, when you get gifts the night before?

ANDERS: We go to church, a service before dawn. We go with torches, and with Christmas songs.

M. C.: The golden light! The light again, my friends, just blazed before us in the studio.

ANDERS: Beg pardon, sir?

M. C.: I'm sorry. Please go on . . . you have a minute yet. What else, my boy?

ANDERS: I want to say we put out sheaves for birds at Christmastime, in our country, atop high poles, so they can have a feast. We feed the stock more hay . . . because we feel good will for all the creatures, big and small, when Christmas comes. And now, "God Jul" to you from all of us in Sweden.

M. C.: The same to you! And now to Austria . . . to Franz and Lisa in the mountains there. (*Pause.*) Hello! Hello! (*Pause.*) Hello, in Austria. The signal's dead. I'm sorry, folks, but I have something here to interest you: a note about a famous Christmas carol an Austrian composed, a priest named Josef Mohr. He wrote it for a festival at church, and had a neighbor make a tune for it. The time was long ago, but Mohr's song spread.

(CHORUS *begins to sing softly, "Silent Night."*) And now it's sung in more than sixty languages. (CHORUS *sings more loudly, at least two stanzas.*)

The light has come again. The strangest thing! It touched that song from Austria with gold. . . . Well, we've a carol ourselves, our very own, American, that's rather famous too. A bishop by the name of Phillips Brooks composed the song, one year, for Sunday Schools. (CHORUS *sings several stanzas of "O Little Town of Bethlehem."*)

And once again the light has come and gone! Can anyone explain it? If you can, please wire or call the studio at once. . . . The engineer has signaled me just now; he has the circuit through to Amsterdam, to Hilda, waiting at the microphone.

HILDA: This is Hilda speaking.

M. C.: Good enough. And how is Christmas there?

HILDA: Why, some of it was over days ago—getting gifts, I mean. We get our presents in the Netherlands December 6th. St. Nicholas, or Sinterklaas, arrives the eve before (you call him Santa Claus). We don't hang stockings up, but use our shoes instead, and line them up beneath the mantelpiece with hay in them for Sinterklass's horse; and in the morning all the hay is gone and there are gifts instead.

M. C.: Imagine that! And on the 25th, on Christmas Day, what happens then?

HILDA: We go to church, and then there's visiting, and we remember it's the Christ child's day.

M. C. (*Softly*): The light again! Well, thank you, Hilda. Thank you very much. . . . We took the Santa Claus idea from them, the Hollanders. They brought the legend to New Amsterdam when they came over in the early days. The Saint who loved the children! We adopted it, and now St. Nick is popular, for sure. You know that famous poem by Clement Moore. (*Child from* CHORUS *recites "'Twas the Night Before Christmas."*)

M. C.: I see the engineer is warning me that France is standing by: Jeannette and Jean are ready to report on Christmas there. Come in, you two.

JEAN: I'm Jean.

JEANNETTE: And I'm Jeannette. We wish you all could see the manger scene, the crèche, we helped to fix. I'm sure St. Francis would approve of it—he was the first to make a crèche, you know, a long, long time ago, to help make people understand about the birth of Christ.

JEAN: The figures in our crèche are made of clay and very brightly painted, most of them. This year we added several extra sheep, and two new angels, and a new black King. The other broke.

JEANNETTE: We brought in moss and lichens and some laurel to make the setting. And little stones, as well. And Grandma sprinkled flour so it would look like snow.

JEAN: The child lies in the manger on real hay, and Mary kneels close by, and Joseph, too.

M. C.: The light! The light!

JEAN: We light it up with little candles, sir.

M. C.: Oh no, not that. I'm sorry I broke in. Now tell us something more . . .

JEANNETTE: We don't have Santa Claus in France, you know. But every Christmas Eve the Christ child comes, Petit Noël, we call him, and he fills our shoes with presents. The grownup's day is January first—for giving gifts, and hanging mistletoe!

JEAN: Let's not forget the Yule log. Is there time?

M. C.: Yes, time enough.

JEAN: The Yule log is a famous ritual—the family all take part. We bring it in, and carry it around the room three

times, for luck, you see. We try to get a log that's big
and firm, so it will last a week, from Christmas Eve.

JEANNETTE: We light it with a piece of last year's log we
kept for that. And every night we smother out the
flames to make our Yule log last.

M. C.: Thanks so much! Good holidays to all of you in
France! We switch you in a moment, friends, to Spain
. . . Diego . . . are you there?

DIEGO (*Very faintly*): Hello, hello.

M. C.: The signal isn't clear. I'm sorry, folks. We can't
get through to Spain. But I have something here about
the way the Spaniards celebrate the holidays. One moment, please. . . . Ah, here it is: The Spaniards always
go to Midnight Mass on Christmas Eve. (That baffling
light just flashed its rays across the studio!) They go to
Mass, I say, and after that they have processions in the
streets, and celebrate. The children get their gifts on
January 6th, the night the Wisemen are supposed to
pass, en route to Bethlehem. The children put their
shoes on balconies with straw inside to feed the Wisemen's camels, and, next day, the straw is gone, and
there are gifts instead.

The channel's open now to Germany. Stand by, my
friends. The singing you now hear is coming from a
German children's choir, to praise a fir tree with its tall
green spire. (CHORUS *sings "O Tannenbaum" but they
don't quite finish the first stanza when the connection
apparently fails. Singing stops abruptly.*)

M. C.: The signal failed, it seems. The engineers are trying to get it back. And meanwhile, friends, I'm sorry to
report our time runs short. We won't have time, I see,
to switch to Poland, with its famous puppet shows and
lovely carols for singing Christmas Eve; or Finland . . .
where the old-time custom was to plait the ceiling with
a canopy of straw and spread straw on the floor inside

the house, to call up visions of the manger scene. Or
Denmark . . . with its kindly little gnome, instead of
Santa Claus, a gnome that likes rice pudding Christmas
Eve, and brings the children gifts, and watches over all
the house all year. (CHORUS *singing "O Tannenbaum"*
heard again.)

M. C. (*As* CHORUS *comes on*): There's Germany again.
Ah, good enough! (CHORUS *finishes song, and* M. C.
continues.) That song's appropriate because, they say,
the Christmas tree originated in Germany. Who'll tell
us how it started? Someone . . . please . . .

FRIEDA: I'm Frieda. And I know of several tales about the
Christmas tree: how people, many, many years ago at
Christmas time would bring a fir tree in, and make it
bloom with paper flowers, and fruit, to show that spring
at last was on its way.

The story I like best is different, though. It tells how
Martin Luther, one cold night, was walking home—it
was on Christmas Eve—and as he passed a snowy, winter
wood (his mind upon the gospel that described the
birth of Christ), he looked up through the branches of
the firs, and saw the stars, like candles on the boughs.
Like stars of Bethlehem! He hurried home, and fixed a
Christmas tree—a little fir with candles on the boughs,
and woke his children up, and had them see . . .

M. C.: We saw a light ourselves! But brighter far than
candles, or the brightest silver star. . . . Well, thank
you, Frieda. That's a pretty tale. But time is getting
short, too short to take us *half* the places left. We won't
have time to visit Switzerland—where animals are said,
on Christmas Eve, to kneel and pray at midnight, at the
hour the Child was born. We won't have time to go to
South America, I fear. December comes in summer
there, you know. Imagine flowers in bloom, and summer heat—it's like July with us! The Christmas of the

South Americans is a religious holiday 'most everywhere, without a Santa Claus, or gifts . . . without a Christmas tree.

And now, Antonio, in Italy, is standing by with news of Christmas in that sunny land. Antonio . . .

ANTONIO: Buon Natale! We have no Santa Claus, or Christmas tree, but we have La Befana.

M. C.: Who is that?

ANTONIO: She brings us gifts on Twelfth Night, which, you know, is January 6th.

M. C.: Why then, Antonio?

ANTONIO: It's quite a story: Years and years ago when Jesus lay inside the stable, off in Bethlehem, three Kings set out to bring him gifts and praise. They passed Befana's house, and asked for help and hospitality. But she was much too busy with her work! And so she said, "Come back some other time." The Wisemen went away and never came again. Now every year Befana waits for them, on January 6th, and in remorse for her unfriendliness she leaves small gifts for girls and boys—if they've been good, of course!

M. C.: That story makes me think of one the Russians used to tell about Babouscka . . . very similar. But what, Antonio, of Christmas Eve and Day?

ANTONIO: On Christmas Eve the shepherds from the hills come down to towns and villages, and play—on bagpipes—simple country tunes in honor of the Child.

M. C.: The magic light has flashed again, my friends. We hope that someone will explain it soon. . . . What else, my boy? I'm sorry I broke in.

ANTONIO: Of course there's Midnight Mass in every church, and Christmas music. It is wonderful.

M. C.: I'm sure it is. And now, goodbye, Antonio. Our time is almost up, and still . . . how can we leave the air until we solve the mystery of that light? Does any-

body know what it could be? You members of the
chorus, can you say? Or someone in the audience who's
watched the broadcast in the studio today? What was
the light that flashed so many times? (*Pause.*) Did someone raise a hand? That child down there. . . . Yes?
Yes? Come up and tell us in the microphone. My
friends, a little girl, perhaps she's eight—she can't be
more than that—is coming up to speak. Perhaps she
knows; perhaps some deeper sight helps her to see the
light behind the light!

GIRL: I think the light is easy to explain.

M. C.: You do!

GIRL: It's what makes all the Christmases alike, no matter
where they are.

M. C.: Alike, you say? I didn't think they were alike at all.
I thought they all were different.

GIRL: They're alike in the *important* thing: the thing that
makes the light flash on like that.

M. C.: And what is that?

GIRL: Why, everybody knows! The Christmases are all
alike because they celebrate the Christ Child's birth, you
know. That's when the light flashed on; it flashed on
every time . . . for Him.

M. C.: Why, so it did. It flashed on, I remember, when
they sang, "O Come, Let Us Adore Him"; then again,
when Pedro spoke the little Christmas prayer; and when
we heard Edwina say they liked to go to church to hear
about the Christ Child and the star . . . and Anders,
too; and during "Silent Night" . . . and when they
sang "O Little Town of Bethlehem," as well, and all the
other times. . . . Why, yes, you're right: the light of
Christmas *is* the same, of course, throughout the Christian world.

GIRL: Without the Christ Child, Christmas wouldn't *be*.

M. C.: The legends, and the customs, and the tales, the

gifts, and Santa Claus . . . they change from time to time and place to place, but underneath it all, the same light shines, the light of lights that came into the world that winter night in Bethlehem.

And now, my friends, our time is up, I fear. So Merry Christmas, in a score of languages! Whoever you are, wherever you live, we of the Globeview Network, U.S.A., send you our Christmas greetings . . . send you our wishes that, throughout the year, the light of Christmas will stay close and clear.

THE END

On Such a Night

Characters

OLD WOMAN
OLD MAN
CHILDREN'S CHORUS
SHEPHERDS
THREE WISE MEN

TIME: *A few nights before Christmas.*
SETTING: *A farmhouse kitchen.*
AT RISE: *The* OLD WOMAN *is sitting in a rocker near the stove, knitting. The* OLD MAN *sits with his pipe, occasionally poking the fire, putting a rug in front of the door to keep out the wind, or looking out the window into the night.*

OLD WOMAN: Still snowing, you say?

OLD MAN: Still snowing.

OLD WOMAN: And cold?

OLD MAN: And cold. With a bitter wind.

OLD WOMAN (*Sighing*): Without the wind we might have gone.

OLD MAN: No. I told you, the car will not start. The engine won't turn over. Besides, how could we make the hill with the snow drifting? And four miles to the school-house.

OLD WOMAN: It is the first time we have missed in nineteen years.

OLD MAN: Eighteen. The first time in eighteen years.

OLD WOMAN: Nineteen! We missed the year Elma Hendriksen finished eighth grade. We missed hearing her sing "Silent Night" for the last time. And they say she never sang better. But you remember what a night it was.

OLD MAN: The year of the big snow. Eighteen years ago.

OLD WOMAN (*Shrugging*): All the same, all the same. Eighteen or nineteen—at our age it makes little difference. (*Dreamily*) What a voice Elma had! Head and shoulders above the others, I always said. (*Looks up from knitting*) Listen!

OLD MAN: Listen to what? The wind blowing? Is that it?

OLD WOMAN: Can't you hear? (*In the background* CHILDREN'S CHORUS *slowly crosses the stage singing "Silent Night." One voice is loud and clear above the others.*)

OLD MAN: Hear what? (*Cocks his head*) My ears are not what they once were.

OLD WOMAN: Head and shoulders above the others, I always said. (*The* OLD MAN *shrugs, puffs his pipe.* OLD WOMAN *listens intently. The* CHORUS *sings several stanzas, moving slowly offstage.*) Beautiful! Like old times.

OLD MAN: What are you talking about?

OLD WOMAN: The song, "Silent Night." (*Pause*) Perhaps . . . we could walk.

OLD MAN: On such a night? With the road covered with snow and the wind blowing? And four miles to the schoolhouse? Not for me.

OLD WOMAN: I could do it.

OLD MAN: You! If you got as far as Hendriksens', you would do well.

OLD WOMAN: There would still be time to walk. The

program does not start so early this year. Now the school is so small, children from town will come out to help, after their own program.

OLD MAN: So you have said. They will come out from town to help.

OLD WOMAN: I remember years there were eighteen, even twenty children in the school.

OLD MAN: Twenty-one even. I remember twenty-one, the year Carl finished.

OLD WOMAN: So many? (*Pause*) I remember Carl was always one of the shepherds.

OLD MAN (*Chuckling*): So he could follow the Star silently. So he would not have to speak. Afraid of his own voice, he was. (*In the background several boys dressed as* SHEPHERDS *come in. They see the Star, point at it in wonder, follow it offstage.*)

OLD WOMAN: I can see Carl still, following the Star. (*Sighs*) And now only five children in the school. Let me see, that would be . . . Mary . . . Joseph . . . and three shepherds.

OLD MAN: Why not three Wise Men instead of three shepherds?

OLD WOMAN: The Wise Men were later. You remember. They came after the shepherds, seeking the Christ Child.

OLD MAN (*Shrugging*): Well, no matter. There are still only five. It is no wonder they need help from town.

OLD WOMAN (*After a pause*): Still snowing?

OLD MAN (*Going to look*): Still snowing.

OLD WOMAN: And the wind?

OLD MAN: Still drifting the snow.

OLD WOMAN: It is just like *that other night.*

OLD MAN: What other night?

OLD WOMAN: The night of the play they had on the program, ten years ago.

OLD MAN: What play did they have?

OLD WOMAN: You don't remember? It was the story about the Wise Men who came knocking at the old woman's door, asking the way. In Russia.

OLD MAN: Not Russia. Surely not Russia. Italy!

OLD WOMAN: I remember, Russia. Just such a winter night as this, when the three Wise Men knocked on the door. The woman's name . . . I forget it now. But it began with "B" . . . (*Shrug*) "Ba . . . Ba . . ." She had a bright fire on the hearth and she had just cleaned the house, I remember.

OLD MAN: Yes, you would remember she had cleaned the house.

OLD WOMAN: Inside, warmth and comfort. Outside, cold and wind and snow.

OLD MAN: Like tonight.

OLD WOMAN: Just as I said.

OLD MAN: No. Wait a minute. How would there be so much cold and snow in Italy?

OLD WOMAN: In Russia, I tell you. And the woman—why do I forget her name? It began with "B."

OLD MAN: Now I too remember it began with "B" . . . but in Italy.

OLD WOMAN: She heard the knock at the door, and opened it. And there were the three Wise Men standing in the cold. They entered, carrying their gifts for the Christ Child. Gold, frankincense, and myrrh.

OLD MAN: In Russia?

OLD WOMAN: They were lost, you see. They were seeking their way through the storm to Bethlehem. The Star they followed was buried in the snowy sky. They asked the old woman to show them the way, but she would not leave the warmth and comfort of her house to guide them!

OLD MAN: Are you saying we should leave the warmth and comfort of our house and walk to the school? Is that it?

OLD WOMAN: She would not leave her warm fireside to guide them, and they went on alone through the night. Ever after she was filled with great regret.

OLD MAN: Only a story. Who would come, or go, on such a night?

OLD WOMAN: And ever after at Christmas time she went searching, searching all over Russia, looking for the Christ Child. She looked in all the children's faces, and left them little gifts. But she never found Him, the One she sought.

OLD MAN: Just a story, I say.

OLD WOMAN: A story of regret. (*There is stomping at the door, then loud knocking.*)

OLD MAN: What! On such a night, who can it be? (*Goes toward door*) Come in! (*Opens door.* THREE BOYS *enter. They are dressed as* WISE MEN, *under snowy jackets*)

OLD WOMAN (*Staring*): Can I believe my eyes? (*Goes to* BOYS, *peers at costumes*) The Wise Men. The three Wise Men.

OLD MAN: You think so?

1ST BOY: Yes, that's right.

2ND BOY: Can you show us a way? The road is so drifted the driver can't make the hill.

3RD BOY: Is there a way around?

OLD WOMAN: On such a night, as I said, the Wise Men came!

1ST BOY: The road is not too bad, if we could only get around the hill.

3RD BOY: There must be a way. . . .

OLD WOMAN (*Excited*): *Around.* Yes, yes. (*To* OLD MAN) The Wise Men have come, and I will show them the way. I will not be like the one in the story. I will not stay home in warmth and comfort. Where are my over-shoes? (*Goes into other room, mumbling*)

OLD MAN (*Following her*): What are you thinking of?

1ST BOY: They can't put on the program if we don't get there. Only five in the school. You can't have much of a Christmas program with only five.

2ND BOY (*Nodding toward other room*): The old lady seems to have an idea. Maybe there's a way around, all right.

OLD WOMAN (*Coming back, bundled up*): I will show you.

OLD MAN (*Tagging after*): And what star do you intend to follow?

OLD WOMAN (*Suddenly, turning to* OLD MAN): I have thought of it! I knew it began with "B." Babouscka! That is it—Babouscka.

OLD MAN: I have thought of it too. Befana! With "B." In Italy.

OLD WOMAN: Babouscka, I say . . .

1ST BOY: Did you think of a way? We don't want to be late.

OLD WOMAN: I will show you. The car can go roundabout —across our field to Hendriksens'. The snow does not drift there, and it misses the hill.

OLD MAN (*Excited*): Yes, of course. I know the way even in the dark. (*Begins to put on wraps*) We swing around Hendriksens' hayfield to the creek, then follow the fence back to the road. There is even a gate. We will show you.

OLD WOMAN: We?

OLD MAN: We will take you right to the schoolhouse. (*There is a sound of singing offstage.*)

OLD WOMAN: Listen! (*Opens door a crack*) All of you, listen. On such a night, music! Is it out of heaven itself?

1st Boy (*Laughing*): Oh, it's just the angels, practicing their song.

2nd Boy: Singing to keep warm.

Old Woman: Wise Men at the door, angels in the yard. That is even more than came to Babouscka. (*They start out.*)

Old Man: To *Befana.*

Old Woman: Every year we go to the Christmas program.

Old Man (*Pulling down ear-flaps*): Every year. We have not missed in eighteen years.

Old Woman: Nineteen! But no matter. Come, Wise Men. We will show you the way.

(*Curtain*)

THE END

Nine Cheers for Christmas

Characters

JOHN
JANE
CHORUS *of four boys and four girls*

NINE CHILDREN, *representing the nine letters which spell*
CHRISTMAS.

TIME: *The present.*
SETTING: *Bare stage.*
AT RISE: *The* CHORUS *is lined up in two rows at the back
of the stage.* JANE *and* JOHN *step out and come to the
front at the right side of the stage.*

JOHN: We went through the village
  And knocked at each door;
JANE: We asked everybody
  What Christmas was for.
JOHN: And one said . . .
1ST BOY: For getting a trinket or toy!
JANE: And some said . . .
1ST GIRL: For giving.
2ND BOY: For peace.
2ND GIRL: And for joy.

108

JOHN: We asked every stranger
And person we knew.

JANE: We said, "What's the meaning
Of Christmas to *you?*"

JOHN: And one said . . .

3RD BOY: For feasting!

JANE: And one said . . .

3RD GIRL: For mirth.

JOHN: And one said . . .

4TH BOY: For singing.

4TH GIRL: For gladness on earth.

JOHN: And so we wrote Christmas
A letter, saying, "Please . . .

JANE: "Just *what* do you stand for,
Since no one agrees?"

JOHN: "Just *what* is your meaning?"
And Christmas replied,
(*He takes out a letter; they both look at it, and read slowly.*)

JANE *and* JOHN: "Each letter means something.
I'm sending a guide.
I don't stand for *one* thing,
I stand for a lot.
Just follow my spelling
To know what is what."
(JOHN *puts letter back in pocket.*)

1ST BOY: Each letter means something!

1ST GIRL: And CHRISTMAS . . . let's see . . .
(*Counts on fingers*)
Has nine different letters.

2ND BOY: Nine things it must be!

JANE: We've asked all the letters
To come and explain.

JOHN: They should have arrived
On the six-o'clock train!

2ND GIRL (*Pointing to wings at left*):
Oh, look! They are coming.
3RD BOY (*Peering toward wings*):
The letters, all nine,
With "C" as a leader,
Are waiting in line.
JANE (*Tiptoeing back to* CHORUS):
Now if we keep quiet . . .
JOHN (*Tiptoeing back to* CHORUS):
And listen with care . . .
CHORUS: We'll learn why each letter
In Christmas is there.
(*A* GIRL *with a large letter* C *on her headband comes skipping in gaily from left. Eight other children are ready in the wings to come in, each with a bright card-board letter on headband.*)
C: I am C!
I stand for Carols.
I bring you joy—
Just barrels and barrels.
(*Curtsies joyfully*)
My music sounds
Across the snow;
It loops the globe
By radio;
And during Christmas
Holidays,
I'm sure to be
In lots of plays!
(*Looks around, sees* CHORUS)
I stand for songs of Christmas cheer . . .
Haven't I some helpers here?
CHORUS (*Eagerly*): Yes. Yes!
(*With* C *leading them, they sing a joyful carol, such as "There's a Song in the Air," or "Joy to the World!" or*

"Hark! the Herald Angels Sing." At the end of the carol, c sits down on the floor in front of the chorus, at the far right of the stage. h comes in with a holly wreath. NOTE: *any evergreen wreath with red ribbon will do.)*

H: H is for Holly—
The colors of Christmas
From pole to pole
And from gulf to isthmus.
Colors of red
And green together,
For light and life
In winter weather.
Hang up the wreath!
(*Goes to hang it near* CHORUS)
And all those near it
Soon feel the tingle
Of Christmas spirit!

CHORUS (*Looking at wreath and calling merrily*):
Merry Christmas! Merry Christmas!
(H *sits down next to* c, *as* R—*a boy—comes prancing in from left.*)

R: R is for Reindeer Santa Claus drives.
On Christmas, we have the time of our lives!
(*Prances around*)
We're very unusual; we race through the sky
And never fall down . . . though you mustn't ask why!
You know what we are? The fun and frolic
Of Christmas Eve . . . so away we rollick!
(R *prances to his place next to* H, *and* I *comes in softly and slowly from left.*)

I: I stands for Infant
Born in a manger,
In a land that was strange,
On a night that was stranger.
At an hour that was silent,

A place that was lowly,
An infant was born,
And His birthday is holy.
(*The* CHORUS *sings softly "Away in a Manger" as* I *tiptoes to her place next to* R. *When the song is over,* S *comes in, carrying a sack of toys over his shoulder.*)

S: S is for Santa—a jolly good fellow,
With a smile as broad as a violoncello!
(*Makes a big gesture.*)
With a heart as kind and full of devotion
As there are drops in a great big ocean!
With a sack full of gifts, for—as you're living—
Santa Claus means the spirit of giving.
(S *opens sack and distributes miscellaneous gifts to the* CHORUS, *amidst their "Oh's," "Ah's," and "Thank You's." Then* S *takes his place next to* I. T *comes in with a small Christmas tree on a stand, which he places left center. The tree is sparsely trimmed with bright balls and tinsel, leaving room for the stars which the letter* S *brings in later.*)

T: T is for Tree:
The spruce, or fir,
Fragrant as frankincense
And myrrh,
Its branches green as snow is white,
Its speartop pointing toward the light.
Out of the cold
We bring the tree,
And set it here
Where all can see
Its sun-like balls and tinsel-rays,
That brighten up our holidays.
(CHORUS *sings "O Tannenbaum" in English as* T *takes his place next to* S. M *comes in with a handful of Christmas cards.*)

M: M is for Message;
   I am starred
   On every tag and Christmas card.
   (*Begins to look through cards and distribute them to*
   CHORUS *and to* JOHN *and* JANE.)
   Message of joy.
   Message of cheer.
   Message of hope throughout the year.
   I bring you merry words—just dozens—
   From aunts and uncles and friends and cousins!
   (*Children in the* CHORUS *look at their cards and read
   out messages, one at a time.*)
JANE: May Christmas happiness and cheer
   Be yours throughout the coming year.
1ST BOY: Merry Christmas! Hip, hooray!
   And here's to fun on New Year's Day!
1ST GIRL: This lighted candle that you see
   Is flashing joy to you from me.
2ND BOY: The ocean's not so full of fishes
   As this card is of Christmas wishes!
2ND GIRL: I hope your Christmas will be glad—
   In fact, the best you've ever had.
3RD BOY: My fondest wish I now divulge:
   I hope your Christmas sock will *bulge.*
3RD GIRL: Words are much too small and few
   For all the things I wish for you.
4TH BOY: I'm making tracks, as you can see,
   To wish you Christmas jollity.
4TH GIRL: I hope your Christmas will be bright
   As tree lights twinkling in the night.
JOHN (*Looking at audience*):
   Christmas greetings to you all—
   Young and old, and big and small.
   (M *takes place next to* T, *while* A *comes in slowly.*)
A: A is for Angel

Who dazzled the sight
Of shepherds who watched
In the cold of the night—
An Angel with tidings
Of peace and good will,
On a night that was holy
And wondrous and still.

CHORUS (*Recites slowly, in the manner of choral reading,
Luke, 2:8-12, while* A *quietly takes her place next to*
M.):
"And there were in the same country shepherds abiding
in the field, keeping watch over their flocks by night.

And, lo, the angel of the Lord came upon them, and
the glory of the Lord shone round about them: and they
were sore afraid.

And the angel said unto them, Fear not: for, behold,
I bring you good tidings of great joy, which shall be to
all people.

For unto you is born this day in the city of David a
Saviour, which is Christ the Lord."

(S *comes in, carrying some tinsel stars.*)

S: S is for Star
In the eastern sky,
Which wise men saw
And were guided by.
(*He goes to the tree and puts on stars.*)
And S is for stars
That we all see
Shining each year
On our Christmas tree.
(S *sits down next to* A. *The* LETTERS *should now be sit-
ting across the stage so* CHRISTMAS *is spelled out for
the audience.* JOHN *and* JANE *come forward to stand at
extreme down right corners of the stage.*)

JANE: We went through the village

And knocked at each door;
JOHN: We asked everybody
What Christmas was for.
JANE: And one said for that thing,
And one said for this;
JOHN: And here we see nine things
That no one should miss!
CHORUS: Nine cheers for Christmas—
A cheer for each letter!
Three cheers are usual,
But *nine* cheers are better!
JANE: The letters in Christmas
Are needed, each one.
JOHN: They stand for its spirit . . .
(H *for Holly, and* T *for Tree stand up.*)
1ST BOY: Its story . . .
(I *for Infant,* A *for Angel, and* S *for Star stand up.*)
1ST GIRL: Its fun!
(R *for Reindeer stands.*)
2ND BOY: They stand for its message . . .
(M *for Message stands.*)
2ND GIRL: Its gifts . . .
(S *for Santa stands.*)
3RD BOY: And its song.
(C *for Carols stands.*)
CHORUS: We need all the letters,
And we did right along!
JANE: And now that we're certain
We have them all right,
Let's sing one more carol;
Let's sing "Silent Night."
(*Everyone on the stage joins in singing "Silent Night,"
as the curtain falls.*)

THE END

Sing the Songs of Christmas

Characters

MASTER OF CEREMONIES
PEASANT
TWO WOODCARVERS
APPRENTICE WOODCARVER
FRANCIS OF ASSISI
THREE SHEPHERDS
JEANETTE
ISABELLA
CHILDREN
MARTIN LUTHER
CATHERINE LUTHER

LUTHER'S SONS
LUTHER'S DAUGHTER
WAITS, *roving singers*
THREE INDIAN BRAVES
THREE INDIAN CHIEFS
ISAAC WATTS
JOSEPH MOHR
FRANZ GRUBER
PHILLIPS BROOKS
LEWIS REDNER
CHORUS

SETTING: *The stage is decorated gaily for Christmas.*

AT RISE: *The* CHORUS *stands upstage.* MASTER OF CERE-MONIES *comes in briskly, carrying a script, and goes to a reading stand at one side.*

M. C. (*To audience*): Merry Christmas! (*To* CHORUS) Merry Christmas!

BOY IN CHORUS: In FRANCE it's Joyeux Noël.

GIRL: In China it's Tin Hao Nian.

Note: Words and music to the carols in this program may be found in *A Treasury of Christmas Songs and Carols,* edited by Henry W. Simon, Houghton Mifflin, Boston, 1955; or in *Fireside Book of Folk Songs,* edited by Boni, Lloyd, and Provensen, Simon and Schuster, New York, 1947.

BOY: In Italy it's Buon Natale.

GIRL: In Germany it's Froeliche Weinachten.

BOY: In Sweden it's God Jul.

GIRL: In Mexico it's Felices Pascuas.

M. C.: But wherever you are, however you say it, it means the same thing: Merry Christmas!

ALL: Merry Christmas! (CHORUS *begins to march around gaily, singing the first two stanzas of "Deck the Halls." As they march they throw sprigs of fir or small red paper bells around the stage. At the end of the second stanza,* M. C. *stops them.*)

M. C.: Wait a minute! Wait a minute! I'm afraid you're starting at the wrong place. "Deck the Halls" shouldn't come at the beginning of the program. You'll be getting everybody all mixed up. (*All* CHORUS *members, except one* GIRL, *go back to their places.*)

GIRL: But it's such a merry song, and we were just talking about a Merry Christmas! (*She does a little jig as she sings.*) "Fa-la-la-la-la, la-la, la-la."

M. C.: Merry, yes, but we have to have some order here, not just a jumble of carols. (*Thumbs through script*) "Deck the Halls" doesn't come until page ten.

GIRL (*Jigging again merrily*): Fa-la-la-la-la, la-la, la-la.

M. C. (*Back at stand, ignoring* GIRL): Ladies and gentlemen, a great deal of obscurity surrounds the origin of many of our favorite Christmas carols, but we are going to do our best to put them in their places. (GIRL *begins to jig again.* M. C. *gently but firmly puts her back in her place in* CHORUS, *then returns to stand.*) In the first place, people have been singing Christmas carols for hundreds and hundreds of years. Let's go back to 1223 A.D., more than seven hundred years ago. It is Christmastide in Assisi, a town in central Italy. The day is cool, but fair, with a gleaming jewel of sun in a clear sky. A peasant approaches, carrying a queer wooden box and a bundle of hay. (PEASANT *enters with box and hay, looks around curiously, puts down box and shrugs.*) Something is obviously wrong. He doesn't seem to know what he is here for. Well, here comes a woodcarver. Perhaps he will know. (1ST WOODCARVER *enters. He carries wooden figures of animals. He looks around.*)

1ST WOODCARVER: Is this the place?

PEASANT (*Shrugging*): Each man has his own place, so they say. What place do you mean?

1ST WOODCARVER: I was told to come to the edge of town near a certain olive tree.

PEASANT: Here's an olive tree, that's certain. What have you there?

1ST WOODCARVER: An ox, an ass and three sheep, carved of wood and painted according to instructions.

PEASANT: You, too, had instructions?

1ST WOODCARVER (*Nodding*): From Brother Francis. (*Looks at* PEASANT's *box and hay*) But I am afraid I do not perceive the meaning of *your* instructions. A box of hay?

PEASANT: Box, indeed! Have you never seen a manger?

1ST WOODCARVER: Oh, a manger. *One* manger for an ox, an ass, and three sheep? I do not understand.

M. C.: Now, a second woodcarver approaches. He recognizes the first. (2ND WOODCARVER *comes in briskly, carrying wooden figures.*)

2ND WOODCARVER: Good morrow to you. Where is Brother Francis?

1ST WOODCARVER: Who can say?

2ND WOODCARVER: I can say I'd like to know the meaning of all this. Hay. A wooden box. Animals of wood. And my carved figures.

PEASANT: What figures?

2ND WOODCARVER: A middle-aged man, a young mother, and a child. At first I hesitated to carve the child. "Such a child as the Christ Child might have been," Brother Francis instructed me. How could I carve such a child? How would a stern Judge who fills us with fear and awe look as a child, I wondered. Ah, it was as if Brother Francis read my thoughts.

1ST WOODCARVER: How's that?

2ND WOODCARVER: "Not a Judge!" he told me. "People think of Christ wrongly. I must show them they are mistaken. He is not a dreaded Judge. He is as a friendly, loving child. Can you carve him so?" (APPRENTICE WOODCARVER, *carrying other figures, enters, and stands listening.*) So I carved a smiling child, like my own son in the cradle! So! (*Holds up figure. Sees* APPRENTICE WOODCARVER.) Who are you?

APPRENTICE WOODCARVER: I am an apprentice woodcarver. My master is ill. He was unable to bring the three kings to the appointed place. (*Puts kings down, takes angels from pocket*) And the angels. (*Somewhat embarrassed*) Brother Francis asked me, a mere apprentice, if I could carve angels. Are they all right?

1ST WOODCARVER (*Appraisingly*): A little small, I should say.

2ND WOODCARVER: On the contrary, not small enough.

PEASANT: Here comes Brother Francis. He will know what is large enough and small enough! (FRANCIS OF ASSISI *enters joyously.*)

FRANCIS: So you are all here, brothers. Ah! I see you have brought what I asked. Now I can teach the people what they must be taught, and in a simple way. I can teach that Christ is not a stern Judge, but a little Child to be loved. (*Bends over box*) The manger is just as I wanted it—not too fine and fancy. (*Puts in some hay*)

PEASANT (*Awed*): The Christ is not to be feared, you say?

FRANCIS: No, no. He is to be loved. Here you see the whole story. (*Gestures at manger and figures*) We shall carry the story into the church and light it with candles, so everyone in Assisi can see.

1ST WOODCARVER: See what, Brother Francis?

FRANCIS (*Laughing*): You do not understand? Then watch me. (*He begins to set up the crèche.*) Here is the manger in Bethlehem, the city of David, where Joseph, who was of the house of David, went to be taxed. Here, brothers, are the humble, friendly beasts in the stable, giving of their warmth that winter night so long ago. (*Places animals around the manger*) This is the little donkey Mary rode from Nazareth, she being great with child. Blessed Mary! (*Places her near the manger*) "And she brought forth her first-born son, and wrapped him in swaddling clothes, and laid him in a manger, because there was no room for them in the inn."

PEASANT: Now I see the need for the manger! And hay for the bed!

FRANCIS: "And there were shepherds in the same district living in the fields and keeping watch over their flock by night." (*To* 1ST WOODCARVER) Your cloak will make an excellent field, brother, being of such a good earthy color. (*Puts cloak to one side, places shepherds on it*) "And behold, an angel of the Lord stood by them . . ."

APPRENTICE (*Holding out angel*): Here is the angel, Brother Francis. Is it too small? Or too large, perhaps?

FRANCIS: Just right, my boy! (*Places angel near shepherds*) "And the glory of the Lord shone round about them."

2ND WOODCARVER: The candles in the church are like the glory of the Lord.

APPRENTICE WOODCARVER (*Intent on the story*) : The shepherds were afraid. But the angel told them not to fear, didn't he, Brother Francis?

FRANCIS (*Nodding*): "Behold," he said. "I bring you news of great joy, which shall be to all people. For today in the town of David a Saviour has been born to you, who is Christ the Lord. You shall find Him wrapped in swaddling clothes, lying in a manger."

PEASANT: Aye, a manger.

FRANCIS: "And suddenly, there was with the angel, a multitude of the heavenly host praising God . . ." Come, brothers, we must praise God. We must circle around the manger of God's Son and sing our praises. Christmas is a time of joy, brothers! Christmas is a time for singing. Come, join hands, and sing for the Christ Child in the manger on the holy eve of Christmas. Sing with joy! (*They join hands and circle around the crèche singing "Angels We Have Heard on High."*)

PEASANT, WOODCARVERS, FRANCIS:
"Angels we have heard on high,
Sweetly singing o'er the plains," etc.

CHORUS (*Joining in*): "Gloria," etc.

PEASANT, WOODCARVERS, FRANCIS (*Circling the crèche as they sing*): "Shepherds, why this jubilee," etc.

CHORUS: "Gloria," etc. (PEASANT, WOODCARVERS *and* FRANCIS *begin to move the crèche to back center stage where it will be out of sight behind* CHORUS. CHORUS *parts, standing on both sides temporarily.*)
"Come to Bethlehem and see
Him whose birth the angels sing"; etc. (*If the crèche has not been completely moved by the end of the third stanza,* CHORUS *sings fourth stanza, "See Him in a manger laid."* PEASANT, WOODCARVERS *and* FRANCIS *exit behind* CHORUS.)

M. C.: That was the beginning of Christmas caroling, more than seven hundred years ago—the singing for joy around the first crèche of St. Francis of Assisi! That was the beginning. After St. Francis made religion more human by his little drama of the story of the Nativity, special Christmas songs sprang up among the people. In many places in Italy, peasants and shepherds came down out of the hills at Christmastime, to sing and play their pipes in the villages. Townsfolk who wished to celebrate Christmas would place a wooden spoon outside their door as a signal. (BOY *from* CHORUS *puts out a wooden spoon. In a moment* THREE SHEPHERDS, *rather frightened, come running in.*)

1ST SHEPHERD: What a woman!

2ND SHEPHERD: Chasing us down the road like that with a stick!

3RD SHEPHERD: Wake her baby, indeed! With our singing? As if her baby wouldn't be lulled to sleep by our singing!

1ST SHEPHERD: Aye. (*Sees spoon*) Look, a spoon. (*Looks back toward wings*) Is it safe? Has she gone? (*Picks up spoon, uses it for baton*) Come, lads, let's give them a song of rejoicing. "O Come, O Come, Emmanuel."

THREE SHEPHERDS: O come, O come, Emmanuel, And ransom captive Israel," etc.
(SHEPHERDS *move out at the end of two or three stanzas, taking the spoon with them.*)

M. C.: Rejoice! Rejoice in other countries, too, as well as in Italy. In France, too, songs were being sung to celebrate the Christ Child's birthday. Noël, they called it. Noël for the Christmas birthday! Joyeux Noël! And we still sing one of the shepherd carols of medieval France, "The First Noel."

BOYS IN CHORUS: "The first Noel the angel did say," etc.

CHORUS: "Noel, Noel," etc.

BOYS IN CHORUS: "Then let us all with one accord," etc.

CHORUS: "Noel, Noel," etc. (*All five stanzas of "The First Noel" may be used if desired. During the last chorus, several* CHILDREN *carrying flashlight torches hurry across the stage.*)

M. C.: What was that? Lights? Torches? Yes, of course.

We are still in France in the Middle Ages. We are in Provence, in southeastern France, at Christmas time. There must be a crèche for Christmas Eve in Provence. (CHORUS *parts, so crèche shows.*)

GIRL IN CHORUS (*Calling out*): "Torches here, Jeanette, Isabella! Torches here to His cradle run!" (JEANETTE *and* ISABELLA, *followed by other* CHILDREN, *come running in again with lights. They stand near the crèche to light it while singing "Bring a Torch, Jeanette, Isabella."*)

GIRL IN CHORUS: "This is Jesus, good folk of the village, Christ is born, 'tis Mary calling."

JEANETTE, ISABELLA *and* CHORUS (*Loudly, crowding to look*): "Ah! Ah! Ah! What a lovely mother! Ah! Ah! Ah! What a lovely Child!"

GIRL IN CHORUS (*Shushing them*): "Wrong it is, when the Baby is sleeping,

Wrong it is to shout so loud."

(OTHERS, *chagrined, shrink back*)

GIRL IN CHORUS: "Now you there, and you others, be quiet!

For at a sound our Jesus wakens."

JEANETTE: Hush!

ISABELLA: Hush! Hush!

CHORUS: "He is sleeping so soundly.

Hush! Hush! Hush! Do but see Him sleep!"

(*All look at the crèche. Softly* CHORUS *begins to sing the stanza beginning "Softly now in the narrow stable . . ."* JEANETTE, ISABELLA *and* CHILDREN *who followed them take a final look, then tiptoe out with their torches as* CHORUS *finishes the song. A* GIRL *comes back quietly and stands looking at crèche, her curiosity mixed with awe. She begins to sing "What Child Is This?"*)

GIRL: "What Child is this, who, laid to rest,

On Mary's lap is sleeping?
Whom angels greet with anthems sweet,
While shepherds watch are keeping?"

CHORUS: "This, this is Christ the King," etc.

GIRL: "Why lies He in such mean estate,
Where ox and ass are feeding?"

CHORUS: "Good Christian, fear," etc.

GIRL (*Speaking*): The Babe, the Son of Mary!

CHORUS: "So bring Him incense, gold and myrrh," etc.
(CHORUS *goes to stand in front of crèche.* GIRL *stands
behind* CHORUS.)

M. C.: "Joy, joy, for Christ is born!" Joy—and rejoice—
those are the words for Christmas, over and over again.
Good Christian men, rejoice! That takes us to Germany. "Good Christian Men, Rejoice" is a German
carol of the Middle Ages. At that time, half of it was
written in German and half in Latin, but for more than
four hundred years we have been singing it in English.
Rejoice, good Christian men, at Christmas time!

CHORUS: "Good Christian men, rejoice
With heart and soul and voice," etc. (*At least two
stanzas, more if desired*)

M. C.: Good Christian men in Germany were the first to
rejoice around a Christmas tree, as the Italians were the
first to rejoice around a crèche. It may be just a legend,
but a famous German pastor, Martin Luther, is credited
with bringing home the first Christmas tree. He also
wrote several Christmas songs. (CHORUS *begins to hum
very softly, "Away in a Manger" as background.*) It is a
snowy Christmas Eve in the 1530's. Martin Luther is
walking home through the woods, thinking of the comfort of home ahead, yet not unmindful of the beauty
around him. He sees stars caught in the branches of the
fir trees. He thinks of the star that shone down on a
stable in Bethlehem on just such a sparkling night many

years ago. Why, he wonders, can we not bring some of that light into a home on Christmas Eve? Eagerly, he cuts a small fir tree by the roadside and hurries home. (LUTHER *comes in with fir tree.* CHORUS *stops humming.*)

LUTHER: Wife! Wife! My dear Catherine, see here!

CATHERINE (*Stepping from* CHORUS): Sh, Martin. You will wake the children.

LUTHER: Wake the children! Yes, indeed, by all means, I will wake the children, so they may see, too.

CATHERINE: See what?

LUTHER: The glory of Christmas Eve! The light of the star! The light of the Christ Child! (*He sets the tree in a pot or stand.*) Have you some small candles, my dear Catherine, so we can bring the starry heavens right into the house?

CATHERINE: Candles for stars? Why, yes. I made some little candles from the last beeswax.

LUTHER: Let us tie them to the tree! (CATHERINE *starts out for candles.*) And one candle larger than the rest, even as the star of Bethlehem dominated the heavens that night. (*She goes, he admires the tree. She returns with a string of white lights.* LUTHER *and* CATHERINE *put the lights on the tree, with one larger light near the top.*) Under the tree we must arrange the manger scene. Stars above to light the heavens, and Jesus below to light the world!

CATHERINE (*Excited*): How did you ever think of it?

LUTHER: Walking through the woods, meditating on the Nativity. (*They finish lights, then arrange the manger scene.* CHORUS *parts so they can arrange it.*) Now call the children, Catherine! (*He continues to work on the crèche while* CATHERINE *goes to get their* SONS *and* DAUGHTER, *who are very sleepy. They are awed by the lighted tree, and are quickly awake.*)

1ST SON: Where did the shining tree come from?

DAUGHTER: What is it, Father?

2ND SON: It shines like stars in the night.

LUTHER: Do you hear, Catherine? Like stars in the night.

1ST SON (*Looking at manger scene*): I know. You have brought in the stars to shine above the Christ Child's head on his birthday!

DAUGHTER: A birthday tree.

1ST SON: A Christmas tree. (*They join hands and circle around the tree singing "The Christmas Tree."*)

DAUGHTER: Now we must sing your song, Father, the one you wrote for us. (*She begins to sing "From Heaven High."*)

"From heaven high I come to you

To bring you tidings strange and true.

SONS (*Joining in*): "Glad tidings of great joy I bring

Whereof I now will say and sing."

LUTHER *and* CATHERINE (*Joining in*): "To you this night is born a child

Of Mary, chosen Mother mild," etc.

(*CHORUS joins in, marching slowly around stage to give the LUTHERS a chance to replace crèche and go out with the Christmas tree.*)

CHORUS: "Glory to God in highest heaven,

Who unto us His Son hath given!" (*CHORUS may repeat a stanza to give plenty of time for LUTHERS to exit. CATHERINE rejoins CHORUS.*)

M. C.: Carols from Italy, carols from England, carols from France and Germany. (*GIRL steps out from CHORUS.*)

GIRL: What about America? Didn't we make up any carols of our own?

M. C.: Yes, but first we must go back to England.

GIRL: Back to England?

M. C.: We must go back to Elizabethan England, always

remembering that England gave us most of our Christmas carols.

GIRL (*Jigging*): "Fa-la-la-la-la, la-la, la-la."

M. C.: As a matter of fact, "Deck the Halls" is an old Welsh carol, full of the spirit of England under the first Queen Elizabeth. In England, as time went on, Christmas became more and more a great festival of merry-making. The halls of the lords were decked with holly.

CHORUS (*Singing*): "Deck the halls with boughs of holly," etc., (*To end of first stanza.* GIRL *jigs on the refrain*)

M. C.: Elizabethan England was gay with feasting and singing and games and wassailing at Christmas time. Masked actors called *mummers* presented pantomimes. Roving bands of singers called *waits* went about the streets singing Christmas carols, and hoping to be paid for their efforts. (*A group of* WAITS *come in. They are gaily singing "Wassail Song." They turn toward the audience.*)

WAITS: "Here we go a-wassailing
Among the leaves of green," etc. (*Turning to* CHORUS, *holding out little leather purses*)
"We have got a little purse
Of stretching leather skin," etc. (WAITS *gather a few coins and replace purses.*)
"Bring us out a table,
And spread it with a cloth," etc. (*They pantomime hungrily.*)
"Good Master and good Mistress,
While you sit by the fire," etc. (WAITS *go out, annoyed that they haven't been treated better.*)

M. C.: Christmas in old England! The Yule log—roast goose—plum pudding—singers in the streets—holly and ivy!

GIRL: *Now* do we go to America? To jolly young America?

M. C.: Just a minute! In the early days Christmas was anything but jolly in America.

GIRL: Anything but jolly?

M. C.: The Puritans were opposed to such frivolous sport as singing carols. Early New England colonists even forbade the celebration of Christmas. In 1644, the Puritans declared December 25th to be a market day instead of a holiday, and forbade anyone to have plum pudding or mince pie. Later, they even fined anyone who stopped work or feasted on Christmas Day.

GIRL: So we didn't have any carols in the early days? Or any holiday? Or any mince pie?

M. C.: That's right. But strangely enough, about that very time, the first American carol was born. Not in New England. In New France. The time is around 1640. Father Jean de Brebeuf, Jesuit missionary to the Huron Indians on the neck of land between Lake Huron, Lake Erie, and Lake Ontario, is rehearsing a group of Indians for the celebration of Christmas just a few days off. He has composed a carol for them in their own language. But he has no organ. The Indians have only tom-toms and rattles. So Father Brebeuf used words that would fit a tom-tom accompaniment. Here is the English translation. (*Several members of the* CHORUS *begin to beat muted drums to the rhythm of "God Rest You Merry, Gentlemen." A* BOY *who has slipped on an Indian headdress steps from* CHORUS *to chant words of the carol.*)

BOY: " 'Twas in the moon of wintertime,
When all the birds had fled,
That mighty Gitchi Manitou
Sent angel choirs instead.
Before their light the stars grew dim,
And hunters heard the hymn:

CHORUS (*Joining chant*): "Jesus, your King, is born;
Jesus is born,

In Excelsis Gloria!" (*Several* INDIAN BRAVES *with bows and arrows come in from wings. They kneel in reverence.*)

1ST INDIAN BRAVE: "In the lodge of broken bark
The tender babe was found;
A ragged robe of rabbit skin
Enwrapped his beauty round.
And as the hunter braves drew nigh,
The angel song rang high:

CHORUS (*Joining chant*): "Jesus, your King, is born;
Jesus is born,
In Excelsis Gloria!" (THREE INDIAN CHIEFS *enter from wings. They carry pelts, and kneel and offer their gifts.*)

2ND INDIAN BRAVE: "Earliest moon of wintertime
Is not so round and fair
As was the ring of glory
On the helpless infant there,
While chiefs from far before him knelt
With gifts of beaver pelt."

CHORUS: "Jesus, your King, is born," etc.

3RD INDIAN BRAVE: "The children of the forest free,
O sons of Manitou,
The Holy Child of earth and heaven
Is born today for you.
Come kneel before the radiant boy
Who brings you peace and joy:

CHORUS: "Jesus, your King, is born;
Jesus is born,
In Excelsis Gloria!" (CHORUS *repeats chorus as* INDIANS *exit.*)

M. C.: The first American Christmas carol! Few of us have ever heard it sung. The Christ Child in a bark lodge instead of in a manger! Wrapped in a rabbit skin instead of swaddling clothes! Wandering hunters instead of shepherds hearing the angel choir! Indian chiefs coming from afar with their gifts of fox and beaver skins, instead of three Wise Men with gold, frankincense and myrrh! Christmas in the New World!

As America was settled, of course, the Puritans were outvoted. Carols from the "old country" came over with the settlers, and Christmas became a joyous occasion up and down the Atlantic seaboard.

Meanwhile, the English produced another famous Christmas carol. It was written by the great English hymn writer of the eighteenth century, Isaac Watts. He was working on a book, telling the psalms of David in his own words, when his inspiration came. He was reading the 98th Psalm. (ISAAC WATTS *enters with Bible, reads aloud.*)

WATTS: "Make a joyful noise unto the Lord, all the earth: make a loud noise, and rejoice, and sing praise. Sing unto the Lord with the harp; with the harp, and the voice of a psalm. For he cometh to judge the earth; with righteousness shall he judge the world, and the people with equity." (*Looks up*) Make a joyful noise, for he cometh! What a text for a song! A Christmas song of joy. (*Hums*) Joy to the world! The Lord is come—

CHORUS (*Taking up carol, "Joy to the World"*): "Let earth receive her King," etc.

WATTS (*Singing second stanza as solo*): "Joy to the world! The Saviour reigns," etc.

CHORUS (*Singing third stanza as* WATTS *goes out*): "He rules the world with truth and grace," etc.

M. C.: Carols from Italy, carols from France, carols from England and Germany! But we have to go to Austria for one of the most beloved carols of all. (GIRL *steps out from* CHORUS *and starts to jig.*)

GIRL: To Austria we go! Fa-la-la-la-la la-la, la-la. (*Others pull her back.*)

M. C.: We go to the little town of Obendorf in the Austrian Alps. It is a sparkling cold night, just before Christmas, 1818. The mountains are covered with snow, the air is clear, almost brittle, the sky bright with stars. Joseph Mohr, 26-year-old vicar of the little church, is hurrying down the village street to call on his friend Franz Gruber, the schoolmaster, who plays the organ at church. Father Mohr has a piece of paper in his pocket to show the schoolmaster-organist. Now he is at his friend's door. Now he is ushered into the house, to warm himself at the stove. (FATHER MOHR *and* FRANZ GRUBER *enter.*)

GRUBER: A cold night to be abroad, Father.

MOHR: But calm and bright. I was struck by the brightness when I returned to my room after meeting with the children of the parish. (*Smiles*) The same children you know and teach, my dear Franz.

GRUBER: Ach, and their minds full of nothing but Christmas!

MOHR: I am afraid that is the state of my mind, too. Soon we shall be celebrating the Nativity. My thoughts were full of it as I walked home. I wished for some new way to celebrate, something a little different for the boys to sing in church on Christmas Eve. (*He takes the paper from his pocket, thrusts it at* GRUBER.) Here, tell me what you think, Franz, as a schoolmaster and organist, not as a friend who might be prejudiced.

GRUBER (*Reading aloud*): "Silent night! Holy night! All is calm, all is bright . . ." (*He reads in silence for a moment then looks up excitedly.*) Why, it is beautiful, Father. Where did it come from?

MOHR: I—well, I wrote it. Do you think the words could make a song, Franz?

GRUBER: Yes, yes, indeed, yes. (*Looks at words, beats time to imaginary tune.*)

MOHR (*Urgently*): Can you do it, Franz? You can play the

organ; you have instruction in music. Can you set it to music right away, for the Christmas celebration? I know there is little time, but will you try?

GRUBER: I will try. (*Looks at words again, becomes absorbed.* FATHER MOHR *smiles and tiptoes out.*)

M. C.: Franz Gruber, the 29-year-old schoolmaster, wrote music for the vicar's words, but when he went to try the song on the organ, the organ refused to play. It was old and there were mice in it! Still, Father Mohr must have his new song for the Christmas festivities. So the schoolmaster taught the children to sing the song with only a guitar for accompaniment. (GRUBER *turns to* CHORUS *and directs the singing of "Silent Night," either a cappella or with only a guitar accompaniment.*)

SOLO BOY: "Silent night, holy night,
All is calm, all is bright
Round yon Virgin Mother and Child,

CHORUS (*Softly*): "Holy Infant so tender and mild,
Sleep in heavenly peace,
Sleep in heavenly peace."
(*Second and third stanzas also should be sung with solo parts and* CHORUS. *During the last chorus,* GRUBER *exits.*)

M. C.: Gradually, Father Mohr's wonderful song spread through Austria and Germany. It became popular wherever it was heard. Twenty-five years after it was written, "Silent Night" was sung at a Christmas concert in Leipzig. From that time its fame was assured. Now it belongs to the world!

Carols have come from Christians of all nationalities and races—from the Czechs, the Chinese, the Croatians; from the Scandinavians, the Sicilians, the Poles; from the Puerto Ricans, the Russians, and even from Negro slaves in the United States before the Civil War. Here is one of the carols the slaves gave us:

BOY (*Swinging into "Rise Up, Shepherd, and Follow"*):
"There's a star in the East on Christmas morn,"

CHORUS: "Rise up, shepherd, and follow." (*Throughout the spiritual, CHORUS comes in only on "Rise up, shepherd, and follow." BOY carries the other lines.*)

M. C.: And now here is a strange coincidence. In Austria, Father Mohr and his church organist produced "Silent Night" as something different for the children of the parish to sing for Christmas. Fifty years later, an Episcopalian rector in Philadelphia and his organist composed a new carol for the children of *their* Sunday School to sing as something different. The song was as speedily written and as speedily set to music as was "Silent Night." It, too, became world famous. The American rector's name was Phillips Brooks; his organist was Lewis Redner. (BROOKS *and* REDNER *enter.*)

REDNER: A cold night to be abroad, isn't it, sir?

BROOKS: But calm and bright, Redner. As I walked home from the meeting at the church, I was struck by the brightness. On just such a night three years ago, I was in the Holy Land. I will never forget it. I was riding horseback from Jerusalem to Bethlehem, following the stars.

REDNER: How does Bethlehem look by starlight? I've often wondered.

BROOKS: It's on a hill, you know. Just five miles from Jerusalem. By day it isn't much of a town, but at night — (*Takes paper from pocket*) Redner, you know I have been wishing for some new way to celebrate Christmas this year, something a little different for the children to sing. (*Holds out paper*) Here, tell me what you think of this. Do you see anything in it?

REDNER (*Taking paper, reading aloud*): "O little town of Bethlehem,
How still we see thee lie!

Above thy deep and dreamless sleep
The silent stars go by;
Yet in thy dark streets shineth
The everlasting Light . . ." (*Looks up*) Where did you find it?

BROOKS: I wrote it. Perhaps I should say it wrote itself, out of my memories. Do you think it would make a song?

REDNER: I should say it would! (*Studies words, drumming rhythm*)

BROOKS: Will you do it, Redner? Will you set it to music right away? I know there isn't much time. This is Saturday evening. Tomorrow is the last day of Sunday School before Christmas.

REDNER: I will try. A tune is opening up already. (*He is engrossed with the paper.* BROOKS *smiles and tiptoes out.*)

M. C.: Sure enough, the church organist had his rector's words set to music in time for Sunday School the next morning, and the song has been heard at Christmas time ever since. (REDNER *directs* CHORUS *in "O Little Town of Bethlehem," all four stanzas if desired. At the end of the song, he joins* CHORUS.) Hundreds of Christmas songs and carols have been written over the centuries. We couldn't begin to sing them all on one program, but we still have time for one of the oldest and most famous of all Christmas songs. The tune is attributed to St. Bonaventura, who lived in the thirteenth century. The song has been translated into more than a hundred languages and dialects, and every year it is sung in Christian churches throughout the world. "Adeste Fidelis— O Come All Ye Faithful."

CHORUS: "O come, all ye faithful, joyful and triumphant;" etc. (M. C. *gestures for audience to join in.* CHORUS *and audience sing at least two stanzas.*)

THE END

Setting Santa Straight

Characters

TINKER, *Santa's handyman*
MISS MERRY, *Santa's secretary*
GROOMER, *Santa's stableman*
MRS. SANTA CLAUS
SANTA CLAUS
TECK ⎫
TUCK ⎪
PECK ⎬ *interviewers*
PUCK ⎭
JEFFRY, *child in the first corner of the world*
SUSAN ⎫
LINDA ⎬ *children in the second corner of the world*
ROBIN ⎭
RUTH, *child in the third corner of the world*
GILBERT ⎫
CHUCK ⎬ *children in the fourth corner of the world*

TIME: *A few days before Christmas.*
SETTING: SANTA'S *office in his house at the North Pole.*
AT RISE: TINKER *is working furiously on a huge TV set, with tools, wire, tubes, etc., scattered on the floor around him.* MISS MERRY *is at a desk or table on the other side of the room engulfed in mail, trying to sort the letters into stacks.*

MISS MERRY (*Looking up*): How is it coming, Tinker?

TINKER: Sometimes I think it was a crazy idea, trying to get television up here at the North Pole. Then again, I think it might work. How much time is left?

MISS MERRY (*Looking at watch*): I asked Santa to come to the office at 2:30 sharp. I told him we would have a surprise for him. You still have a little time, Tinker. Don't get nervous.

TINKER: Don't get nervous, she says, when a connection like this has never been tried before! Just keep as cool as a cucumber on an iceberg! (*Looks at* MISS MERRY *desperately*) What if it doesn't work, Miss Merry, after all our trouble?

MISS MERRY: *Something* has to work. Santa can't go on like this. (*Looks at cluttered desk and sighs*) If only children wouldn't write so many letters asking for expensive presents! Santa's afraid the "gimme" epidemic has gone so far it's blotted out the spirit of Christmas. I tell him it isn't that children are more demanding than they used to be—it's just that there are more children. More children, more letters! (TINKER *nods, then squirms under set to do some adjusting.* MISS MERRY *goes back to her work. In a moment,* GROOMER *staggers in with a sack of letters.*)

GROOMER: Picked up some more, Miss Merry. Never saw the likes—the way they keep drifting down.

MISS MERRY: Oh, dear, more letters—and everyone asking for preposterous presents. I'm afraid Santa will lose another ten pounds.

GROOMER: Isn't he any better yet?

MISS MERRY: He's worse, if anything, Groomer. He's just never been like this before. It isn't that he's really sick, but he's lost all his energy, all his gusto.

GROOMER: What's Santa without gusto? Has his wife tried giving him blackstrap molasses? Brewers' yeast? Wheat germ? Yogurt? Vitamin C and calcium? That's how I keep the reindeer in trim.

MISS MERRY: Santa's wife has tried everything, including a double dose of old-fashioned sulphur and molasses. Nothing seems to help.

GROOMER: What about a massage? I could give him a good rubbing, the way I do the reindeer.

MISS MERRY: Mrs. Santa has used the electric vibrator on him morning, noon, and night for the past week, and it hasn't pepped him up a bit.

GROOMER: What's the solution, Miss Merry? Christmas comes on Thursday.

MISS MERRY: I don't know. The elves are beside themselves trying to get all the toys finished and painted. Even if they do finish, who's going to deliver them, unless Santa has a change of heart?

GROOMER (*Shaking his head*): Nobody could ever take Santa's place. Well, do you want me to leave the rest of the letters out there in the snow, or shall I keep picking them up?

MISS MERRY: Better pick them up, Groomer. Shall I send one of the elves to help?

GROOMER: They're busy enough in the workshop. I've got time on my hands today, you know, with four of the reindeer gone on that gallop poll.

MISS MERRY: That's right. (*Looks at watch*) If all went well with the reindeer, the four reporters should be stationed in the four corners of the world by now. And if all goes well on *this* end, Tinker will have things fixed so we'll be able to see the boys and girls being questioned, on television.

GROOMER: Sounds like reaching for the Northern Lights to me.

MISS MERRY: Hurry and catch up with the letters, Groomer, and then slip in to watch the program.

GROOMER (*Eagerly*): Thanks, Miss Merry. (*Hurries out*)

TINKER (*Scrambling out from under TV set*): I'll give her a try now just to see if she's in focus. (*Turns knobs. SUSAN, LINDA, and ROBIN appear on TV stage, wobbling around, as they sing "Jingle Bells" quaveringly. As TINKER works with knobs, the girls gradually straighten up and their voices clear.*) There!

MISS MERRY: That's fine, Tinker. (*Girls exit at end of song.*)

TINKER: Now to clear the circuits to the walkie-talkies.

MISS MERRY: Don't get nervous. I'll have to talk to Santa first, anyway, and show him some of the letters. (*Both work quietly for a minute. Then MRS. SANTA CLAUS comes in, stops near door and speaks urgently over her shoulder.*)

MRS. SANTA: Come on, dear. I'm sure the surprise is something besides letters. After all, they're no surprise at this time of year.

SANTA (*Entering tentatively*): Gimme this, gimme that! I tell you, I'm putting my foot down! (*He puts his foot down so hard he hurts his toe. Hops in on one foot. When he sees the TV set, he stops and looks in amazement.*) What's that thing doing in my office?

MRS. SANTA: I'm as much in the dark as you are. They wouldn't let me in here all day. It must have something to do with the surprise.

SANTA: What is it, Miss Merry?

MISS MERRY: Something that's never been tried before at the North Pole. Perhaps Tinker had better explain. He's underneath. (*Calls*) Tinker!

SANTA (*Loudly*): Tinker!

TINKER (*Sticking his head out*): Yes, sir?

SANTA: Is this supposed to be a surprise?

TINKER: It certainly is, sir. If it works I'll be as surprised as you are! We'll see in a few minutes. (*Ducks under TV set again*)

SANTA: What's it all about, Miss Merry?

MISS MERRY: An experiment, Santa. With this life-size television we hope to show you that children in the world *haven't* really changed. Maybe they do ask for a lot of things in their letters, but they haven't lost the Christmas spirit. (*Tentatively*) We hope!

SANTA: How is this contraption going to prove that?

MRS. SANTA: I love experiments, whether they prove anything or not!

MISS MERRY: Tinker fixed up four sets of walkie-talkie-picture transmitters, and four of your helpers went off with them before dawn this morning to the four corners of the world.

SANTA: How?

MISS MERRY: They rode four of the reindeer. We had a hard time persuading Groomer to cooperate, but he finally agreed.

SANTA: I still don't get the point, Miss Merry.

MRS. SANTA: Oh, I do. It's a practice run, dear. So if you *still* feel too discouraged on Christmas Eve, the others can take over your job.

MISS MERRY: No, no. Nobody could ever take over Santa's job. Our idea is quite different. We feel that the "gimmes," as Santa calls them, are only skin deep. *Inside* the children are just as eager to give as to get. So Teck and Tuck and Peck and Puck have gone to the four corners of the world to take a poll. They are due to begin their interviews in a few minutes. (GROOMER *appears at door with more letters. He stands listening.*)

SANTA: Hummmp! So you think the "gimmes" are just skin deep, do you? You think the children still know that Christmas means giving as well as getting? I contend that they have such highfalutin ideas of what they want these days, they haven't time to think of anyone else. Are there any letters that haven't been filed?

GROOMER (*Coming in*): Letters! Here's the latest collection, and they're still arriving. (*Dumps letters on top of others*)

SANTA: Now, Miss Merry, pick a couple of letters at random and read them to me. We'll see who's right.

MRS. SANTA: Let me pick them! Miss Merry has worked hard enough today. (*Hurries to desk*) Eeney, meeny, miney, mo. (*Picks out two letters*)

SANTA: All right. Read them.

MRS. SANTA (*Opening first letter, reading*): "My name is Henry, and I am nine years old. I want an atomic engine that I can hitch to my bicycle. I want an electric train with enough track to go around the living room twice. If you handle ponies up there, I'd like a brown one with a white mark on its nose. Of course, I'll need a saddle, too. Your friend, Henry."

SANTA: Such big ideas! You must admit children have changed.

MRS. SANTA: Times have changed, too, dear. It's next to impossible to buy a fur lap robe for your sleigh these days. (*Opens second letter and begins to read*) "Dear Santa, have you heard about those new wrist watches that don't need winding? I hope you bring one to put in my stocking . . ."

SANTA: Put in her stocking indeed! What does she think I'm made of—solid gold diamonds?

MISS MERRY: It's almost time for the telecast, folks. Perhaps we'd better get seated. (MISS MERRY *and* GROOMER *arrange four chairs in front of the TV and put a chair near the set for* TINKER.)

TINKER: Keep your fingers crossed, everyone. (*To* MISS MERRY) Teck was to come on first, wasn't he?

MISS MERRY: Yes, from the first corner of the world, at exactly 2:35 our time. Just a second or two from now.

TINKER: The dials are all set— (TECK *walks onto TV stage.*)

TECK (*Softly*): Calling the North Pole, calling the North Pole.

TINKER: A little more volume ought to do it. (*Turns knobs*)

SANTA: Well, I never thought I'd sit in on anything like this—life-sized television!

TECK (*Full voice*): I have the automatic transmitter all set up. I'll stop the first girl or boy who passes by and ask some questions. It's a bright December day here in the first corner of the world. The streets and stores are all decorated for Christmas. The air tingles with excitement. Wait, here comes a youngster. He seems to be in a hurry, but I'll try to get him to talk. (JEFFRY *hurries on TV stage.*) Just a minute, sonny, what's the hurry?

JEFFRY: I have something for my sister. Look! (*Holds up pen*) A retractable pen—red and gold!

TECK: How old is your sister?

JEFFRY: Not quite four.

TECK: She uses a retractable pen?

JEFFRY: No. It's like this, see. We had a grab-bag at school, and everyone drew a present. I got a bag of marbles. But since I deliver papers after school, I never have time to play marbles. So I traded for a harmonica. But my Dad isn't very musical, so I traded again for this retractable pen.

TECK: I don't see what your Dad's being musical has to do with it.

JEFFRY: That's easy. My sister doesn't have anything to give my Dad for Christmas. She's too young to earn money, of course. So I'm giving her the pen to give to Dad.

TECK: It sounds rather involved.

JEFFRY: Not at all. It's just a case of figuring things out, so the right present gets to the right person.

TECK: But where do you come in?

JEFFRY: Me? (*Laughs*) I certainly didn't need a bag of marbles. (*Pulls Christmas seals from pocket*) Say, Mister, have you bought your Christmas seals yet? I'm selling them. Just a penny apiece, and it's for a good cause. How many will you take? A hundred? Two hundred?

TECK: I—I forgot to take any money when I left home this morning.

JEFFRY (*Looking at him skeptically*): *Everybody* buys seals. It's part of Christmas.

TECK: Look, what's your name?

JEFFRY: Jeffry.

TECK: I'm going to put in a good word for you with Santa Claus, Jeffry.

JEFFRY: Say, are you kidding? (*Goes out*)

TECK (*Softly into mike*): Have you been listening, Santa Claus?

SANTA: Well! That boy Jeffry didn't have himself on his mind at all, did he? He was thinking about others more than about himself.

MISS MERRY: Now it's time to switch to the second corner of the world, where Tuck is waiting. At least, I hope he's waiting.

TINKER (*Tinkering*): So do I. (TUCK *comes on TV stage.*) Ah, there he is.

TUCK (*Into mike*): Are you there? Am I getting through to you? The equipment's all set up, ready to go. Here come three girls walking down the street. I'll ask a few questions. (SUSAN, LINDA, *and* ROBIN *enter.*) Just a moment, girls. I'm a roving reporter. Tell me, have you any plans for Christmas?

SUSAN: Plans for Christmas? Well, I should say.

LINDA: We're the Three Carolers. We won't have a free minute from now till Christmas night.

TUCK: What do you mean?

ROBIN: We're singing carols at all the hospitals, the railroad station, and the Retirement Center, and on Christmas Eve we're going from house to house to sing for our friends and neighbors. (*Begins singing a carol; others join in for a few lines.*)

TUCK: You'll be giving folks a lot of pleasure, I can see that. Do you get paid for it?

SUSAN: Sometimes. Not because we want it, but people just naturally like to give at Christmas time. We turn the money over to the Women's Service Club for Christmas baskets. That way everybody's happy.

LINDA: By the way, wouldn't you like to contribute a little something for the Christmas Basket fund?

TUCK: I—I didn't bring a cent with me today.

LINDA: We'll be singing at the Community Hospital this afternoon, if you should find some change in your pocket! (*Girls go out.*)

TUCK (*Into mike*): Did I get through to you, Santa? I feel like two cents, without even enough to buy a chicken leg for one of those Christmas baskets! (*Goes out*)

SANTA: Hmmmm. What's happened to the gimme epidemic all of a sudden? I hope one of the reporters remembers to ask about the *letters*.

MISS MERRY: Maybe Peck will. He's next. (TINKER *is working the dials.*) In the third corner of the world. (PECK *walks on TV stage.*) Look, there he is, big as life!

PECK (*Into mike*): Can you hear me? Can you see me up there at the North Pole? Whew, it's warm here in the third corner of the world! You'd never know it was December. But the excitement of Christmas is in the air just the same. I'm standing here on a street corner, waiting to question the first boy or girl who happens by.

Hold on, it looks as if it's going to be a teen-ager. (RUTH *enters.*) Would you mind answering a few questions for a special television audience, Miss?

RUTH: If it won't take too long. I'm on my way to work.

PECK: What kind of work? How old are you?

RUTH: I'm 14 going on 15. I baby-sit for women in the neighborhood. Everyone wants to go Christmas shopping these days, so I'm very busy.

PECK: Do you get paid for baby sitting?

RUTH: Oh, yes.

PECK: What do you do with your money—buy things for yourself?

RUTH: Mostly I've been saving it for Christmas, to buy presents for my family.

PECK: Of course, you're too old now, but did you ever write a letter to Santa Claus asking for presents?

RUTH (*Laughing*): Did I ever? I *still* write him letters, sometimes a dozen a day!

PECK: You do?

RUTH: It's a wonderful way to entertain the children when I baby-sit. We think of all the presents imaginable, write them down in a letter to Santa, and send the letter whisking up the chimney.

PECK: You mean—you do it to entertain the kids? You don't really expect to get all those things?

RUTH: It's a sort of game, you see. Nobody expects to get a rocket to the moon!

PECK: I'll be switched! I'll bet Santa Claus never thought of *that* angle.

RUTH: Now if you don't mind, I have to hurry along. Merry Christmas!

PECK: Merry Christmas! (*Voice fades and he exits as* TINKER *turns dial.*)

SANTA (*Laughing*): So that's why I get so many letters!

The joke's on me. Baby sitters. So some of the *gimmes* are gimmicks!

MRS. SANTA: You get more useful every year, dear.

TINKER (*Turning dials*): Now for the last corner of the world, where Puck is stationed. Let's see what he comes up with. (PUCK *appears on TV stage, swaying from side to side*.) Not a very good connection. Just a minute. (*Makes adjustments*, PUCK *straightens up*.) That's better.

PUCK: Good afternoon, up there. Sorry I have to be so abrupt, but someone's coming already. Two boys with their arms full of toys. (GILBERT *and* CHUCK *enter carrying toys*.) Hello. You must have been Christmas shopping.

GILBERT: No. These toys aren't new; they're old ones we collected. The firemen down at the station fix them for the orphanage.

CHUCK: We help all we can—sandpapering, painting, varnishing, gluing. We've been working for more than two weeks, after school.

GILBERT: It's fun helping the firemen get them working again. Do you have any old toys to give, sir?

PUCK: Er—not old ones, I'm afraid, but I certainly admire your spirit. Merry Christmas!

BOYS: Same to you. (*They hurry out*.)

PUCK: Same to you up there at the North Pole! (TINKER *turns off TV*. SANTA *jumps up, full of energy*.)

SANTA: Merry Christmas to everyone, from one corner of the world to the other. What are we sitting here for, watching television in the middle of a busy afternoon? We have stacks of toys to finish and pack. We have to shine up the old sleigh and polish the harness. What are we waiting for? We can't disappoint those millions of youngsters bubbling over with Christmas spirit.

MRS. SANTA: It's good to see you full of the Old Nick again, Santa.

SANTA: Tinker, we can use you in the workshop, in the motor and engine department. Groomer, with four of the reindeer gone, you can help out with the hobbyhorses today. Miss Merry, get my address book up to date, will you, please? And you, Mrs. Santa Claus—

MRS. SANTA: What can I do?

SANTA: Throw out all that old sulphur and molasses and come help wrap the Christmas candy. Let's get going, everyone! We've a job to do—a wonderful, exciting, satisfying job to do! (SANTA *hurries out with* MRS. SANTA *and* GROOMER. TINKER *holds back a moment.*)

MISS MERRY: Well, it worked, Tinker.

TINKER (*Nodding happily*): All goes to show, Miss Merry, that Christmas is still Christmas, after all! (*Curtain*)

THE END

Mother Goose's Party

Characters

MOTHER GOOSE
OLD WOMAN WHO LIVES IN A SHOE
JACK AND JILL
BO PEEP
BOY BLUE
MARY QUITE CONTRARY
POLLY FLINDERS
SIMPLE SIMON
TOM TUCKER

TIME: *Just before Christmas.*

SETTING: MOTHER GOOSE'S *house, decorated for Christmas.*

AT RISE: MOTHER GOOSE *is sitting at a big table piled high with presents, wrapping paper, ribbons, boxes, etc. She is writing gift tags and not having an easy time, judging from the way she screws up her face and looks off into space, thinking. Suddenly there is a knock at the door and* MOTHER GOOSE *hurries to answer it.*

MOTHER GOOSE (*At door*): I'm so glad you got my message and could come to the rescue. As the Old Woman Who Lives in a Shoe, you'll surely know what to do.

OLD WOMAN: Always glad to oblige, Mother Goose.

MOTHER GOOSE: Come in, take off your wraps. We'll have to hurry. (*Hurries* OLD WOMAN *in and helps her take*

off her coat and hat) It took me so long to decide on a
gift for everyone, I'm way behind with the wrapping.
And time is short. The first guests are due to arrive in a
few minutes.

OLD WOMAN (*Efficiently*): I'll tend to the wrapping.
Where's the paper? And the stickers? Where's the ribbon? The scissors? The presents?

MOTHER GOOSE (*Taking her to table*): Everything's right
here. You wrap, and I'll attach the cards and hang the
gifts on the tree.

OLD WOMAN (*Wrapping furiously*): Big party?

MOTHER GOOSE (*Attaching cards*): Yes, indeed. Let's see,
now. *This* one is for Polly Flinders, and this for Tom
Tucker.

OLD WOMAN: Who else is coming?

MOTHER GOOSE: Jack and Jill, Mary Quite Contrary . . .

OLD WOMAN: Think *she'll* come?

MOTHER GOOSE: Oh, yes. Mary is never contrary at this
time of year.

OLD WOMAN (*Chuckling*): 'Course. Children are regular
angels just before Christmas. Have to keep looking at
their shoulders to see if they're sprouting wings. I draw
the line at a halo, though. Just another thing to keep
polished.

MOTHER GOOSE: Little Boy Blue is coming, and Bo Peep.

OLD WOMAN: Shouldn't be any lost sheep with them
around.

MOTHER GOOSE: And Simple Simon—that's about all the
invited guests.

OLD WOMAN: It's been so long since I've seen those
youngsters, I don't believe I'd know one from the other.
(*Looks at all the presents, baffled*) But if nobody else is
coming, Mother Goose, what are all the presents for?

MOTHER GOOSE: Oh, there'll be other guests, too. **Only
they won't know till the last minute.**

OLD WOMAN: How'll they get here in time if they don't know?

MOTHER GOOSE: They'll get here. They're really almost here already! Stay for the party, Old Woman Who Lives in a Shoe, and you'll see what I mean.

OLD WOMAN: Just can't figure out how unexpected guests get expected. Be something to tell my children when I get home. Yes, I'll stay.

MOTHER GOOSE (*Nervously, looking at clock*): How many gifts do we have left?

OLD WOMAN: Dozen or so.

MOTHER GOOSE: Then with luck we'll finish in time. (*They work fast.* MOTHER GOOSE *hurries to put the last gifts on the tree; switches on tree lights. Laughter and singing are heard off stage.*)

OLD WOMAN (*Trying to whisk materials out of sight*): Here they come.

MOTHER GOOSE (*Going to door*): I hope they don't notice we're out of breath. (*Opens door*) Come in, come in, and Merry Christmas! (*A jumble of shouts and greetings comes from the boys and girls.* MOTHER GOOSE *beckons* OLD WOMAN *to come forward.*) You remember the Old Woman Who Lives in a Shoe, don't you? But she's not sure she remembers you. Introduce yourselves, won't you, by giving a little description of yourselves? (*Children step forward in turn, bow to* OLD WOMAN, *and introduce themselves by a phrase from their nursery rhyme.*)

JACK *and* JILL: "Up the hill."

OLD WOMAN (*Mystified*): Up the hill?

JACK *and* JILL: That's where we went.

OLD WOMAN: Oh! You're Jack and Jill!

BO PEEP: "Dragging their tails behind them."

OLD WOMAN: So you're the little girl who lost her sheep, Bo Peep!

BOY BLUE: "Under the haystack."

OLD WOMAN: Fast asleep? Did you enjoy your nap, Boy Blue?

BOY BLUE: Yes, but folks are still talking about it.

MARY QUITE CONTRARY: "With silver bells."

OLD WOMAN (*Confused*): Let's see, do you have rings on your fingers and bells on your toes?

MARY QUITE CONTRARY: No, I have silver bells and cockle shells.

OLD WOMAN: Oh! You're Mary Quite Contrary, aren't you?

POLLY FLINDERS: "Nice new clothes."

OLD WOMAN (*Admiring* POLLY's *clothes*): They certainly are nice.

POLLY FLINDERS: Except when I start spoiling them.

OLD WOMAN: Polly Flinders, you sit among the cinders!

POLLY FLINDERS: Only when my feet get cold.

SIMPLE SIMON: "Going to the fair."

OLD WOMAN: Goodness, I suppose all of you go to the fair at one time or another.

SIMPLE SIMON: "Let me taste your ware."

OLD WOMAN: You're Simple Simon, and you met a pie-man!

TOM TUCKER: "White bread and butter."

OLD WOMAN: Sing for your supper! I know who *you* are. You're Tom Tucker.

MOTHER GOOSE: Now take off your wraps, everyone. Pile them right here on the couch. How nice to see you all! (MOTHER GOOSE *and* OLD WOMAN *help children off with their wraps. While their backs are turned,* BOY BLUE *quietly slips to the tree and hangs a package on it, then quietly slips back to others.*)

SIMPLE SIMON: We thought of a riddle, Mother Goose. See if you can guess. We thought of someone whose initials are S.N., K.K. and S.C.—and it's all the same person.

MOTHER GOOSE: One person with three sets of initials? I never heard of such a thing. (*To* OLD WOMAN) Did you?

OLD WOMAN: Not in all my born days.

OTHERS: Yes, you did. Give up?

MOTHER GOOSE: Give up.

SIMPLE SIMON: St. Nicholas, Kris Kringle, and Santa Claus.

OTHERS: All the same person!

MOTHER GOOSE: Well, I never.

MARY QUITE CONTRARY: *I'm* thinking of something we couldn't get along without for Christmas—something besides Santa Claus. There are two words to its name. The first begins with an ocean and the second begins with something to drink.

MOTHER GOOSE: There isn't such a word!

MARY QUITE CONTRARY: Oh, yes, there is. There's one right in this room. (MOTHER GOOSE *and* OLD WOMAN *look around baffled.*)

OLD WOMAN: Begins with an ocean? In this room?

MOTHER GOOSE: Has something to drink?

OTHERS (*Laughing*): Christmas Tree! (MOTHER GOOSE *and* OLD WOMAN *are still puzzled.*)

MARY QUITE CONTRARY: *Christmas* begins with a C, and a sea is an ocean, isn't it? And *tree* begins with a T, and tea is something to drink.

MOTHER GOOSE: Get along with you, you scalawags! (TOM TUCKER *starts toward Christmas tree, singing, and others join in. They circle the tree, singing.*)

CHILDREN: Here we go round the Christmas tree, Christmas tree, Christmas tree; here we go round the Christmas tree at Mother Goose's party. Everybody is full of glee, full of glee, full of glee; everybody is full of glee at Mother Goose's party.

MOTHER GOOSE: All right, now, sit down, everyone . . . while I "ocean" what's on the Christmas tree for you!

(Goes to tree, looks at tags. As each name is called, guest comes forward, reads tag aloud, opens gift and shows it, and returns to seat.) Let's see, now. Here's something for Jack and Jill. *(Takes twin packages from tree.)*

JACK AND JILL *(Reading card together)*:
Jack and Jill, when at the hill
To fetch a pail of water,
Use a CANE, and then it's plain
You won't go tumbling after.
(Children clap as JACK *and* JILL *unwrap their gifts and find large candy canes.)*

MOTHER GOOSE: I'm not the best poet in the world, but you get the idea! *(She picks up another gift.)* Little Bo Peep.

BO PEEP *(Reading card)*:
Little Bo Peep
You lost your sheep,
But now you'll always find them,
For here's a pup to round them up
And hurry home behind them.
(Bo PEEP *unwraps parcel to find a stuffed toy dog.)*

MOTHER GOOSE *(Taking down another gift)*: Simple Simon.

SIMPLE SIMON *(Reading)*:
Simple Simon, when a pieman
Has a heart of stone,
Here's a *mix* so you can fix
A pie that's all your own.
(SIMPLE SIMON holds up a package of pie mix.)

MOTHER GOOSE *(Finding another gift)*: Little Polly Flinders.

POLLY FLINDERS *(Reading card)*:
Little Polly Flinders,
Forget about the cinders.
They ruin your nice new clothes.

These slippers will be handy
And ought to work just dandy
For warming your pretty little toes.
(POLLY FLINDERS *holds up a pair of woolly slippers.*)

MOTHER GOOSE (*Holding out another gift*): Little Boy Blue.

BOY BLUE (*Reading*):
Little Boy Blue, you went to sleep—
The cow got out and so did the sheep.
Here is a story to keep you awake
And save you from making the same mistake!
(BOY BLUE *holds up a book with a bright-colored jacket.*)

MOTHER GOOSE (*Taking down another gift*): Mary Quite Contrary.

MARY (*Reading*):
Mary, Mary quite contrary
How does your garden grow?
With carrots, beans, and spinach greens,
And cabbages all in a row!
(*She holds up packets of seeds.*)

MOTHER GOOSE (*Looking at tree*): Let's see. Here's one for Tom Tucker.

TOM TUCKER (*Reading card*):
When little Tom Tucker
Sings for his supper,
What will he eat?
White bread and butter.
Who will have baked it?
Somebody's wife.
How will Tom cut it
Without any knife?
(TOM TUCKER *opens parcel and is delighted with his new jackknife.*)

MOTHER GOOSE: And now, Old Woman Who Lives in a

Shoe, here's something under the tree for you. (*Holds out bulky package.*)

OLD WOMAN: For me? (*Reads card*)

Be cheery, Old Woman Who Lives in a Shoe,

Here's something in up-to-date housing for you:

A house that is honest-to-goodness and real

And not just a shoe that's run down at the heel.

(OLD WOMAN *opens package to find a bright cardboard doll's house.*)

BOY BLUE (*Coming up and pointing to the package he put on the tree when no one was looking*): And now, Mother Goose, please look and see what's in *that* package on the tree.

MOTHER GOOSE (*Surprised*): Did I forget someone?

BOY BLUE: You certainly did. (*Takes down package and hands it to her*) It has your name on it.

MOTHER GOOSE: Mine? How in the world did it get there? (*Reads*)

"Dear Mother Goose, we're all agreed

Without you we'd be lost indeed,

So on a day as nice as this is

We give you lots and lots of kisses!"

MOTHER GOOSE: Kisses? (*Opens wrapper to find a box of candy kisses.*) How sweet! (*Passes them around*) And now I have a surprise for you. You notice there are still some gifts on the tree? (*Children nod.*) And others beneath the tree? (*Children nod again.*) They're for our unexpected guests.

CHILDREN (*Looking around*): Our unexpected guests?

SIMPLE SIMON: Do you mean someone is hiding around here?

MOTHER GOOSE: Not exactly hiding, but out of sight.

CHILDREN: Where?

MOTHER GOOSE: Very close. Behind the veil that divides the real world from the make-believe.

POLLY FLINDERS: I don't see any veil anywhere.

OTHERS: I don't either.

MOTHER GOOSE: But there is one, a big one, right out here in front of us. And since it is so close to Christmas, I can cast a spell and magic it away. (*Stands before audience blowing at "veil" and making gestures.*)

TOM TUCKER: Why, look, there are boys and girls sitting there watching us!

BO PEEP: Where did they come from?

MOTHER GOOSE: They've been there all along, only you couldn't see them.

OLD WOMAN: Well, I never!

MOTHER GOOSE (*Beckoning to audience*): Come, join the party, join the fun. We have a gift for everyone! (*As* MOTHER GOOSE *goes to the tree, where storybook characters help her, children from audience begin to file up for their gifts. They sing "Jingle Bells, Jolly Old St. Nicholas" and other songs during the gift-giving.*)

THE END

The Christmas Tablecloth

Characters

GRAM
MOTHER (MARGARET)
KATHY
RICK
DAD

TIME: *Christmas Day, late in the afternoon.*

SETTING: *Living room of a comfortable old farmhouse, decorated for Christmas. There is a Christmas tree in one corner, and an unlighted red Christmas candle in front of the window.*

AT RISE: MOTHER *is knitting.* GRAM *sits near a table on which lies a big half-opened tablecloth full of names and dates embroidered in red.* KATHY *is on the floor drawing pictures in colored chalk on large pieces of wrapping paper.*

GRAM: It's been a nice Christmas, hasn't it? Except for the tablecloth . . .

MOTHER: I'm sorry about that tablecloth. It means so much to all of us. But this is just one of those days when plans didn't work out.

KATHY: It hasn't stopped snowing for twenty-four hours! (*Brightens*) But one of *my* plans worked out—getting this box of colored chalk for Christmas. (*Holds up picture*) Do you recognize this, Mom? See, Gram? It's

156

the way our house looks in summer when the lilacs are in bloom. If I drew it the way it looks *now,* all I'd need would be white chalk.

MOTHER: Not bad, Kathy.

KATHY: I can do a better one. (*Goes back to drawing*)

MOTHER: I can't help wondering if Don and Phyllis started to come and got stuck. With the telephone out, there was no way to warn them. A snow-laden branch must have snapped the wires.

GRAM: Maybe the repair crew has been out by now, even if it is Christmas Day.

KATHY (*Jumping up*): I'll see. (*Picks up receiver, listens*) There's still that terrible ringing noise. I couldn't hear a word if anyone answered.

GRAM (*With a sigh, beginning to fold the tablecloth*): Well, I might as well fold up the tablecloth.

KATHY: Don't, Gram. Don't give up. Christmas isn't over yet.

GRAM: But nobody can possibly come in such a storm, Kathy.

KATHY: You can't be *sure.* Dad and Rick are out shoveling.

MOTHER: Just to the barn, remember. And even if they got as far as the road, the snowplow hasn't gone through. Nothing short of a helicopter could reach us today!

KATHY: I'm for not giving in until the very, very last minute. (*Goes back to drawing*)

GRAM (*Hesitates, then stops folding*): It's the first time in forty years somebody hasn't signed the tablecloth.

MOTHER: That long, Mother? I thought thirty-eight or -nine.

GRAM: Forty years today. I got the idea five years before you were born, Margaret. Your father fell right in with it . . . said it would make a wonderful heirloom for our grandchildren.

KATHY: That's Rick and me!

GRAM: I remember the Christmas I started the tablecloth we had Aunt El and Uncle Dave over for dinner. (*Finds place on cloth*) See, here are their signatures. I embroidered them over later in red floss. And here's the date underneath. 19— (*Fill in date, forty years before present year*) The next Christmas we had ten guests for dinner.

KATHY: It's good you didn't always have ten guests, or there wouldn't be any room for them to sign. (*Holds up picture*) How's this for a sprig of holly, Mom?

MOTHER: Very good, Kathy! Why don't you cut around it and pin it on the curtain?

KATHY (*Jumping up, starting for corner where Christmas tree stands*): Where's your work basket? Where's the scissors? Where's a pin? The table's gone, to make room for the Christmas tree!

MOTHER: Oh, of course. Look in my bedroom, Kathy. Dad carried the table in there when we put up the tree. (KATHY *goes out.*)

GRAM (*Still looking at tablecloth*): The year of the flu epidemic we nearly missed getting a signature. But old Dr. Herrington came in the afternoon and I remembered to have him sign. How I ever remembered with three of you down in bed is a mystery.

MOTHER: The tablecloth has always meant so much to you, that's why. (KATHY *comes back with pin, scissors, and an envelope.*)

KATHY (*Holding out the envelope*): What's this, Mom? It was sticking out from under your work basket. It's addressed to Gram.

MOTHER: Mercy goodness, I forgot all about that letter!

GRAM: For me?

MOTHER: It's from your old friend Addie, Mother. Her

daughter wrote me several weeks ago asking for my date-bar recipe, and enclosed this Christmas letter for you. She asked me to hold it until nearer the holidays, and I forgot all about it when we moved the table. I'm sorry.

GRAM: I'm not, Margaret. Now I have it to read on Christmas Day. There couldn't be a better time to have a visit with Addie. (*Takes letter, opens it, adjusts glasses, reads.* KATHY *cuts around picture, pins it on curtain and stands back to admire it. Goes back to window and stands looking out.*) Her son Arnold has another boy, born on Halloween. His name is Peter, but Addie calls him Punkins. Sounds just like Addie! (*Goes back to letter.*)

KATHY: The path to the barn is filling in already. Rick and Dad had better hurry with their chores or they'll have to shovel their way back to the house again. (*Sighs*) Well, it does look as if nobody can get through to us today.

GRAM: Weren't you the one who wasn't willing to give up until the very, very last minute? (*Puts down letter*) Well, I must say reading Addie's letter was just like having a visit with her face to face. Just as if she'd been right here.

KATHY (*Suddenly inspired*): Gram, did she sign it?

GRAM: Of course, she did. Signed it "Your old friend, Addie."

KATHY: If it was just like having a visit with her, why couldn't you trace her signature on the tablecloth to embroider? Then you wouldn't break the record, Gram.

MOTHER: That's an idea!

GRAM (*Considering*): Trace it on the tablecloth? (*Shakes her head*) No, it wouldn't do. I'm afraid it wouldn't be fair. All the others have signed in person, crossed our threshold and been right here with us. No, it wouldn't be the same. I guess we'll just have to leave a blank space for 19— (*Fill in present year. Stamping feet are heard at back door.*)

KATHY: There's Dad and Rick.

MOTHER (*Calling out*): Shake your coats and caps on the porch. And take off your overshoes so you won't track up the floor.

KATHY: I bet they look like snowmen. (*Gets up and runs to kitchen, her voice trailing after her*) Did your hands freeze? How deep is the snow? Did you remember to take the yardstick, Rick?

DAD (*Coming in, rubbing hands*): A good day to stay home, and a good night to go to bed early. There'll be a lot of shoveling to do in the morning. (KATHY *and* RICK *come in.*)

KATHY: How deep is it?

RICK: Almost thirty inches, and still coming down.

DAD: It's slackening a little, though. Sky ought to be bright and clear by morning. But I doubt if the snowplow will reach us for a few days. (*Looks around, goes to turn on tree lights*) Well, this is what I call a nice cozy family Christmas. It doesn't often happen we're alone on Christmas.

GRAM: Only once in forty years!

RICK: Poor Gram, there hasn't been any company to sign her tablecloth. And Christmas is almost over.

KATHY: It's dark enough now to light the candle in the window, isn't it, Mom?

RICK: Why light the candle? Nobody's going to see it.

KATHY: *We'll* see it. Let me take your matches, Dad. (*He hands her a little box of safety matches, and she lights the candle.*)

RICK: What's for supper, Mom? I'm starved in eight languages.

MOTHER: After all that turkey you ate this noon, Rick?

KATHY (*Suddenly*): Listen! I heard something.

RICK: Just the nice quiet snow falling, that's all.

KATHY: No, I heard a funny sort of squeak. Listen! (*All are quiet for a moment. A faint squeaking noise is heard.*) There! On the window sill! Look, someone *did* see the Christmas candle!

DAD: Why, it's that little stray cat we saw out at the barn. I thought I told you to shut her in, Rick.

RICK: She must have slipped out with us when we finished the chores.

KATHY: I wonder whom she belongs to. She's cold and hungry and lonesome, poor little thing. Mom, I'm going out to get her.

MOTHER: Just open the back door and call, Kathy. She'll probably come. (KATHY *hurries out, and can be heard calling, "Here, kitty, kitty, kitty." In a moment she returns with the cat in her arms.*)

KATHY: She's shivering and purring at the same time.

GRAM: Poor little mite.

MOTHER: Get her a saucer of warm milk, Kathy. And put the saucer on a paper so she won't drip on the floor. (KATHY *goes to kitchen with kitten.*) Whose do you think it is?

DAD: Probably one of Sandersons'. They have about a dozen.

RICK: Well, Gram, we did get some company, after all, didn't we? It's just too bad cats can't write on tablecloths.

MOTHER: Yes, it is. To think that after forty years— (KATHY *comes back with saucer and cat.*)

KATHY: I'll put her down on one of my old pictures, so I can pet her while she drinks. Nice kitty. There! Enjoy your Christmas supper.

DAD: It's a good feeling to have the cows under cover on a night like this.

RICK: And the chores done early.

KATHY (*Suddenly excited*): Gram!

GRAM: Goodness, Kathy, you made me jump. What's the matter?

KATHY: Gram, look. Come here, everyone. Look! (*They crowd around.*) The cat stepped on the lilac bush in my picture and look!

MOTHER: The colored chalk dust stuck to her paw, and she's made a purple footprint, like a little rose

GRAM: What a pretty little print!

RICK: Only roses don't come in purple.

KATHY: The color doesn't matter, Rick. It's the *idea.*

RICK: What idea?

KATHY: Don't you see? It can be a signature . . . without having to be traced. A signature for Gram's tablecloth. We can hold the kitten up to put its footprint on the cloth, for Gram to embroider.

GRAM: Why, Kathy, you're right. The only visitor who crossed our threshold today! And the little print will be one of the nicest signatures of all.

KATHY: So the record will go on unbroken, won't it? And the print of a little red rose will mark a Christmas we'll never forget! (*Curtain*)

THE END

PLAYLETS AND SPELLDOWNS

Standing Up for Santa

Characters

BRUCE
BARBARA
TEN BOYS AND GIRLS
CHILDREN IN AUDIENCE

SETTING: *A stage.*
AT RISE: BOYS *and* GIRLS *come in singing "Jolly Old St. Nicholas." Each carries behind his back a large red letter. As* BOYS *and* GIRLS *near end of first stanza of song,* BRUCE *and* BARBARA *enter. They stand near front of stage, listening.*

BOYS *and* GIRLS: "Christmas Eve is coming soon;
Now, you dear old man,
Whisper what you'll bring to me;
Tell me if you can."
BRUCE (*To audience*): Why, it sounds as if they believe in Santa Claus! Can you feature that!
VOICE (*From audience*): I believe in him, too.
2ND VOICE: I don't. What about you, Barbara?
BARBARA: Yes . . . and no.
BRUCE: Believe in Santa Claus! (*Mimics singers*) "Whisper what you'll bring to me." Did anyone ever *see* Santa Claus, I'd like to know . . . let alone get close enough to hear him whisper? (*Points to boy in audience*) Did

you ever see him? I mean the Santa Claus who's supposed to drive reindeer . . . not the one in a department store.

BOY (*In audience*): No-ooo.

BRUCE (*Pointing to girl in audience*): Did *you* ever see him?

GIRL: Almost . . . once. But I fell asleep just before he came.

BRUCE: Well, I never saw him, either. And I won't believe in anything I can't see.

BARBARA: But you believe in . . . in liberty, Bruce. You can't see that.

BRUCE: But liberty *means* something. I believe in what it stands for. What does Santa Claus stand for, I'd like to know?

BARBARA: Sh, Bruce. They want to finish the song.

BOYS *and* GIRLS (*Singing*):
"When the clock is striking twelve,
When I'm fast asleep,
Down the chimney broad and black,
With your pack you'll creep . . ."

BRUCE (*Interrupting*): You're way behind the times. Most houses don't have chimneys broad and black any more. Ours hasn't. Barbara's hasn't. Half the houses in our block haven't. People cook with electricity these days, and heat with oil. They don't need chimneys broad and black.

BARBARA: We cook with gas and heat with gas, and you don't need much of a chimney for that.

BRUCE: Anyway, who'd want to creep down a chimney broad and black? (*Points to boy in audience*) Would you?

BOY: No, not exactly.

BRUCE (*Pointing to girl*): Would you?

GIRL: Oh, I should say not. I'd get all dirty.

BRUCE: So would Santa Claus. All in all, I can't believe that anyone wants to crawl down a broad black chimney. Santa Claus!

BARBARA: Not so loud, Bruce.

BOYS *and* GIRLS (*Singing again*):
"All the stockings you will find
Hanging in a row;
Mine will be the shortest one,
You'll be sure to know."

BRUCE: As if he could see with soot in his eyes.

BARBARA: Shhh!

BOYS *and* GIRLS (*Singing*):
"Johnny wants a pair of skates;
Susy wants a sled . . ."

BRUCE (*Interrupting, to audience*): Did you ever try to push a nice big *sled* down a chimney?

BOYS *and* GIRLS:
"Nellie wants a picture book;
Yellow, blue and red."

BRUCE: And black. Don't forget a little chimney black!

BOYS *and* GIRLS:
"Now I think I'll leave to you
What to give the rest;
Choose for me, dear Santa Claus,
You will know the best."

BRUCE (*Mimicking*): "Choose for me, dear Santa Claus, you will know the best." (*To* BOYS *and* GIRLS) So you really believe in him!

GIRLS: Of course, we do.

BOYS: You believe in him too, Bruce, only you won't admit it. So does Barbara.

BARBARA: I do admit it . . . sort of.

BRUCE: Well, I don't. And all the king's horses and all the king's men can't make me.

BOYS *and* GIRLS: Don't be so sure.

BARBARA: But how can *you* be so sure?

BOYS *and* GIRLS: Because of what he stands for.

BRUCE: Stands for? What does Santa Claus stand for?

BARBARA: Yes, what?

GIRLS: He stands for the spirit of Christmas.

BOYS: He spells out the joy of Christmas-time.

BRUCE: How, I'd like to know? (BOYS *and* GIRLS *begin to "spell out" SANTA CLAUS. As each says his lines, he takes a step forward and shows his letter. A space should be left between the two words.*)

1ST: S for shopping, and surprises,
secrets of all shapes and sizes.

2ND: A for adding once again
to peace on earth, good will to men.

3RD: N for night of new-found glory
pictured in the Christmas story.

4TH: T for trees, and tunes, and toys,
and oh, such *thoughtful* girls and boys.

5TH: A for all who are aware
of something special in the air.

6TH: C for cheer for friend and stranger,
and for Christ Child in the manger.

7TH: L for lights of red and green
dressing up the winter scene.

8TH: A for angels softly singing
of the tidings they are bringing.

9TH: U for using thought and care
to scatter pleasure everywhere.

10TH: S for star and stable near it,
and for sparkly Christmas spirit.

BOYS *and* GIRLS (*Holding letters high*): That spells SANTA CLAUS.

BRUCE: Well, so it does. What do you know?

BARBARA: I know I believe in everything the letters stand for. Don't you, Bruce?

BRUCE (*Hesitating*): I can't remember.

1ST: Surprises . . . secrets.

BRUCE: I believe in those any old time.

2ND: Acting with good will.

BRUCE: Oh, sure.

3RD: The night of the first Christmas—you believe in that, don't you, Bruce?

BRUCE: Yes, I do.

4TH: Trees . . . tunes . . . and toys.

BRUCE: You bet!

5TH: Being aware of something special.

BRUCE: I guess nobody can miss *that* at Christmas time.

6TH: Cheer. Lots of cheer.

BRUCE: Yes.

7TH: Lights.

BRUCE: On Christmas trees and in the shops—well, I should say!

8TH: Angels bringing tidings of great joy.

BRUCE (*Nodding*): "And on earth peace, good will to men."

9TH: Using care to make others happy. You believe in that?

BRUCE: What would Christmas be without it?

10TH: Star . . . stable . . . Christmas spirit.

BRUCE: Everybody believes in them.

BOYS *and* GIRLS (*Laughing*): You see!

BRUCE: What do I see?

BOYS *and* GIRLS: You believe in everything Santa Claus stands for.

VOICES (*From audience*): So do we!

BARBARA (*To* BRUCE): In spite of all the king's horses and all the king's men, you believe in Santa Claus.

AUDIENCE: Santa Claus!

BOYS *and* GIRLS (*Holding letters high*): Santa Claus!

BRUCE: Well . . . when you put it that way . . . who

wouldn't believe in him! (*He and* BARBARA *join* BOYS *and* GIRLS *and they march around singing "Jolly Old St. Nicholas." Curtain*)

THE END

What's for Christmas?

Characters

MASTER OF CEREMONIES (M. C.)
BOYS AND GIRLS
MESSENGER
TWO PORTERS
TEACHER *or* GROUP LEADER

Everyone in the room or group should be prepared to take part in this Christmas program, although no one knows who will get a chance to perform or in what order the acts will come!

One child may like to prepare a little dance, representing a snowflake, mechanical man, toy monkey, or some other toy. Another may want to sing a Christmas song. Another may be good at speaking a Christmas piece or doing a monologue. Several may like to work together and act out a pantomime, or skit. If any children have special musical or artistic talent, they might like to use it in some act that could be tied in with Christmas.

The program begins when the Master of Ceremonies comes in, at front of room or stage, ringing a bell.

M. C.: Merry Christmas, everyone! You are about to attend a most unusual Christmas program—one where the audience picks the show! We have here actors from

(*Insert grade and school, or name of group*). Each one is ready to perform his part in this Christmas program, and yet no one knows whether he will get a chance to act or not! No one knows just what this entertainment is going to be like. It's all up to the audience! (M. C. *picks up a big net Christmas stocking from table nearby and holds it up.*) This stocking, my friends, holds the key to our Christmas program. In it are the names of all our actors, written on slips of paper and folded up. All the slips look alike. You, the audience, will choose the acts! (M. C. *walks down into audience, stopping at some seat and holding out the stocking.*) Will you kindly draw a slip? Will you choose the first act? (*Member of audience draws a slip, hands it to* M. C., *who reads the name on it.*) My friends, our Christmas program this year begins with an act by ——. (*Reads name, or names, on slip. Performer does act. When the first act is over, performer returns to his seat in audience, as audience applauds.* M. C. *takes up Christmas stocking again, rings bell for silence, and goes down into audience.*)

M. C.: The audience picks the show, my friends! And now we are ready for the second act on our program. (*Stops and offers stocking to someone in audience.*) Would you like to choose it? (*Acts are all handled in this way, with members of the audience pulling slips from the stocking. It would be more fun for the children if they did not know what acts the others had prepared. After all acts have been given, a* MESSENGER *suddenly rushes into the room from the back, and hurries through the audience. As he goes he calls loudly:*)

MESSENGER: Call for ——. (*Name of teacher or group leader.*) Call for ——. (*Repeat several times.*)

TEACHER (*Stepping in front of audience*): For me! What in the world can it be?

MESSENGER: Are you ——? (*Insert name.*)

TEACHER: Yes, I am.

MESSENGER (*Holding out pad and pencil*): Sign here, please. Special delivery letter. And two large parcels. (*Turns and calls back to* PORTERS.) Bring the packages in here, boys. Here's the person we're looking for. (*Hands letter to* TEACHER.) Here's the letter!

TEACHER: This is a big surprise. Why, it's from Santa Claus! Return address: Santa Claus & Co., North Pole. (*As she opens the envelope, two* PORTERS *bring up a big box and sack through the audience to the stage.*)

MESSENGER: Put them right there, boys. That'll be all. Well (*Turns to* TEACHER) . . . Merry Christmas!

TEACHER: Merry Christmas to you. (MESSENGER *and* PORTERS *exit, going down through audience.*)

TEACHER (*Opening letter and reading*):

"Dear —— (*Insert name.*) Would you kindly do me a favor? I have been unusually busy this year, and I still have a thousand and one things to do before Christmas. I know you will understand when I tell you it would rush me too much to attend your Christmas program this year. But I have thought of a great plan! By special messenger I am sending a box containing one of my extra outfits, so *you* can dress up like me. No one will probably ever know the difference! Also, I am sending a special bag of gifts for your boys and girls. Thanks a lot for helping me out. You can't imagine how much this means to me. Merry Christmas! Your old friend, Santa Claus.

P. S. Be careful how you stick on the whiskers. Don't sneeze, or they might fall off!" (*Looks up.*) Well, so I am to be Santa Claus this year! I hope the costume will fit me. Let's see . . . : (TEACHER *opens the box containing the costume, takes out the various items one by one. Box contains whiskers, beard, false hair, two small pillows for padding, red coat trimmed in white cotton, red cap, belt for coat, and a huge pair of overshoes with white cotton glued around the tops. Trousers are omitted, which makes the costume look even funnier. TEACHER dresses up as Santa Claus in front of the audience, putting on each thing deliberately and rather rakishly.*)

TEACHER (*When she has finished dressing up*):
There! Now don't forget I'm Santa Claus! (*Picks up sack of toys and puts it over shoulder; walks back and forth for a short time.*) That was quite a trip coming down from the North Pole, specially for this Christmas program. I wouldn't want to miss it for anything, though. I had some anxious moments when Dasher shied at one of those new-fangled weather balloons. But here I am! Santa Claus in person. (*Shakes finger at audience.*) Don't ever let anyone tell you there isn't a Santa Claus! (*Takes bag off shoulder, and looks in.*) Now, let me see . . . as I remember there are some little things in here for certain girls and boys with names like . . . (*Begins to take out gifts and call names. As each name is called, children come up from audience for their presents, then return to their seats. When the bag is empty, and shaken out, M. C. comes running in, ringing bell.*)

M. C.: And now, before Santa Claus dashes back to the North Pole, let's all stand up and sing "Jolly Old St. Nicholas."
(*Everyone sings, and on that note, the program ends.*)

THE END

Christmas in Quarantine

(A pantomime with one speaking part, which may be read)

Characters

MOTHER
GWEN
GERALD
DANNY

TIME: *Christmas afternoon.*

SETTING: *May be presented with or without a stage set. Action takes place in the living room of a family home decorated for Christmas. A door at the back leads to the kitchen; another door (at the side) to other rooms of the house. On the other side of the living room are windows facing the street.*

AT RISE: MOTHER *sits near the windows writing a letter at a desk or table. Close by,* DANNY *is curled up in a big chair with a lap robe over him. He is looking at the pictures in his Christmas books. His actions should make it obvious that he is just recuperating from an illness.* MOTHER *reads letter aloud as she writes it.*

MOTHER *(Slowly, as if writing)*:
My dear, dear husband: How I have missed you this Christmas afternoon—our first Christmas apart in four-

teen years! And the children have missed you, too. I
tried to make it a happy Christmas for them, but I'm
afraid I haven't succeeded too well. Being quarantined
just doesn't seem to go with Christmas, does it? And
there you are over at Carlson's, wanting to be home as
much as we want to have you!

Danny continues to get better and stronger. He is
sitting near me in the big chair as I write, looking at his
Christmas books. In fact, he is so much better, I have a
hard time keeping him still. (DANNY *drops one of his
books, throws off lap robe, and starts to go after book.*
MOTHER *turns from letter, hands him the book, and
tucks him in again, shaking her finger at him as a warning for him to keep quiet. Then she goes back to her
writing.*)

MOTHER (*Continuing*) : Doctor says that in a day or two,
for sure, the quarantine sign can come down, and we
can all be together again. It's been such a long time!
Not quite three weeks, but it seems like ages. Gwen and
Gerald have been getting on each other's nerves, I am
sorry to say. Right this minute I hear a frightful racket in
the kitchen. I do hope they don't *break* anything. You'd
think that on Christmas afternoon all would be peaceful
and happy. But no. Gwen and Gerald have been teasing
each other and quarreling ever since dinner. I suppose
I can't blame them *too* much. They have been cooped
up here in the house for so long, and you know how full
of energy and high spirits they are!

Everything was quite gay and jolly this morning, with
the novelty of the presents and all. And the Christmas
tree looks lovely. You were a dear to take care of everything, and have all those packages left at the door, and
the tree, and greens, and all.

Well, as I was saying, this morning was a jolly time.

But now that it's getting along in the afternoon . . .
(*As* MOTHER *writes,* GWEN *and* GERALD *come in, quarreling.* MOTHER *stops reading her letter aloud as the children pantomime.* GWEN, *wearing an apron, has a book, evidently a cookbook, which* GERALD *wants.* GERALD *keeps pulling* GWEN'S *apron strings, as she holds the book away from him. They make faces at each other, and hop about. Finally,* GERALD *knocks the book down.* DANNY, *excited, slips off his chair to get the book.* MOTHER *leaves her writing and comes to break up the quarrel. She sends* GWEN *back to the kitchen and* GERALD *out the other door. After getting* DANNY *settled in his chair again, she goes back to her writing.*)

MOTHER: As I was saying, Gwen and Gerald are very restless. It's the first time in their lives they haven't been out with their friends on Christmas afternoon, or had some of their friends here. Oh, well, in a few more days they will be able to use up their energy outdoors. And *you* will be back home again! (GWEN *comes in with her new Christmas shoe skates. She sits near the windows and tries them on, while* DANNY *and* MOTHER *watch. Then* GWEN *looks longingly out the window, sighs heavily, sadly takes off the skates, and goes out.* MOTHER *returns to her writing.*)

MOTHER: It is hard for the children, of course, to see their nice new outdoor gifts and not be able to use them. Everything is so near and yet so far this Christmas. Here you are only three blocks away from us, and you might as well be *miles.* Though it was nice of you, dear, to walk past the house twice this morning and wave to us and leave those extra Christmas greetings. (GERALD *comes in with his new skis. He puts them on, adjusts straps, bends over and balances himself as if he were sliding down a steep hill.* MOTHER *and* DANNY *watch.*

GERALD *goes through other make-believe skiing antics;* *then, with a great sigh, takes off the skis, picks them up sorrowfully, and exits.*)

MOTHER: Gerald has just been practicing some skiing steps (do you call them *steps?*) in the middle of the living-room floor. He is so proud of the new skis, and I must say they are much nicer than I expected—for the price. He can't *wait* to try them out on the hill, any more than Gwen can wait to try out her skates. I tell them they can be glad they didn't catch scarlet fever from Danny, or they'd be cooped up for some more weeks! (GWEN *and* GERALD *come sauntering back into the living room, with time hanging heavy on their hands. They are just beginning to pick at each other again when* DANNY, *looking out of the window, waves frantically.* MOTHER *looks.* GWEN *and* GERALD *hurry over and wave too.* MOTHER, *standing at the window, nods and smiles.* GERALD *rushes out the door like a thunderbolt.* MOTHER *goes back to writing.*)

MOTHER: How sweet of you to walk past again just now, dear, and to throw another letter on the porch for us. Gerald is just getting it. But, really, you should wear your woolen muffler on a cold day like this . . . and your *overshoes,* even if the walks *are* shoveled. (GERALD *runs in with the letter.* MOTHER *opens it, and the children huddle around to read it.* DANNY *obviously has the hardest time understanding, since he is the youngest.* MOTHER *smiles and nods.* GWEN *and* GERALD *look at each other questioningly. Then* GERALD *shrugs as if to say it's all right with him.* GWEN *blinks and grins. And all of a sudden everyone is overwhelmingly gracious to each other!* GWEN *and* GERALD *bend over backward trying to be nice. They pass each other fruit and candy. They insist on each other having the most comfortable chairs, etc. Then* GWEN *jumps up and begins to decorate the coffee table with sprigs of spruce, and cones.* GERALD *pulls up chairs. They bring a new book for* DANNY *to look at, and a pillow for* MOTHER. MOTHER, *meanwhile, goes on with her letter.*)

MOTHER: However did you think of it? *Just* when we needed it, too. We've all fallen right into the spirit of your marvelous idea, and I'm sure it's going to make all the difference for the rest of the day. Why, it's going to be perfectly jolly! Gwen and Gerald are fixing up the coffee table right now for "company" refreshments. They have taken to your suggestion like ducks to water. How *did* you think of it! And what a nice way you put it. (MOTHER *picks up father's letter and reads from it.*)

"Since you're spending Christmas in quarantine, and can't have company, my four great big dears, why don't you make believe you're *all* company . . . and treat each other like guests? It ought to be amusing . . . and very dramatic." (*At that moment,* GWEN *and* GERALD *indulge in an ultrapolite drama of putting the finishing touches to the refreshment table. Then with a flourish, they escort* MOTHER *and* DANNY *to their chairs, and everyone sits merrily nodding and smiling at each other as the curtain closes.*)

THE END

Shoes and Stockings and Solomon

Characters

READER
SHOE
STOCKING
SOLOMON (*the Teddy Bear*)

AT RISE: SHOE *and* STOCKING *are sitting absolutely still when* READER *comes in with book and begins to read:*

READER: Along about the first of December each year, the Right Shoe and the Left Stocking—to say nothing of the Left Shoe and the Right Stocking—always used to get into a frightful argument. They did it for years. Every night of the Christmas month they started quarreling exactly at midnight, which, as you know, is the charmed hour for people like shoes and stockings and Teddy Bears. "Time to wake up, time to wake up, time to wake up," the clock would say as it struck twelve. And then the talk would begin! (*Sound of gong or triangle struck twelve times.*)

STOCKING (*Sitting up suddenly, looking at* SHOE): As I was saying . . . I'm certainly glad I was born a Stocking instead of a Shoe. It's almost Christmas! Soon I shall come into my own, and I don't mean into my own shoe either. Soon I shall be the most important person around here!

SHOE (*Making a face*): But in the long run, Miss Stocking, you know perfectly well you'd never get anywhere without me. You better not treat me like a heel.

STOCKING (*Excitedly*): In a few days it will be Christmas Eve. And then I shall be hung in the place of honor at the fireplace, while you cool your heels under the bed, Mr. Shoe.

SHOE (*Sadly*): You sometimes talk as if you hadn't any sole, Miss Stocking.

STOCKING: Oh, the thrill of it! To be hanging at the fireplace when Santa Claus comes down the chimney!

SHOE: Do you mean to say you really believe that story?

STOCKING: Why, of course. I've heard it from ever so many of my relatives—before they became dust-rags. Just think, Mr. Shoe, I shall be hanging there waiting when Santa comes. And then he will fill me with all kinds of wonderful things . . .

SHOE (*Stifling a yawn*): Ho, hum.

STOCKING: Nuts and candy and toys and an orange. . . . Isn't it exciting? Oh, I must say I was lucky being born a Stocking instead of a Shoe, because I have such an important part to play at Christmas time.

SHOE: You're certainly head over heels in love with yourself, aren't you?

READER: And so the talk would go on between the Right Stocking and the Left Shoe, or the Left Stocking and the Right Shoe, if you prefer. Every night, right up till Christmas itself, the Stocking would boast of her importance; and every night the poor Shoe had his toes stepped on.

Then one night, three days before Christmas, Solomon Grundy, the Teddy Bear, accidentally walked into the argument. Solomon usually stayed with his friends in the playroom, but this particular night the noise in the bedroom was so loud, Solomon came to see what he could do about it. (SOLOMON *enters, stands waiting*.)

Now, Solomon Grundy was an unusually wise Teddy Bear. His button eyes shone with a special glint of intelligence. Which is why he was named Solomon in the first place, after wise King Solomon. Well, for a moment Solomon stood there watching the sparks fly, and then he spoke:

SOLOMON: Miss Stocking, have you perchance ever traveled in Spain?

STOCKING: Spain? No, I can't say that I have. And what's more I have no desire to set foot on foreign soil!

SOLOMON: Then you have never traveled in France, Holland, or Norway either?

STOCKING: Assuredly not.

SOLOMON: And, I presume, you have never read a travel book either?

SHOE (*Chuckling*): If she tried to open a book, she'd put her foot in it!

STOCKING: What is the point of all this, Solomon, may I ask?

SOLOMON: Oh, just that . . . in Spain, on Twelfth Night, the children put their *shoes* between the gratings of the window, and Balthazar, one of the Three Wise Men, always finds them and fills them with sugar plums.

SHOE *and* STOCKING: Their shoes!

SOLOMON: Quite so. And many French and Dutch children leave their shoes to be filled with Christmas presents. In Norway the whole family put their shoes together in a row on Christmas Eve, as a sign that everyone will get along well together during the coming year.

SHOE *and* STOCKING: Their shoes!

SOLOMON: Yes, their shoes. They don't even think of their stockings!

STOCKING: Th-th-they d-d-don't?

SOLOMON: No, and I think, my friends, that this little misunderstanding between you has gone quite far enough. Now if you, Miss Stocking, will put yourself in your friend's shoes, you'll see that you have done him a grave injustice, and if you, Mr. Shoe, will remember what I have just told you, it will never again be necessary for you to feel run down at the heel. Besides, my friends, Christmas is the season of peace and good will. Without that, you miss the whole point of everything. Come, now, shake hands and be friends. (SHOE *and* STOCKING *shake hands violently.* SOLOMON *nods and smiles.*)

READER: And so the argument was settled once and for all. And ever since, shoes and stockings have been on such good terms with each other that it really doesn't matter if you put your Right Stocking into the Left Shoe, or your Right Shoe over the Left Stocking, or your Right Stocking into the Right Shoe, or whatever you do, because the hearts of both shoes and stockings are now full of Christmas spirit. Especially at midnight!

THE END

Say It with Rhymes

(A spelldown for fifteen boys and girls)

Each child has a red cardboard letter, and all fifteen letters spell out MERRY CHRISTMAS! *The exclamation mark is on the 15th card. Along the front of the stage, there are numbers on the floor to show where children should stand when they step forward, since they will not step forward in order. There should be more space between the 5th card* (Y) *and the 6th Card* (C) *to separate the words* MERRY *and* CHRISTMAS. *The audience should be kept guessing what is being spelled out as long as possible. Everyone keeps his letter concealed until the proper time comes for him to step forward, and stand on his number. He holds up his letter as he recites his verse.*

7TH CHILD: H is for shiny green, red-berried holly,
  Whose brightness and color make Christmas more jolly.
2ND CHILD: E is for evergreen—symbol of life
  In weather that blusters and cuts like a knife.
5TH CHILD: Y is for Yule log that crackles and blazes
  And makes people tingle with holiday praises.
10TH CHILD: S is for Santa who comes in a sled
  Long after children are snoozing in bed.
12TH CHILD: M is for mistletoe hung from the ceiling,
  Giving its measure of Christmas-y feeling.

11TH CHILD: T is for tinsel, for tree, and for toys,
And thoughts of good will among all girls and boys.

4TH CHILD: R is for reindeer—"Now, Prancer and Vixen!
On, Comet! On, Cupid! On, Donder and Blitzen!"

14TH CHILD: S is for star on the tree, shining bright,
Recalling a star in Judea one night.

3RD CHILD: R is for redness of bell and of berry
That gives Christmas color and helps make it merry.

15TH CHILD: This is for something we need at the end,
To make it more hearty for neighbor and friend.

6TH CHILD: C is for Christ Child whose birth we remember
With reverence and joy every year in December.

13TH CHILD: A is for angel who came down to earth
With tidings of Jesus and news of his birth.

9TH CHILD: I is for icicles all strung together
Like fringe on the eaves in this cold Christmas weather.

8TH CHILD: R is for ribbons, gay-colored and bright,
Tied around presents to keep them from sight.

1ST CHILD: M is for music the season is bringing,
Gay songs of Christmas that carolers go singing.

ALL (*Holding letters high*):
And now that our message of Christmas is clear,
MERRY CHRISTMAS TO ALL! AND A HAPPY
NEW YEAR!

(*They sing a merry Christmas song.*)

The Week Before Christmas

Characters

BOY
GIRL
NINE BOYS
NINE GIRLS

AT RISE: BOY *and* GIRL *are on stage.*

GIRL (*Gaily*): Christmas is coming,
and laddies and lasses
are wearing the rosiest
rose-colored glasses.
BOY (*Glumly*): Christmas is coming . . .
as slow as molasses!
GIRL (*Gaily*): Christmas is coming—
it's very exciting,
with presents for wrapping
and greetings for writing.
BOY (*Glumly*): But waiting and waiting
is not so inviting!
GIRL (*Gaily*): Christmas is coming—
it's thrilling to tell it,
to see it and hear it
and sniff it and smell it.
BOY (*Glumly*): But oh, it is poky
however you spell it! (*Nine pairs of* BOYS *and* GIRLS

186

enter in turn, each pair with a letter to spell Christmas.
They may stand side by side or, if the stage is small, one
behind the other. They pantomime their parts as much
as possible.)

1ST BOY (*Carrying C, munching cookie*): C . . . for
crunching cookie crumbs,

1ST GIRL (*Shaking head over calendar*): And counting
days till Christmas comes!

2ND BOY (*Carrying H and holly sprig*): H . . . for hanging holly high,

2ND GIRL (*With clock*): And hoping time will hurry by!

3RD BOY (*Carrying R, and packages for mailing*): R . . .
for rushing gifts galore,

3RD GIRL: Then reading, "Christmas—eight days more!"

4TH BOY (*Carrying I*): I . . . for idling near each gift,

4TH GIRL: And itching for the twenty-fifth!

5TH BOY (*Carrying S, and gaily wrapped presents*): S . . .
for sealing secrets well,

5TH GIRL: And shush-ing sister not to tell!

6TH BOY (*Carrying T*): T . . . for trusting old St. Nick,

6TH GIRL: But thinking he's more slow than quick!

7TH BOY (*Carrying M*): M . . . for making plans complete.

7TH GIRL (*Marking time*): And marking time with restless
feet.

8TH BOY (*Carrying A, and holding gilt halo over head*):
A . . . for acting nice as pie,

8TH GIRL: And aching for the days to fly!

9TH BOY (*Carrying S*): S . . . for seeing snowflakes pelt,

9TH GIRL: And shouting for them not to melt!

ALL: That spells CHRISTMAS . . .
Hold your thumbs,
Hold your halo . . .
Here it comes!

Stable at Midnight

Characters

RONNIE
LINDA
FATHER

SETTING: *A stable at midnight, very dimly lit. Screens may be used to indicate stalls. The light is dim throughout.*
TIME: *Christmas Eve, near midnight.*
AT RISE: *The sound of a door creaking and footsteps are heard. A flashlight blinks on.* RONNIE *and* LINDA *come into the stable.*

RONNIE: They didn't hear us leave the house.
LINDA: But how the stairway squeaked!
    We tiptoed quiet as a mouse,
    And still our footsteps creaked.
RONNIE: Well, anyway, we're safely here.
LINDA: You're sure the clock was right?
RONNIE: It isn't midnight yet.
LINDA: How queer
    The stable looks at night.
    I wonder what the folks would say . . .
RONNIE: Well, *Grandma* must believe
    That cows get on their knees and pray
    At midnight, Christmas Eve.
    She told the story several times.

LINDA: I know. But is it true?

RONNIE: She says that when the church bell chimes
It's what the cattle do.

LINDA: But Grandpa never said a word.
And Father only smiled—
Perhaps *he* tried it when he heard
The story, as a child.

RONNIE: Well, Mother says it may be so.
She says some folks believe
That roosters give a lusty crow
At midnight, Christmas Eve,
To celebrate the Christ Child's birth.

LINDA: But how would roosters know?

RONNIE: They tell the news to all the earth.

LINDA: They speak in Latin, though!

RONNIE: Well, anyway, I'm glad this year
We've come to Grandpa's farm.
I'm also glad we stole out *here*. . . .

LINDA: It can't do any harm.
Let's turn the flashlight on the coop.
(*They go to one side of the barn, open a door, and turn
the light into the next room.*)

RONNIE: It's quiet as can be.

LINDA: Those chickens are a sleepy group.

RONNIE (*Suddenly, excited*): The rooster looked at me!
I think he *just* was going to crow.
I bet we scared him out!

LINDA (*Doubtfully*): Perhaps he doesn't even know
What Christmas is about.
Besides, it's not quite midnight yet.
Let's watch the cows instead!
We'll *hear* the rooster, don't forget,
If it's as Mother said.
(*They come back into the stable and flash the light
around.*)

RONNIE: Three cows are up, and one is down.

LINDA: Give me the flashlight, please.

RONNIE (*Excited*): Oh, look! The white cow marked with
brown
Is going to her knees!
You see? She's really kneeling down . . .
(*There is a loud noise outside, and* FATHER *comes into
the stable with a lantern.*)

FATHER: What goings on are these?

LINDA: Father . . .

RONNIE: Oh!

FATHER: I *thought* I heard the stairway creak.
I *thought* I heard a door . . .
Your beds were empty. Come, now, speak—
What did you do it for?

LINDA: We hoped we'd hear the rooster crow,
And see the cattle kneel.

RONNIE (*Disappointed*): Our flashlight scared the rooster,
though.

FATHER: I know the way you feel.
But nothing really works, you see,
When *people* are about.

RONNIE: But I am sure as I can be
The cow, without a doubt,
Got down upon her knees to pray—
That white one marked with brown.

FATHER (*Softly*): My son, that is the usual way.
She does, when she lies down.
I came here one time years ago . . .

LINDA: You mean, you don't believe?

FATHER: Of course, I do. You see, I know
It's part of Christmas Eve!
But such things aren't for human eyes
Or human ears at all . . .
You will not watch if you are wise

Or hide beside the stall,
You will not pick the myths apart
To see if they are right,
You just must know that *every* heart
Is glad this holy night.
LINDA *and* RONNIE: We just must know that every heart
Is glad this holy night.

THE END

A Gift for Old St. Nick

*(A musical skit to be sung to the tune
of "Jolly Old St. Nicholas.")*

THREE BOYS *and* THREE GIRLS *are on stage. They hold
large cardboard letters behind their backs, showing
them as they sing their individual lines.*

GROUP: Jolly old St. Nicholas,
    Lend your ear this way,
    We have something on our minds
    That we'd like to say:
    You have given us so much,
    Old St. Nick, it's true
    We would like to give a gift
    Labeled just for you.
BOYS: What we give is just a word,
    Not so very long.
    But we give it from our hearts
    With a merry song.
GIRLS: Every letter of the six
    Stands for what you do,
    But, together, they spell out
    What we give to you!
1ST BOY: T is for the toys you leave
    Every Christmas-tide.

1ST GIRL: H is for the happiness
That you scatter wide.
2ND BOY: A is the amount of love
You bestow on all.
2ND GIRL: N is for the needs you fill—
Very big or small.
3RD BOY: K is for the kindliness
That you always bring.
3RD GIRL: S is for the Christmas songs
People like to sing.
CHORUS: So, for all you give to us,
And for all you do,
We give THANKS, St. Nicholas,
(*Each child holds up letter.*)
Many thanks to you!

Something in the Air

CAT, *a girl with a cat's mask*
DOG, *a boy with a dog's mask*

SETTING: *A room decorated for Christmas.*
AT RISE: *The* CAT *is admiring the tinsel on the Christmas tree when the* DOG *enters. It is early Christmas Eve.*

CAT (*Arching her back*): Fffifftt!

DOG: Don't fifftt me. I'm not going to bite you.

CAT (*Warily*): "Dogs begin in jest and end in earnest."

DOG: Not tonight, Kit. Come on, relax. I haven't a single design on any of your nine lives tonight. In fact, I feel actually friendly toward you for once. I can't understand why, but it's true. Shake, pal.

CAT: "Give a dog a finger, and he'll want your whole hand."

DOG: Oh, I don't blame you for being cautious. All those times I chased you and tormented you! But tonight . . . haven't you noticed there's something different in the air?

CAT (*Tentatively*): "A dog is a dog, whatever his color."

DOG: Look, what do you make of it all? (*Gestures toward wreath in window and decorated tree*) What's it all about? That bunch of green stuff hanging there with the red bow. And this evergreen tree. I've seen enough trees to know that they grow in yards and parks, not in houses. With all those fingle-fangles hanging from it, and those boxes and packages under it, what does it mean? Come on, tell me—you're an intelligent creature.

CAT (*Still cautious*): "There are more ways of killing a cat than choking her with cream."

DOG (*Sniffing*): There's something in the air lately, I tell you. Smell it? Feel it? Something cheerful, fragrant, exciting, jolly, expectant! Surely you must have noticed.

CAT (*Sniffing*): There *is* something about it, all right.

DOG (*Sniffing again*): Ah!

CAT (*Softening*): Maybe your bark *is* worse than your bite, Dog. For the time being, at least.

DOG: The way I feel tonight, I wouldn't hurt a flea. Mind you, Kit, I can't figure it out. But it's there. It's the way I feel. Do you think all this greenery and fingle-fangle in the house might have something to do with it?

CAT: Could be. (*Softly*) "And the wolf also shall dwell with the lamb, and the leopard lie down with the kid." Where'd I get that idea?

DOG: Everything's wonderfully strange tonight. It's not for us to understand the reason, I suppose.

CAT: I suppose not. (*Begins to purr*)

DOG: Would you like to chew on my bone a while, Pal? (*Takes bone out of pocket and offers it*)

CAT: Would you like a taste of my catnip? (*Takes out catnip and offers it*)

BOTH: Whatever it is, it's a pretty nice feeling for a change, isn't it? It must have something to do with this thing called Christmas!

Up a Christmas Tree

Characters

MOTHER
FATHER
BONNY ⎱
DONNA ⎰
WALLY ⎱ *their children*
DICK ⎰

TIME: *Several days before Christmas.*
PLACE: *A living room.*
SETTING: *A simple living-room set, with two doors—one at left and one at right. When the curtains open, MOTHER is sitting in a chair, sewing; and FATHER is reading the newspaper.*

MOTHER: They asked what gifts we'd like,
        With Christmas Eve so near.
FATHER (*Laughing*): I trust you said a bike,
        Or roller skates, my dear.
MOTHER: I answered no such thing.
        I told them all, what's more,
        The nicest gift they each could bring
        Was not sold in a store.

NOTE: If desired, this skit may be presented as a miniature "musical comedy." The play has been written to the rhythm of the verse and chorus of "Jingle Bells."

BOTH: Christmas gifts, Christmas gifts!
We shall not deny:
What we really want the most
Our children cannot buy!

(MOTHER *and* FATHER *go out left. In a minute,* BONNY *and* DONNA *come in from right. They seem puzzled.*)

DONNA: I asked Mom several times.

BONNY: And I asked Daddy, too.

DONNA: I said we'd saved our dimes
To buy them something new.

BONNY: But Mother shook her head,
And slyly winked her eye,
And said, "Give us a gift, instead,
That's not the kind you buy."

BOTH: Christmas gifts, Christmas gifts!
What did Mother mean?
Oh, we're "up a Christmas tree"
Because we are so green!

(*They sit down on the davenport and appear deep in thought.* WALLY *and* DICK *come in from right.*)

WALLY: She said both she and Dad
Knew something they would like.

DICK: She said they'd both be glad
If we could guess it right.

WALLY: It's nothing we can *get.*

DICK: I'm surely stumped, aren't you?

WALLY: I wonder what it is . . . (*Suddenly*) I bet
It's something we can *do!*

(BONNY *and* DONNA *join the boys.*)

ALL: Christmas gifts, Christmas gifts!
What do parents mean?
Oh, we're "up a Christmas tree!"
We *wish* we weren't so green!

(*They all begin to pace the floor, thinking hard. Sometimes they are so lost in thought that they bump into each*

other. MOTHER *and* FATHER *peek in at the door left, and watch; but the children are too concerned to notice them.*)
WALLY (*Excitedly. Stops pacing so suddenly, the others stop, too.*):
    I know! I'll write a pledge!
    I'll promise not to tease.
    I'll sign it at the edge,
    And mind my q's and p's!
(MOTHER *nods to* FATHER *at the door.*)
BONNY (*Eagerly*): I'll write a promise, too:
                To hold my temper in!
                Instead of getting mad or blue,
                I'll take things on the chin.
(FATHER *nods to* MOTHER *at the door.*)
WALLY *and* BONNY: Christmas gifts, Christmas gifts!
                How can we go wrong?
                If we give what can't be bought,
                And give it all year long!
DICK: I know! I'll write a rhyme!
    I'll promise, cross-my-heart:
    Instead of wasting time,
    I'll always do my part.
(MOTHER *and* FATHER *nod at each other.*)
DONNA: And I will be like you:
    I'll start to practice thrift.
    I'll save my time and money, too . . .
    And that will be my gift.
(FATHER *and* MOTHER *nod, smile happily, and tiptoe away.*)
CHILDREN: Christmas gifts, Christmas gifts!
                It won't be a cinch—
                Sticking to our promises.
                But we won't budge an inch!
WALLY: Let's fix our pledges now.
BONNY: Let's make them Christmas-y.

DICK: Let's draw a holly bough.

DONNA: Or paint a Christmas tree.

WALLY (*Going out right*): Our folks will be amazed!

BONNY (*Going out right*): And glad, I bet my hat.

DICK (*Going out right*): They ought to be a little dazed.

DONNA (*Going out right*): To get such gifts as that.

(MOTHER *and* FATHER *come back, and stick their heads in door at left. They are beaming.*)

MOTHER *and* FATHER:

Christmas gifts, Christmas gifts!

Aren't our children smart?

All those things we wanted most . . .

They knew them all by heart!

THE END

Christmas Spelldown

(Children show letters as they speak their lines.)

1ST: C for candles, carolers, chimes.
2ND: H for holly, happy times.
3RD: R for red—red bow and berry.
4TH: I for inn too full for Mary.
5TH: S for Santa, songs, and shops.
6TH: T for trees with tinseled tops.
7TH: M for Magi bringing gold.
8TH: A for angel saying, "Behold!"
9TH: S for star, the sign of glory.
ALL: That spells out the old, old story:
CHRISTMAS, MERRY CHRISTMAS!

Trimming the Tree

(For any number of boys and girls)

AT RISE: *The tree is waiting to be trimmed. Lights have been connected and strung but are not switched on.* CHILDREN *stand on either side with ornaments; or, in a classroom, have ornaments at their desks.*

LEADER *(Holding up a large tinsel star and facing Christmas tree)*: You bring us the fragrance of the woods, Christmas tree. In every needle of every twig of every branch you have locked the tang of wind and sun and snow and rain and life-giving earth. You bring us the freshness of the outdoors, the essence of life everlasting. Here is a star for your top, Christmas tree, to keep you from being lonesome for the stars in the sky. *(Attaches star to top of tree.)*

GIRLS *(Coming forward with yellow balls of ornaments)*: And here are golden suns, Christmas tree, to make up for the great sun that shone above your head by day. *(They attach the balls.)*

BOYS *(Coming forward with silver balls)*: And here are silver moons, to replace the changing one that sailed above your head by night. *(They attach the ornaments.)*

GIRLS: And here are other shining balls of color to remind you of rainbows, and sunrises in the east, and sunsets in the west, and Northern Lights flitting across the sky.

(They hang bright balls of red, green, blue, etc., on the tree.)

BOYS: And here are ornaments of many colors to take the place of the flash of bird wings in your branches. *(They hang other ornaments.)*

GIRLS: And here is tinsel, like rays of sunlight, like the glitter of ice, like the sparkle of water. *(They put on tinsel.)*

LEADER *(As* BOYS *and* GIRLS *put on the rest of the ornaments)*: You bring us the warmth and wonder of spring, Christmas tree, in the depth of winter. Your branches bloom as with many-colored flowers. You bring us cheer. You bring us promise. You are the symbol of light in darkness, reminding us of the Light that came to the world many years ago in Bethlehem when a Child was born in a manger. *(The lights are switched on and the Christmas tree sparkles.)* You bring us beauty and joy, and the message of hope and faith, Christmas tree. And we are grateful. *(All join in singing "The Christmas Tree" ("O Tannenbaum") or some other appropriate Christmas song.)*

GROUP AND
CHORAL READINGS

Songs of Christmas

(For a speaking chorus and a singing chorus)

SPEAKING CHORUS: Years and years ago—
And years ago again,
The angels sang of peace on earth
And of good will to men.
They sang upon a winter night
To all the waiting earth,
They sang a joyous Christmas song
About the Christ Child's birth.

SINGING CHORUS *sings "Angels We Have Heard on High."*

SPEAKING CHORUS: Years ago and years ago—
Six hundred more or less,
The monks wrote simple Christmas songs
Of praise and tenderness:
They sang of Jesus, not as Judge,
But as a friend to all;
They sang of shepherds and of love,
And of a humble stall.

SINGING CHORUS *sings a carol from the Middle Ages, such as "A Babe Is Born," "Unto Us a Boy Is Born," "Adeste Fidelis," "Good Christian Men, Rejoice."*

SPEAKING CHORUS: Years and years ago—
Elizabeth was queen,
The English sang at Christmas time
About the Nazarene,
The boar's head and the mistletoe,

The stable and the star,
For Christmas Eve meant singing
And the songs rang near and far.

SINGING CHORUS *sings any well-known old English carol, such as "God Rest You Merry, Gentlemen," "The Holly and the Ivy," "The Boar's Head Carol," "Deck the Halls with Boughs of Holly."*

SPEAKING CHORUS: Years ago and years ago—
And now as well as then,
We sing of peace at Christmas time
And of good will to men,
For Christmas is the time of year
To which good will belongs,
And what expresses Christmas more
Than Christmas carols and songs?

SINGING CHORUS *sings "Joy to the World," "O Little Town of Bethlehem," "Go Tell It on the Mountain," or some other carols of more recent times.*

And on Earth Peace

GIRL: Really, in a stable?
  But how could he keep warm
  Without a fire, without a hearth
  To hold away the storm?
CHORUS: The warmth of humble creatures—
  Donkey, ox, and sheep—
  Kept the cold from creeping in
  Where Jesus lay asleep.
BOY: Really, after midnight?
  But how could Mary see
  With just a little lantern flame
  That flickered nervously?
CHORUS: The light of fifty candles,
  Ablaze, could not compare
  With that unearthly brilliance
  That lighted up his hair.
GIRL: Really, in a manger?
  But how could Jesus lie
  Without a quilt or eiderdown
  On brittle hay and dry?
CHORUS: The shepherds brought a blanket
  Of wool to spread above,
  And he was wrapped in radiance
  And tenderness and love.
BOY: Really, in the morning?
  But how did people know

A Child was born to be their King,
And where they ought to go?
CHORUS: The brightest star of ages
Hung high above the stall,
And angels from the sky itself
Proclaimed the news to all:
ANGELS: "Glory to God in the highest,
And on earth peace,
Good will to men."
(*If desired,* ANGELS *sing the Gloria from "Angels We Have Heard on High."*)

The Christmas Pig

(A humorous reading for two small choruses,
three boys, and two girls)

1st Chorus: Oh, there was a jolly farmer
And his name was Uncle Sig.
He came home from town one summer
With a wriggly little pig.
And he called his wife named Carrie,
And his daughter Margaret Mary,
And her brothers Dick and Harry . . .
FARMER: Look-a-here, let's dance a jig!
We'll be eating pork for Christmas,
For I've bought ourselves a pig!
2nd Chorus: They'll be eating pork for Christmas
When they fatten up their pig.
1st Chorus: Then his wife she stopped her jigging
And she gave the pig a look:
Wife: What a darling little duffer
With his pig-tail in a crook.
If he only grows up *homely,*
He'll be easier to cook.
1st Chorus: And the jolly farmer mentioned
That he knew her heart was big,
But she *mustn't* make a pet of
Such a silly little pig.

2ND CHORUS: She mustn't, oh, she mustn't
Pet the Christmas-dinner pig!

1ST CHORUS: Then the daughter Margaret Mary
Gave the little pig a wink:

MARGARET MARY: What a cunning little critter
With a nose of satin pink.
Oh, we'll have to call him Pinkie
When we play with him, I think.

1ST CHORUS: But the jolly farmer shouted
To his family, small and big:

FARMER: You *mustn't* make a pet of
Such a silly little pig.

2ND CHORUS: They mustn't, oh, they mustn't
Pet the Christmas-dinner pig!

1ST CHORUS: Then Harry stopped his jigging
And his brother Dick as well,
And they stroked the little piglet
And they stared at it a spell,
And they scratched its ears with vigor,
Both behind and up in front,
And they thought it most appealing . . .

DICK: It's a friendly little runt.

HARRY: It surely is. I wonder
If it's big enough to grunt.

1ST CHORUS: Then the jolly farmer told them
That they mustn't give a fig
For the looks or disposition
Of a silly little pig.

FARMER: Now, listen, everybody,
I don't mean to be a prig,
But you mustn't spoil or pet him.
If he wants to play, don't let him.
To be brief, you'd best forget him,
Or you won't feel like a jig

When it's time for Christmas dinner
And our feast of roasted pig!
2ND CHORUS: They mustn't, oh, they mustn't
Pet the little Christmas pig.
1ST CHORUS: By fall the pig was husky,
Oh, by fall the pig was fat.
And by fall the pig was petted—
There could be no doubt of that!
His mistress sneaked him tidbits
And he added pound on pound,
And she combed him with a curry
Till he followed her around.
FARMER'S WIFE (*Talking baby talk*):
Pinkie-rinkie-dinkie pig,
If you do not root and dig
Like a common piggy-wig,
I'll bring something nice for you
When my kitchen work is through.
2ND CHORUS: Mustn't pet the pig, mustn't pet the pig.
1ST CHORUS: The farmer's dimpled daughter
Spoiled the piglet left and right.
He wept a shower of teardrops
When she hurried out of sight.
MARGARET MARY: Pinkie, Pinkie, don't you cry,
I'll come pet you by and by.
I've some practicing to finish.
Don't you cry and get all thinnish!
2ND CHORUS: Mustn't pet the pig, mustn't pet the pig.
1ST CHORUS: The brothers Dick and Harry
Had some sport with Pinkie too:
Each day they tried to lift him,
An ambitious thing to do,
For every day the porker
Weighed another pound or two.

DICK: Say, unless we both get stronger,
  We can't lift that pig much longer.
HARRY: Sometimes, Dick, I wonder whether
  You and I and Dad together
  Can lift Pinkie when he's big . . .
2ND CHORUS: Mustn't pet the Christmas pig!
1ST CHORUS: Oh, there was a jolly farmer
  And his name was Uncle Sig,
  And even he . . . yes, even *he*
  Caressed the Christmas pig.
  He called it every mealtime
  With a special kind of shout,
  He fed it fancy rations
  And he stroked its pinkish snout,
  And all the time pretended
  That he didn't give a *fig*
  For the silly little porker
  That would be their Christmas pig.
2ND CHORUS: Mustn't pet the pig, mustn't pet the pig.
1ST CHORUS: At last it was December,
  That exciting time of year
  When voices should be jolly
  With the holidays so near,
  And hearts should all be merry
  With expectancy and cheer.
  But you should see the faces
  Of the family on the farm!
  It seemed the Christmas season
  Didn't hold a bit of charm.
  And, of course, you know the reason
  Why they didn't smile or jig . . .
FARMER'S WIFE, MARGARET MARY, DICK *and* HARRY:
  How can we, oh, how *can* we
  Eat our Christmas-dinner pig!

2ND CHORUS: How could they, oh, how could they
  Eat that silly Pinkie pig!
1ST CHORUS: They didn't feel like presents,
  And they didn't feel like fun.
  They thought of Pinkie Porker
  And his days now almost done.
MARGARET MARY: He likes to root, he likes to dig,
  He's such a *darling* of a pig. (*Sniffs*)
DICK: He always looks so trim and trig.
  He's such a *gentlemanly* pig.
FARMER'S WIFE: He's not a dunce. He's not a prig.
  He's just a *dumpling* of a pig.
HARRY: He's not too fat, he's not too big.
  He's such a nice *well-rounded* pig.
2ND CHORUS: Mustn't pet the pig, mustn't pet the pig.
1ST CHORUS: They didn't feel like singing
  Or like jigging with their feet.
  They only thought that Pinkie
  Was too nice a pig to eat.
2ND CHORUS: Mustn't . . . pet . . . the . . . pig . . .
1ST CHORUS: Then daughter Margaret Mary
  Up and made a drastic plan:
MARGARET MARY: Let's just forget it's Christmas!
  Let's omit it if we can,
  Let's keep the date from Daddy
  And conceal the almanac.
  No Christmas tree, no presents,
  Ought to throw him off the track.
FARMER'S WIFE: And when the day is over
  There will surely be no call
  To have a roast pig dinner
  At all . . .
2ND CHORUS: At all, at all.
1ST CHORUS: Oh, there was a jolly farmer

And his name was Uncle Sig,
And he came from chores that evening
After looking at the pig,
And his face was not as jolly
As his face was wont to be,
For the thought of Christmas holly
Made him sad and melancholy
For, you see, he saw the folly
Of the roast-pig Christmas spree.
But he feared his wife and children
Mightn't dance a Christmas jig
If they didn't get their dinner
After fattening Pinkie pig.
So his frowns were very furrowed
And his sighs were very big.

2ND CHORUS: Oh, his frowns were very furrowed
And his sighs were very big.

MARGARET MARY: Why, Daddy, what's the matter?
What's the *matter?* You look sick.

1ST CHORUS: The farmer thought that maybe
That idea would turn the trick . . .

FARMER: I'll admit I'm not as jolly
As I was some months ago.
Do you think it's my digestion?
Do you think I should go slow?
Oh, I hate to disappoint you
But an *omelet* . . . for me
Would make a better dinner
Than that pig could ever be,
A better Christmas dinner,
If you only will agree.

2ND CHORUS: If they only, if they only, if they only would
agree!

1ST CHORUS: You should have seen the sunburst
On the faces round about.

An *omelet* for Christmas
Would be such a perfect out!
They could have their tree with presents,
They could have their holly sprig,
They could have their Christmas dinner
And still keep their precious pig!

MARGARET MARY: Let's buy our pet a present,
Now we're going to spare his life.

FARMER'S WIFE: He's *not* to get a present
Of a roasting pan and knife!

FARMER: What say we pool our money
And surprise him . . . with a *wife?*
Then maybe in the future
We can dance a Christmas jig
When Pinkie has a family
That is very much too big
For us to make a pet of
Every single little pig!

2ND CHORUS: For them to make a pet of
Every single little pig!

THE END

The Nativity

(*In Song and Scripture*)

Characters

1ST READER (*of Prophecies*)
2ND READER (*of Luke*)
3RD READER (*of Matthew*)
SOLO VOICES
CHORUS

SETTING: *Stage decorated for Christmas.*

AT RISE: *All participants are on stage—*CHORUS *toward back,* 1ST READER *at one side,* 2ND *and* 3RD READERS *at other side.* CHORUS *is singing "From Heaven High," "O Thou Joyful Day* (O Sanctissima)*," or "In Dulci Jubilo" to set the mood.*

1ST READER: "Behold, the days come, saith the Lord, that I will raise unto David a righteous Branch, and a King shall reign and prosper, and shall execute judgment and justice in the earth." (Jer. 23:5) "The Lord thy God will raise up unto thee a Prophet from the midst of thee . . . unto him ye shall hearken." (Deut. 18:15) "With righteousness shall he judge the poor, and re-

---

All songs used in this script can be found in *A Treasury of Christmas Songs and Carols,* Houghton Mifflin Company, Boston: 1955.

prove with equity for the meek of the earth. . . . The wolf also shall dwell with the lamb, and the leopard shall lie down with the kid; and the calf and the young lion and the fatling together; and a little child shall lead them." (Isa. 11:4, 6)

CHORUS *sings "Shout the Glad Tidings." (First two stanzas only).*

1ST READER: "Thou Bethlehem, though thou be little among the thousands of Judah, yet out of thee shall he come forth . . . that is to be ruler in Israel; whose goings forth have been from of old, from everlasting." (Mic. 5:2)

SOLO VOICE *(Female) sings "O Little Town of Bethlehem," first and third stanzas only, beginning "O little town of Bethlehem," and "How silently, how silently."*

1ST READER: "Therefore the Lord himself shall give you a sign: Behold, a virgin shall conceive, and bear a son. . . ." (Isa. 7:14) "The people that walked in darkness have seen a great light: they that dwell in the land of the shadow of death, upon them hath the light shined. . . . For unto us a child is born, unto us a son is given: and the government shall be upon his shoulder: and his name shall be called Wonderful Counsellor, The mighty God, The everlasting Father, The Prince of Peace." (Isa. 9:2, 6)

CHORUS *sings first two stanzas of "A Babe Is Born"—(stanzas beginning "A Babe is born all of a May," and "At Bethlehem, that blessed place.") Or, if preferred,* CHORUS *may sing first stanza of "What Child Is This?"*

1ST READER: "Prepare ye the way of the Lord, make straight in the desert a highway for our God. Every valley shall be exalted, and every mountain and hill shall be made low: and the crooked shall be made straight, and the rough places plain." (Isa. 40:3, 4)

SOLO VOICE *(Male) and* CHORUS *sing the Negro spiritual*

"Go Tell It on the Mountain," the CHORUS *joining in only on the refrain. Since this song is short, it may be repeated if desired, with female* SOLO VOICE *leading.*

2ND READER: "And it came to pass in those days, that there went out a decree from Caesar Augustus, that all the world should be taxed. And all went to be taxed, every one into his own city. And Joseph also went up from Galilee, out of the city of Nazareth, into Judea, unto the city of David which is called Bethlehem . . . to be taxed with Mary his espoused wife, being great with child." (Luke 2:1, 3, 4, 5)

DUET *(Two male voices) sings "Watchman, Tell Us of the Night," all three stanzas.*

2ND READER: "And so it was, that, while they were in Bethlehem, the days were accomplished that Mary should be delivered. And she brought forth her first born son, and wrapped him in swaddling clothes, and laid him in a manger, because there was no room for them in the inn." (Luke 2:6, 7)

CHORUS *sings "No Room in the Inn," (first, second and seventh stanzas only—stanzas beginning, "When Caesar Augustus," and "Then Joseph and Mary," and "O Bethlehem, Bethlehem."*

2ND READER: "Behold, thou shalt . . . bring forth a son, and shalt call his name Jesus. He shall be great, and shall be called the Son of the Highest . . . and of his kingdom there shall be no end." (Luke 1:31, 32, 33)

SOLO VOICE *(Female) sings "The Holy Boy."*

CHORUS *sings one of the following: "Rocking," "Polish Lullaby," "Away in a Manger," "Hush, My Dear, Lie Still and Slumber," or "Sleep, My Little Jesus."*

2ND READER: "And there were in the same country shepherds abiding in the field, keeping watch over their flock by night. And lo, the angel of the Lord came upon them, and the glory of the Lord shone round about them: and they were sore afraid. And the angel said

unto them, Fear not; for, behold, I bring unto you
tidings of great joy, which shall be to all people. For
unto you is born this day in the city of David a Saviour,
which is Christ the Lord. And this shall be a sign unto
you; ye shall find the babe wrapped in swaddling
clothes, lying in a manger." (Luke 2:8-12)

CHORUS *sings one of the following: "The first Noel"
(first and seventh stanzas, beginning "The first Noel,"
and "Between an Ox-stall"); "While Shepherds Watched
Their Flocks by Night" (first four stanzas, beginning
"While shepherds watched," and "Fear not," and "To
you, in David's town," and "The heavenly Babe");
"Hark! The Herald Angels Sing" (first stanza only).*

2ND READER: "And suddenly there was with the angel a
multitude of the heavenly host praising God, and saying, Glory to God in the highest, and on earth peace,
good will toward men." (Luke 2:13-14)

CHORUS *sings the round by Gebhardi, "Glory to God," or,
if preferred, the first stanza of "It Came Upon a Midnight Clear."*

BOYS IN CHORUS *sing all three stanzas of "Angels We Have
Heard on High," with full* CHORUS *coming in on the
"Gloria."*

2ND READER: "And it came to pass, as the angels were gone
away from them into heaven, the shepherds said to one
another, Let us now go even unto Bethlehem, and see
this thing which is come to pass, which the Lord hath
made known unto us." (Luke 2:15)

SOLO VOICE *(Male) and* CHORUS *sing "Rise Up, Shepherd,
and Follow." In this song the soloist sings every other
line, with the group coming in on the words "Rise up,
shepherd, and follow."*

2ND READER: "And they came with haste, and found Mary
and Joseph, and the babe lying in a manger." (Luke
2:16)

GIRLS IN CHORUS *sing "Bring a Torch, Jeannette, Isabella," all three stanzas.*

2ND READER: "And when the shepherds had seen it, they made known abroad the saying which was told them concerning this child. And all they that heard it wondered at those things which were told them by the shepherds." (Luke 2:17)

CHORUS *sings "Silent Night," first two stanzas only.*

3RD READER: "Now when Jesus was born in Bethlehem of Judea in the days of Herod the king, behold, there came wise men from the east to Jerusalem, saying, Where is he that is born King of the Jews? for we have seen his star in the east, and we are come to worship him." (Mat. 2:1, 2)

SOLO VOICE *(Male) sings "The Kings."*

3RD READER: "And lo, the star which the wise men saw in the east, went before them, till it came and stood over where the young child was. . . . And when they were come into the house, they saw the young child with Mary his mother, and fell down and worshipped him: and when they had opened their treasures, they presented unto him gifts; gold, and frankincense, and myrrh." (Mat. 2:9, 11)

THREE BOYS FROM CHORUS *sing "We Three Kings of Orient Are," omitting the fifth-and-last stanza.*

2ND READER: "And the child grew, and waxed strong in spirit, filled with wisdom: and the grace of God was upon him." (Luke 2:40)

1ST READER: "He was a burning and shining light—the true Light, which lighteth every man that cometh into the world." (John 5:35, 1:9)

CHORUS *sings "O Come, All Ye Faithful," all three stanzas. Audience may join in.*

THE END

Signs of Christmas

GIRLS: Shops and songs and smiles and snow
shimmer everywhere we go.

BOYS: Songs and smiles and snow and shops
shine from streets to building tops.

GIRLS: Smiles and snow and shops and songs
dazzle all the merry throngs.

BOYS: Snow and shops and songs and smiles
sparkle now for miles and miles.

ALL: Signs of Christmas—how they glow:
shops and songs and smiles and snow!

The Falconer's Christmas

Characters

READER
RED CHORUS
GREEN CHORUS
THE FALCONER

READER: Once upon a time, when Christmas was much
younger than it is now, in fact when it was very, very
young, there was a bitter dispute among the people in
a certain land of the North. Some of the townsfolk
thought that red should be the color of Christmas.
Others thought that green should be. So bitter did the
argument become that there was little "peace on earth,
good will to men" in that unhappy land at Christmas or
any other time. The Reds and the Greens formed two
hostile camps, and no friendliness seemed possible between them. Only one old man, a Falconer, who lived
on the outskirts of the town, refrained from taking sides.
He alone watched in silence, training his falcons, and
closing his ears to the arguments that drifted his way
when the wind was right. But his heart was sad that such
foolish rivalry should drive out the spirit of Christmas.

Each year for days before Christmas, the Reds would
march up and down the city square insisting that red
should be the color of Christmas. For equally as many

days the Greens would march up and down insisting
that *green* should be the color of Christmas. But they
did not, unfortunately, confine their activities to marching. They shouted back and forth, arguing about the
colors of Christmas.

RED CHORUS:

Red is the color of firelight
Brightening our winter hearths,
The symbol of warmth and brightness
In the midst of cold and darkness.
Red is the color of Christmas!

GREEN CHORUS:

Green is the color of fir trees
Cheering our winter woods,
The symbol of life enduring
In the midst of cold and darkness.
Green is the color of Christmas!

RED CHORUS:

Red is the color of sunrise
Filling the eastern sky,
The symbol of lengthening days,
Of light after winter's starkness.
Red is the color of Christmas!

GREEN CHORUS:

Green is the color of palm leaves
Carried by reverent crowds
In honor of Christ, the Lord,
When he entered Jerusalem.
Green is the color of Christmas!

READER: And so the arguments went. The Reds spoke of
the redness of the Star that showed the way to Bethlehem. The Greens spoke of the greenness of the Tree of
Everlasting Life. There seemed to be no way to settle
the argument.

RED CHORUS: Red!

GREEN CHORUS: Green! (*Repeat several times, at accelerated pace.*)

READER: Then one cold afternoon, the day before Christmas, the old Falconer walked into town, straight to the city square. Between the Reds and the Greens the everlasting bickering was going on. The old man held up his hand for silence. Then he spoke.

FALCONER: My friends, listen to what I have to say. As you know, I take no stand for either the red or the green. But for three nights now I have had the same dream concerning the argument between you. I dream I am seated before my small fire when there is a knock at the door. I open, and there is a stranger. I think he may be bringing me a falcon to train, or perhaps wishing to buy one of mine. But no. He merely says: "Tell them who degrade the Christmas season—tell them to await a sign in the city square on Christmas morning."

VOICES FROM REDS AND GREENS: A sign?
On Christmas morning?
A sign in the city square?
Tomorrow!

FALCONER: For three nights I have had the same dream. And tomorrow is Christmas morning. There will be a sign in the city square. I can only hope that it will put an end to this quarreling.

RED CHORUS (*Confidently*): It will be a sign for *red* as the color of Christmas!

GREEN CHORUS (*Confidently*): No. No. It will be a sign for *green*.

FALCONER: Do you all agree, then, to accept the sign—whatever it may be?

RED CHORUS: We agree. For the sign will be red.

GREEN CHORUS: We shall accept the sign. For we shall win.

READER: And so the old man walked back to his small

house and his falcons. And the townspeople, filled with curiosity and suspense, went home for Christmas Eve, wondering what sign the morrow would bring. Back home, the Falcon spoke gently to the sharpest-eyed of his falcons. He had trained him for weeks in a special way. He had taught him, at the sight of a shining gold coin, to drop whatever he had in his beak when he was on the wing. Later, at home, the falcon would claim a piece of meat as his reward. The old man stroked the head of the sharpest-eyed falcon, and smiled to himself. Next morning, breathing final instructions to his well-trained bird, the old man put a sprig of foliage into the falcon's beak and released him. Then the Falconer walked to the city square. Already the Reds and Greens were gathered there, lined up on opposite sides of the square, awaiting the sign. As they waited, they jeered at each other.

RED CHORUS: The sign will be for red, the color of Christmas.

GREEN CHORUS: For green! It is sure to be green. (*Groups banter back and forth "Red," "Green," etc.*)

READER: Then the old Falconer appeared, and quiet fell upon the crowd.

FALCONER: Good morning, my friends. Have you seen the sign?

REDS AND GREENS: Not yet. Not yet.

FALCONER: Perhaps you have missed it. We must look carefully over every inch of the square, between each smallest crack in the flagstones. Bend over, my friends, and search.

READER: So eagerly did the Reds and the Greens hunt for a sign that might declare them the winner, that they failed to see a falcon high in the sky directly overhead. Likewise, they failed to see the old Falconer open his hand so that a small gold coin glinted in the sunlight and showed to the sharp eyes of the bird above. The falcon did not fail to see! As he had been trained, he dropped the sprig of foliage he carried in his beak, and soared high in the sky in the direction of home. He would claim his reward later. The sprig the falcon carried dropped down, down, down.

FALCONER (*Suddenly, excitedly*): See! See! A sign is falling from the very heavens themselves. Stand back everyone, clear a space so that all may see!

REDS AND GREENS:

What is it?

Where?

It drops from the very sky itself.

A sign from heaven!

READER: Amid murmurs of wonder and awe from the crowd, the Falconer caught the sprig of foliage and held it high.

FALCONER: It is the fulfillment of my dream—a sign of peace and gladness and good will, my friends. The true sign of Christmas. Look! From the heavens has fallen a sprig of holly! The leaves are shining and green, symbol of life everlasting. The berries are crimson as the winter sun that brings light to a dark world. (*Softly.*) And it reminds us that He, whose birthday we celebrate today, was forced to wear a crown of thorns.

REDS AND GREENS:

A sprig of holly!

Red and green. Red *and* green.

FALCONER: Yes, red *and* green. It is a sign, indeed, my friends. You all have cause to celebrate, for you are all winners. From now on, there shall be two colors for Christmas, not one.

RED CHORUS: Heigh-ho for holly!

GREEN CHORUS: Heigh-ho for the red and the green!

ALL: The colors of Christmas. (*Gaily they all either speak or sing the sprightly Welsh carol, "Deck the Halls with Boughs of Holly."*)

THE END

Little Lost Jesus

(Two groups of readers, one on each side of the stage, alternate in reading the lines. The first group is lusty and thoughtless, the second group soft-spoken and thoughtful. The two groups show the contrast in modern attitudes toward Christmas.)

1st Group: String up the tinsel and hang up the holly,
Now is the time to be lusty and jolly:
Christmas is coming! What gift do you choose?
Christmas, you know, is a birthday . . .
2nd Group: But whose?
The little lost Jesus is not in His place,
His manger is empty and bare,
And Mary looks down with a tear on her face—
No little Lord Jesus is there.
1st Group: Garnish the tree with its trinkets and trappings,
Do up the presents in gay-colored wrappings:
Christmas is coming! Be merry, be spry.
Christmas is something that's special . . .
2nd Group: But why?
The little lost Jesus is not in the hay.
The donkey, the ox, and the dove
Stand waiting in vain for the shepherds today
To come with their presents of love.

1ST GROUP: Finish your shopping—the counters are creak-
  ing.
  Bundles and parcels and secrets—no peeking!
  Christmas is coming. It brings such a lot.
  It stands for a special occasion . . .
2ND GROUP: But what?
  The little Lord Jesus is lost in the throng,
  is lost in the glitter and glare,
  is lost in the tumult that surges along,
  is lost in the tinsel somewhere.
  Jesus is lost in the trifles of men.
  Find Him, oh, find Him, oh, find Him again!

Now Is the Time

GIRL: Now is the time for brightest lights
  On shortest, darkest winter nights,
BOY: For red and green and blue and gold
  To liven up December's cold,
GIRL: For secrets hidden way down under,
  And eyes agleam with hope and wonder.
BOY: Now is the time for pointed trees
  To shine with tinsel to their knees,
GIRL: And stars of silver in their tops,
  And fairyland in all the shops,
BOY: For wreaths and candlesticks and holly . . .
  And even lamp-posts looking jolly.
GIRL: Now is the time for "Silent Night,"
  And "shepherds watched" and "all was bright,"
BOY: For wrapping gifts to hide away,
  And watching angels in a play,
GIRL: For snow as white as geese and chickens,
  For chimes and sugar plums, and Dickens.
ALL: Now is the time to sing again
  Of peace on earth, good will to men.

Long Ago on Christmas Morning

GIRL: Once a little Child lay sleeping
  On the manger hay
  While the gentle beasts were keeping
  Watch on Christmas Day,
GROUP: Long ago on Christmas morning,
  Very far away.
BOY: Once a little Child lay quiet
  In a manger bed
  While the shepherds tiptoed by it,
  Bringing fleece and bread,
GROUP: Long ago on Christmas morning
  When the news had spread.
GIRL: Once a little Child lay dreaming
  In a humble stall
  While a golden light was streaming
  Down the stable wall.
GROUP: Peace was born that Christmas morning,
  Peace for one and all.

Getting Ready for Christmas

BOYS: Jerry is merry
    With secrets galore.
GIRLS: Millie and Tillie
    Make cards by the score.
BOYS: Freddy and Teddy
    Are sticky with paste.
GIRLS: Mary is scary
    And hides things in haste.
BOYS: Larry is very
    Involved with the saw.
GIRLS: Polly thinks holly
    Is pretty to draw.
BOYS: Izzie is busy . . .
    Too busy to speak.
ALL: Wouldn't you *know*
    It is Christmas next week?

Star of Hope

(For chorus, two shepherds, three Wisemen)

CHORUS: Like round gray stones on the arid hill,
The sheep loomed up, and the night was still.
A ragged wind that had moaned all day,
Picked up its tatters and limped away.
The night was clear and the air was chill,
And the moon was curved like an ibis' bill.

1ST SHEPHERD: Cold and clear,
Clear and cold!
The grass is sere
As the year grows old.

2ND SHEPHERD: The hills are bare
And dry as bone,
And grass as spare
As a barren stone.
Hunger's a snare
For the lambs, half-grown.

1ST SHEPHERD: Where is the rain?
It's overdue.

2ND SHEPHERD: Where is there grain
For a hungry ewe?
Brother, I fear . . .

1ST SHEPHERD: And I fear, too.

CHORUS: The shepherds hunched on the hard cold ground,
And stared at the sheep and the hills around,
And sighed at the rainless winter sky,

233

And shuddered with fear at the jackal's cry.
Their lips were tight and their dread profound
As they watched their sheep while the stars ticked by.

1st Shepherd: Pasture scant—
And a tax to pay
If you can or can't,
Is the Roman way.

2nd Shepherd: Herod makes
His palace shine
With the tax he takes
From a withering vine,
From a crust of bread,
From a hungry ewe.
Brother, I dread . . .

1st Shepherd: And I dread, too.

Chorus: Out of the night the shepherds heard
The sound of hoofs, and the gray sheep stirred,
And over the hill three Wisemen rode.
The jewels in their camels' bridles glowed,
And the moon was still as a sleeping bird.
The shepherds shouted a friendly word.

Shepherds: Ho, you riders of camels, ho!

1st Wiseman: Hold! Some shepherds. Perhaps they'll
know.

2nd Wiseman: The star in the east . . . have you seen
it glow?

1st Shepherd: Heaven is wide
With stars that shine,
But the grass has dried
Like a cactus spine.
Rain for a week
Would serve us well . . .

2nd Shepherd: The star you seek—
Is there more to tell?

3rd Wiseman: The prophets say on a winter night

A star will blaze with a wondrous light
And give us a sign that the road is right.

1ST WISEMAN: A star in the east will be the guide
To a newborn King, it is prophesied.

2ND SHEPHERD: What matters a King
When the grass has dried?

1ST SHEPHERD: A star? Hold still—
Just over the brow
Of the highest hill
One is rising now!

1ST WISEMAN: Yes! Look! It gleams like a diadem.

2ND WISEMAN: A sudden lantern!

3RD WISEMAN: A priceless gem!

1ST SHEPHERD: It hangs in the sky over Bethlehem.

1ST WISEMAN: Ah, Bethlehem. Then the prophets knew!
The words of Micah will yet come true.

THREE WISEMEN: "But thou, Bethlehem, though thou be
little among the thousands of Judah; yet out of thee
shall he come forth unto me that is to be ruler in
Israel . . ."

2ND WISEMAN: The star in the east is a harbinger
Of a great event that will soon occur:
A King will be born to light the way
Through the dark and dread of wintering day.

CHORUS: The moon was curved as a scimitar,
As the Wisemen road toward the guiding star,
And the shepherds stared at the east with awe—
Could this be a sign, this star they saw?
The sign of hope for a weary land
As parched that night as the desert sand?

1ST SHEPHERD: The grass is dry
As a raveled rope,
But the star hangs high
With the light of hope.

2ND SHEPHERD: This newborn King—

May He come as rain,
As life in spring
To the thirsty plain!
CHORUS: The night went by, and the star went down.
The shepherds dreamed of the distant town
Till the sun rose bright as a daffodil.
And then they stared . . . and their hearts stood still.
The grass was green that had been so brown!
The grass was green over field and hill!
The shepherds smiled, and with tears, knelt down.
The grass was green that had been so brown.

THE END

Where Is Christmas?

GROUP: Where is Christmas?
GIRLS: In the tingle
  Of expecting old Kris Kringle.
BOYS: In the windows of the stores,
  Past the dazzling, magic doors.
GIRLS: In the whispers.
BOYS: In the sight
  Of the lighted trees at night.
GROUP: Where is Christmas?
GIRLS: In the singing
  And the chiming and the ringing.
BOYS: In the labels, "Do not look!"
GIRLS: In the story in the Book.
GROUP: In the dancing winter air.
  In the faces—everywhere!

The Well of the Magi

(A choral reading based on an old legend, for girls' chorus and the three Wisemen)

GIRLS: The Magi riding through the night
  Were full of grave concern:
  The Star they sought had slipped from sight.
  They knew not where to turn.
  The hills around were hunched with cold
  Against the winter sky,
  The withered grass was thin and old,
  The camels' throats were dry.
  Should they go right, or straight, or left?
  The Wisemen wished they knew.
  No water trickled from the cleft,
  Their Star was hidden, too!

CASPAR: "They told us that a well was near,"
  Sighed Caspar to the rest—
  "A double cistern, sweet and clear.
  I think the way lies west."

MELCHIOR: One moment Melchior was still,
  And then his silence ceased.
  He said, "Why not ascend a hill?
  I think the way is east."

BALTHAZAR: Balthazar stroked his camel's head.
  "Our animals must drink,
  And we are tired and cold," he said.
  "Let's go the way they think."

GIRLS: The camels circled to the right
  Across the stony ground,
  Their feet threw pebbles at the night:
  There was no other sound.
  Above, a sea of stars shone down,
  And as a small one fell
  They found the highway to the town,
  And then they found the well!

MELCHIOR: Cried Melchior, "How blessed we are!
  My friends, dismount with cheer.
  We may have lost our guiding Star,
  But there is water here."

GIRLS: The Magi leaned against the stone
  To draw the water out.
  Below, a bright reflection shone . . .
  Their Star! Without a doubt.

CASPAR: "The hill," said Caspar, "hid our Star
  Behind its barricade,
  But in the well where shadows are
  Its guiding light has stayed."

BALTHAZAR: "So now we know the way to go.
  To Bethlehem, ahead!"
  Balthazar watched the image glow:
  "We know the way," he said.

GIRLS: And that is why the Magi took
  The road that climbed the hill.
  The Star was there—they need but look;
  It hovered bright and still.
  And that is how the Magi found
  The newborn King that night . . .
  And we still walk, the world around,
  In His still shining light.

THE END

Christmas All Around

BOYS: You see it in the windows
   Of the houses and the stores
   Where holly wreaths and Christmas trees
   Look in and out of doors,
GIRLS: You smell it in the kitchen
   Where the tangy scent of spice
   Gets mixed with nuts and citron
   And everything that's nice,
BOYS: You hear it in the music
   That echoes down the street,
   And at the crowded counters,
   And in the busy feet,
GIRLS: You sense it in the whisper
   Of secrets in the air,
   And in the happy eagerness
   That twinkles everywhere . . .
ALL: Shiny lights on fir trees,
   Voices that resound,
   Goodies in the oven,
   Secrets that abound,
   You see it and you smell it
   And you hear it all around . . .
   CHRISTMAS!

RECITATIONS

Santa's Christmas Tree

A great many years ago when Santa Claus was just starting out in the business of Christmas, he got into difficulties. And it was because of his difficulties that he accidentally invented the Christmas tree. And what would Christmas be without a Christmas tree? Well, here is what happened:

In that year so long ago, Santa Claus had made a tremendous number of little tin horns for boys and wooden bird whistles for girls. In fact, he had almost forgotten to make anything else. His workshop was full of horns and bird whistles stacked on the shelves and piled from floor to ceiling.

One day Santa's wife came in and looked around the shop in amazement. "Before you go any further," she suggested, "don't you think we ought to paint these? We can't wrap them and pack them till they are painted, and you've already made so many."

"Yes, I have indeed," Santa agreed, looking at the creaking shelves. "I hadn't noticed before. I'll mix up some paint and we can start decorating the toys this very afternoon."

And so Santa Claus mixed up great quantities of red and blue and yellow and green and orange paint. "We'll have to hurry," he said. "I can't afford to let any of this paint dry up."

"I'm ready," Mrs. Santa said cheerfully. "Where shall

we start?" She dipped a brush into the green paint and looked around at the piles and piles of horns and whistles waiting to be decorated.

"You start on the horns," suggested Santa, "and I'll begin on the whistles. Then later we can change off. You know what they say, my dear—a change in time saves nine —or something to that effect." He dipped his brush into the red paint and began to work on whistles from the nearest pile.

And then the trouble began!

Santa and his wife found it very hard to paint such small toys without painting their fingers at the same time. And then the toys stuck to the table when they put them down to dry. And if they didn't put them down to dry, the colors ran together. If they picked them up again or moved them, some of the paint was left behind. Besides, the table was soon full of partly-painted horns and whistles and there was no more room where others could be laid to dry. And to cap the climax, both Santa and his wife knew that if they didn't finish the job within a day or two, the paint would thicken and be ruined!

"Dear me," Santa Claus sighed, staring at his red fingers. "This is very difficult." He rubbed his nose with the hand that held the paintbrush and left a big red smooch.

"What are we going to do?" groaned Mrs. Santa Claus, who already had two smooches on her nose. "And Christmas only a week away!"

Santa stared out of the window, thinking hard. But the more he thought, the more impossible the job seemed. He sighed heavily. Just then a flock of chirpy snowbirds swooped down out of the winter sky and alighted on a fir tree near the window. There were so many of them, they almost filled the tree. Santa Claus smiled. It looked funny to see a tree so full of birds. Then suddenly he jumped three feet into the air and shouted, "I have it!"

Before his wife could say, "Merry Christmas," Santa was into his overcoat and out of the workshop door. Soon he was back with a nice bushy fir tree from the forest. He dragged it into the shop, much to his wife's distress.

"Don't you think it's crowded enough in here?" she asked.

Santa only laughed. He made a crosspiece of lumber and nailed it to the bottom of the tree, and stood the tree near a shelf full of unpainted toys. "Ah," he said. "That will be just perfect."

"For what?" asked Mrs. Santa.

"For a toy-rack, my dear," Santa replied. "It will solve all our difficulties. We'll tie a little string to each of the horns and whistles, so they'll dangle from a twig. That way we can paint them on all sides without having to dry them first. We can hang them all over the tree and they won't take up nearly as much room as on the table."

"How wonderful," his wife gasped. "It will solve everything. Oh, Santa, you're a genius. How did you ever think of it?"

"A little bird told me," Santa smiled, dipping a fresh brush into the yellow paint.

And now you probably wonder what a practical invention like a toy-rack has to do with a Christmas tree. Just this. You see, after Santa Claus and his wife filled that tree full of freshly-painted toys, they were both struck by the beauty of it. It was simply dazzling!

"The green tree and those gay toys," Mrs. Santa gasped. "I never saw anything lovelier in my life."

"It's too good to keep," Santa cried. "I'm going to take this idea down to Earth when I go this Christmas. I'll call it a Christmas tree. Nobody needs to know it started out as a toy-rack."

"A Christmas tree," his wife nodded. "*Everyone* is going

to want one, mark my words. Oh, Santa, you get the best ideas."

And so, you see, that is how Santa's difficulties led in a roundabout way to the invention of the Christmas tree. And the moral of this story is, as Santa would say: Two birds in the bush are worth two in the hand . . . or something to that effect.

THE END

The Christmas Promise

"A promise is a promise," said the Eldest Rabbit, twitching his whiskers. He looked around at his relatives. "And tonight's the night."

"Christmas Eve," said the Quiet One.

"But what if they've changed their minds in the meantime?" asked the Timid One. "They like to sleep all winter. Perhaps they won't thank us for keeping our promise, now there's snow on the ground. Perhaps they'll be very cross at being disturbed."

The Youngest peeked out mischievously from behind a bush. "There'll be more for *us* to eat if we don't have company on Christmas Eve." He said that not because he was greedy, but because he liked to see the Eldest wiggle his nose excitedly.

"Where's your Christmas spirit?" the Eldest demanded between wiggles. "Besides, a promise is a promise. Now, let's see . . ." He became very serious and businesslike. "We promised the Skunk . . . and the Woodchuck . . ."

"And the Bat."

"And the Chipmunk."

"And the Black Bear."

"Oh," the Timid One shuddered. "Did we really promise the Bear?"

"We couldn't get out of it." The Eldest flicked his long white ears. "It was 'way back in September. The Bear overheard us telling the others about Christmas."

"He's never seen a Christmas tree, either," said the Quiet One. "Can you imagine that?"

"These people who sleep all winter!" the Eldest sniffed. "All winter. No wonder they miss things." He counted on his fingers. "That makes five. I thought there were more."

"The Frog," said the Youngest, peeking out again.

"Oh, yes, the Frog. But that was only half a promise. We said we'd wake up the Frog *provided* the pond wasn't frozen over. I hopped by there yesterday and it's quite covered with ice. So we can leave out the Frog."

The Timid One gave a little shudder, thinking of the big Black Bear asleep in his den. "How are we ever going to wake them all? Do you think we can do enough shouting and shaking to make those sleepy-heads understand it's Christmas Eve?"

It *did* take considerable shouting and shaking.

First the rabbits went to the Woodchuck's den under an old stump. They scratched the snow away from his doorway and called down the corridor. Only an echo answered. Finally they had to march down, single file, to the Woodchuck's bedroom and give him a good shaking.

"Christmas tree! Christmas tree! We promised to show you a Christmas tree," the Eldest kept repeating.

"Where?" yawned the Woodchuck.

"On the village green. All decked out with lights and tinsel. Come and see it."

They had an even harder time waking the Chipmunk, because his hallway was so small they couldn't squeeze in to shake him. Fortunately the Chipmunk was not in the habit of sleeping so soundly as the Woodchuck. So he finally heard their shouts.

"Christmas?" he yawned. "Is it Christmas already?"

The Skunk was rather a problem. He had taken over an

old badger's den and was all curled up asleep with his family. It was hard to tell which was which, and the rabbits knew how unwise it was to make a mistake with skunks. But finally they managed to make the Skunk understand.

They found the Bat hanging upside down in a corner of his dark cave. He was very, very sleepy. "Go 'way," he yawned again and again.

"A promise is a promise," said the Eldest Rabbit in a stern voice that made the Bat blink. "Come see the Christmas tree. Remember last summer when you asked us to wake you up at Christmas time. You don't want to miss it now."

It took all the little folk, from the Youngest Rabbit to the Skunk, to wake up the Black Bear. At first he was very cross. But when the Eldest reminded him it was the Bear's own idea to come along, he yawned a friendly, "Oh! Christmas! You don't say. Tell me where it is and I'll break the trail."

"Good," said the Eldest. He explained how to get to the village green where the big Christmas tree stood all alight and sparkling.

"I'll go to the back of the line to be sure no one falls asleep on the way," the Eldest continued. "We rabbits promised to show you a Christmas tree, and a promise is a promise. So let's all be off now. It should not take us long to get there."

Along the creek and through the woods went the strange procession. The night was clear and bright with stars. Underfoot the snow sang as furry paws crunched over it.

The Bat, finding the air too cold for his liking, perched on the Bear's thick warm neck and dozed. The Bear never knew the difference.

"How much farther?" the Bear asked every few minutes. "I'm not as wide-awake as I am in the summer."

"Dear me," said the Quiet One to herself, "I'm afraid we can *never* keep them awake till we get to the village green."

The little Chipmunk's legs were so short he had a hard time running through the snow. When he saw the Bat settle down on the Bear's neck, he jumped up and snuggled down too. And the Bear never knew the difference.

On they went, slowly, through the winter night.

Suddenly there was a loud snort. The Bear had fallen asleep as he walked!

The snort woke up the drowsy little Chipmunk. He opened his eyes and blinked. "Oh, it *is* wonderful," he said.

"What's wonderful?" everyone asked.

"Why, the Christmas tree, of course," piped the Chipmunk. "Lights . . . and tinsel . . . and sparkles . . ."

"Where?" asked the Eldest Rabbit. He was puzzled. They were still a long way from the village green.

"There!"

They followed the Chipmunk's gaze to the top of the hill. There stood a tall fir tree against the starlit sky.

"Oh," gasped everyone except the Eldest Rabbit. He just looked and stammered. "But . . . but . . . the lights?"

"Don't you see them?" whispered the Bat. "All those stars sparkling in the branches!"

"And the tinsel?" the Eldest asked.

"Why, tinsel-sparkles of ice and snow are on every twig," said the Woodchuck.

The Bear held out a huge paw. He looked at the sleepy Bat, the Skunk, the Woodchuck, and the Chipmunk, and he yawned. "I'm glad (he yawned) . . . we didn't have to go all the way to the village green to see such a beautiful Christmas tree. A Christmas tree with lights and sparkles. Just as you promised!"

"Well!" Then the Eldest Rabbit began to smile. "Well, I guess all I need to say is . . . Merry Christmas, everyone. Merry Christmas!"

THE END

The Finch in the Stable

Long, long ago a family of greenfinches lived in the distant land of Judea. The nest was in an olive grove on the side of a rocky hill, not far from a little town. In the nest were four fledglings.

Now it happened that one of the young finches was bolder and greedier than the others. He always managed to snatch more than his share of the insects his parents brought. They noticed that one son was growing strong and handsome, while the other son seemed weak and small, even smaller than his sisters. But the busy parents were too concerned with finding food for their young ones to worry about what was happening in the nest. They simply called one son The Biggest and the other The Least.

For many days the parent greenfinches fed their children. Back and forth, up and down the hillside they searched for worms and insects. Then one summer day, when the fledglings were old enough to try their wings, the parents said to them: "We have been a happy family these many days. Whatever adventures may befall us this summer, let us all meet here at the old nest when cold weather comes, and fly south together."

"Huh," thought The Biggest. "As if I couldn't find my way south by myself."

And so the young finches left the nest and learned to fend for themselves. At first The Biggest sat in the grass and cried, begging his parents to find insects for him. Then he became restless. "There is nothing to see in this olive grove," he said. "I am going to fly to the town."

"Be careful," warned his father. "There are many dangers in a town." But The Biggest was already out of hearing.

"What a handsome fellow he is," the parents said. "Surely he will be a leader among finches." They turned and looked at their other son nearby. "But The Least . . . we must not expect much of him. He is so small and rumpled."

Summer passed quickly. The Least did not stray far from the olive grove. Whenever he found a particularly nice tidbit he liked to call his sisters to share the feast with him. It seemed he never would be able to make up for his poor start!

Meanwhile The Biggest found a mulberry tree near an inn at the edge of town. There life was so pleasant he never once thought of going back to visit his family in the olive grove. He thought only of keeping the mulberry tree as his special preserve. Every day he drove off the smaller birds. He made friends with no one. "I can have more for myself this way," he said.

Then fall came. The weather began to turn cold at night, though the sun was still warm by day. Even when the leaves began to turn yellow, The Biggest was reluctant to leave his mulberry tree. There were still some dried berries, and plenty of grain in the innyard. "No reason to fly south so soon," he told himself, as he pulled his feathers around him to keep out of the wind.

Several afternoons later, when the sky was gray and cold, a small finch flew wearily into the innyard. It seemed very tired. Cautiously it alighted near the stable and began to peck.

"Of all the nerve!" said The Biggest to himself.

"Doesn't that fellow know that I own everything around here?" And with a great lunge he dashed down and knocked the little fellow over, injuring the intruder's wing. Then he saw—it was The Least. It was his own brother.

"Oh, at last I have found you!" cried The Least, without a word about his injury. "I have flown around the town for days, looking for you. It is time to start south; we cannot wait any longer." He gave a deep sigh and closed his eyes. "But you must go on without me. I won't be able to fly again until I have rested."

"Nonsense," said The Biggest. "You can fly. Come, try it."

But The Least sat limply on the ground. "I am too tired, and my wing hurts," he said. "You start south with the others and I'll come later."

The Biggest saw that his brother was in no condition for the long trip south. "Why don't you stay in the stable, then, until you are stronger?" he suggested. "It is warm there with the old ox and the sheep, and there will be plenty to eat."

While his wing was healing and he was gaining strength, the little bird made friends with the old ox in one of the stalls. The ox was a kindly fellow who had lost his partner during the summer and was very lonely. He liked having the cheerful greenfinch to talk to. They spent many happy hours together. The Least told the ox all about his family, and especially about his strong, handsome brother.

"Handsome is as handsome does," the ox muttered. "I know that selfish brother of yours. He hasn't a friend in the world."

Gradually the wing healed, and the day came when the little greenfinch said to the ox, "I feel stronger. Perhaps I should start out tomorrow and try to catch the others."

But the next morning a cold autumn wind whined

around the innyard and banged at the stable door. "You must not go today," said the ox. "This wind would dash you to pieces."

The next day the wind still blew, and then the rainy season began. What with one thing or another, The Least never did fly south that winter. Day after day he talked with his good friend, the ox, and ate seeds from the hay and enjoyed the warmth of the stable.

Then one cold afternoon in December, soon after the shortest and darkest day of the year, a strange thing happened. The stable door opened and the innkeeper came in with a lantern. Behind him were a man and a woman and a small gray donkey.

"This is the best I can do for you," the innkeeper said. "I am sorry. Every room in the inn is taken, but here you can at least keep dry. There is a place for the donkey next to the ox, and here is an empty stall for you, and a manger full of clean hay. This lantern will give you light. It is the best I can do."

"We are grateful for any roof tonight," said the strange man. "My wife is very tired. We have traveled a long way from Nazareth to Bethlehem. I am of the house of David, and we have come to register for the Roman census."

"Yes, of course. That is why the town is so crowded," nodded the innkeeper.

"Thank you, innkeeper," the woman murmured in a faraway voice. "This stable will do well enough. I shall lie on the hay and rest. Joseph, feed the little donkey. He is weary, too."

The innkeeper went out, and the strangers were left in the barn with the ox and the sheep and the little greenfinch, who kept quiet and out of sight.

It was not long after midnight when The Least awoke from sleep with a start. For the first time in his life he wanted to sing! What is even more surprising, he felt he *could* sing, although he was still so young. He wanted to sing more than anything else in the world. And so he opened his mouth, and a cascade of sweet music poured out in that stable in Judea. Never before had such music come from the throat of a greenfinch. The stable was filled with the song of spring, although outside in the innyard the night was frosty-cold.

As the little finch sang, he noticed a strange shaft of golden light pouring in through the single window of the stable, making a path to the empty manger. But the manger was no longer empty! In it lay a new-born child, and nearby knelt Mary and Joseph. The light hovered over the child's head like a golden crown.

On and on sang the finch. And without his knowing it the shaft of light spread out to include his perch, and the gold poured into his feathers.

It was a wonderful night. In the humble stable peace and joy filled every heart.

At dawn The Least fluttered down to say good morning to his friend, the ox. The ox stared at him in wonder. "What has happened to you, my friend?" he asked.

"Happened?" asked the little finch. "Everything has happened. I can sing! Did you not hear me sing?"

"That I did," replied the ox. "And it was like music from heaven. But look at your coat. Never was there a bird with such a handsome coat!"

The Least looked down at his feathers. They were no longer dull and drab, with a tinge of olive-green. They were gold! Bright, shining yellow gold!

"You are no longer a rumpled little greenfinch," said the ox. "You are a *gold*finch now, and wherever you fly you will be a flash of glory. Just as this night has been a night of glory. Wherever you go you will sing from a full heart and bring joy to watching eyes. You are no longer

The Least, my friend. Something new has come into the world this night . . . "he that is least among you all, the same shall be great."

THE END

Investment in Christmas

Once there was an unhappy middle-aged man named Herman Pinchpenny. His mind was pinched, his heart was pinched, and he lived a pinched little life.

Now, there was really no reason why Herman Pinchpenny should be unhappy. He had a good job and a surprisingly large bank account. He owned a big house within walking distance of the office. Yet his life was bankrupt. He never had any fun! And, of course, he didn't believe in Christmas. It cost too much.

There was only one respect in which Herman Pinchpenny was extravagant. That was pencils. When he was a boy he never had enough pencils. Every Christmas he would look in his stocking for pencils, but he never got any. And so he vowed that when he was rich he would carry a vest pocket full of pencils, just to remind himself that he really *was* rich.

No, Herman never pinched his purse or his pennies where pencils were concerned. He bought himself a silver one, a gold one, a black and white onyx one, a mottled green one, a shining blue one, a red and white striped one, a metallic bronze one, a purple and gold one, and a turquoise and silver one. Then he lined up all the nine pencils in his vest pocket. But no one except Herman was ever allowed to touch them. He carried a wooden stub of a pencil in his coat pocket, just in case anyone should ask to borrow one.

And that is the way matters stood one December evening when Herman walked home from the office. Just as he turned into his street he all but bumped into Mrs. Jovial, who lived with her husband and seven children in the smallest house on the block. She was a cheerful woman, although Herman could never figure out why. She obviously had a hard time making ends meet.

"Why, good evening, Mr. Pinchpenny," said Mrs. Jovial, lavishing a broad smile on him. "I haven't seen you in ages. I'm so glad we bumped into each other. I've been wanting to ask you how you expect to spend Christmas this year."

"Spend!" Herman blurted out, with horror in his voice. "I don't intend to *spend* it at all."

Mrs. Jovial laughed. "You have the most unusual sense of humor, Mr. Pinchpenny. But you'll have to spend Christmas somehow, you know. You can't save it. Not that anyone would want to. Christmas is the one season of the year we all spend wholeheartedly." She hesitated, then plunged ahead. "I wonder . . . would you be so kind . . . I mean . . ."

Herman scrunched down in his coat, fearing his neighbor was about to ask for a contribution to the Community Christmas Tree or something. And he couldn't see that such contributions ever paid dividends.

Mrs. Jovial tried again. "I wonder if you would be so kind as to give up a little of your time on Christmas Eve."

"Give!" thought Herman. "That's a word I don't like the sound of at all."

"You see," Mrs. Jovial explained, "my brother has always played Santa Claus for the children on Christmas Eve. But he moved away last summer. And my husband is much too small for our Santa Claus suit. Besides, the children would miss him and suspect something. And I've noticed that you are in the habit of staying up rather late anyway, and you would give us all such a great deal of pleasure . . ."

"*Give*," moaned Herman again, down inside himself.

"It won't take much of your time, Mr. Pinchpenny. My husband will bring over the Santa Claus suit on Christmas Eve and help you put it on, right over your regular clothes." She looked him over. "You'll need a pillow or two in front, I suspect. I'll have the gifts all ready in a sack for you to carry over your shoulder. You just come jingling up to the front door, and we'll be waiting for you. All you have to do is distribute the presents, and . . . well, it might be a rather different way for you to spend Christmas Eve, don't you think?"

"But I'm not a bit worried about spending it, Mrs. Jovial."

"Oh, please, Mr. Pinchpenny. When you see the children all full of wonder and excitement . . ."

"I'm not very good with children," Herman interrupted. "I never know how to act."

"Just act like Santa Claus, and you'll be a great success," Mrs. Jovial beamed.

For the first time in more days than he could remember, Herman Pinchpenny smiled. The idea of his acting like *Santa Claus* was such a nonsensical joke he almost laughed out loud. "All right," he said. "I'll do it."

And so that is how it happened that Herman Pinchpenny, of all people, was spending his Christmas Eve playing Santa Claus at the Jovial house down the street. He didn't feel quite at home in Santa's boots, but there he was, standing before seven wide-eyed youngsters, ranging in age from two to twelve, with a bag of toys to distribute.

"Merry Christmas," Herman said in his best Santa Claus voice. "Did you children invest your time to good advantage this past year?"

The children looked baffled, but Mrs. Jovial hurriedly answered for them. "They have all been very good, Santa Claus."

"I'm glad to hear it," Herman said, taking the bag of toys from his shoulder and opening the drawstring. "Now, let's see. What have we here?"

One by one he took out the gifts, called the names, and watched the children run up eagerly for their presents. They weren't much: a few inexpensive trinkets and the rest all practical gifts like handkerchiefs and mittens and socks. Herman looked down at the children. He'd have been disappointed, not to get a single pencil!

All of a sudden Herman Pinchpenny, for the first time in his life, didn't feel pinched and lonely. He felt, believe it or not, the way he looked—like Santa Claus. It was an amazing feeling. He hardly knew what to make of it.

He cleared his throat and unbuttoned the top two buttons of the red Santa Claus suit. "Now," he said, "I have something for each of you that I didn't want to trust to the toy bag. You know how little things sometimes get lost in the corners. These are very special presents . . ."

He began pulling out his precious pencils. One at a time he passed them around to the children, and it must be said that never in all their lives had the young Jovials felt *so* jovial as when they saw the beautiful pencils. Seven children, seven pencils. Herman Pinchpenny still had the silver one and the gold one left. Then he looked at little Mr. Jovial whose eyes and mouth were wide open. And he looked at Mrs. Jovial whose eyes and mouth were even wider open.

Santa Claus smiled. "I didn't even forget papa and mama this year," he said, handing them the silver and gold pencils.

Such a hubbub. Everyone wanted to write something at once. And then there was a special Christmas supper that

Santa simply had to stay for (after his long trip from the North Pole). And then there were songs to sing. It was the best Christmas Herman Pinchpenny had ever spent in his life.

And so it is time to come to the end of this story. But, here is a funny thing: no one knows for sure how the story is going to end. You see, all *that* happened last Christmas, and *this* Christmas hasn't quite come. And no one can be sure how Herman is going to act. Is he going to play Santa Claus for the Jovials again? Or perhaps will he be Santa Claus down at the big Community Christmas Tree? Or is he planning to take over the entire pencil end of Santa's business? No one really knows. But one thing is certain. Herman is going to *spend* Christmas wholeheartedly, one way or another.

THE END

Not Taking Any Chances

Grownups don't know everything. Take Dad. When I asked him how Santa's reindeer could run through the sky without falling down, he cleared his throat and said he guessed that was something special for *Christmas*. And when I asked how reindeer could come down on roofs without people hearing them, he said people didn't have the right kind of ears. But when I said, "What kind of ears are right?" he couldn't answer that, either.

No, grownups don't know everything. Take Gram. When I asked how Santa Claus could come down the fireplace chimney without getting all sooty, she said perhaps he had a new-fangled nylon suit that didn't show dirt. "Well, why didn't he get dirty *before* he had that new-fangled suit?" I asked. Gram couldn't answer, and she didn't know what happened if there was a fire burning in the grate, either. She just said Dad would be sure to put the fire out before he went to bed, so I shouldn't worry.

No, grownups don't know everything. Take Mom. When I asked her how Santa had time to deliver all those presents on the night before Christmas, she said she was sure his clock wasn't like ours. But she couldn't tell me how it was different. And when I asked how Santa's bag could be big enough to carry all those toys, she said maybe he carried refills. But she didn't know what the refills looked like.

No, grownups don't know everything. But I don't care. I'm going to hang up my stocking where he'll be sure to see it, anyway!

Speaking of Presents

Know what?

I don't like to come right out and *say* what I want for Christmas—because there are quite a few things I want—and I think parents like to think they get ideas themselves. But I figure it doesn't hurt to drop a few hints, beginning about the first of December. After all, it's a long time since Dad and Mom were young. And how can they remember what they wanted for Christmas when they were my age?

Know what?

One Saturday morning a couple of weeks ago I was cracking nuts for Mom's fruit cake. It struck me as a pretty good time to drop a hint, and I thought of a good way to do it. "Mom," I said, "if I were rich, you know what I'd buy you for Christmas?"

"I haven't any idea," Mom said.

"A dog!" I shouted. "A black and white dog—or brown, if you'd prefer. Or spotted. Just so it was a dog."

"Hmm," Mom said. "Then I guess it's just as well you aren't rich, because we haven't room for a dog."

Know what?

During the next few weeks I managed to drop some more hints. I told Mom how we learned in school that fresh air and exercise were absolutely necessary for good health . . . and that anybody who had a *bike* or a *pony* was bound to get plenty of fresh air and exercise.

And what did Mom say? Said experience had taught her

that the best possible exercise was taking a walk on your own two feet. Otherwise the bike or pony got all the exercise.

Know what?

I can't seem to get Mom or Dad interested in wanting one of those new combination pocket knives for Christmas . . . you know, the kind with a wonderful can opener and leather punch and screw driver and corkscrew in addition to a big and little blade. Mom says she has a much better can opener already, and she wouldn't have any use for the leather punch. And Dad says he has at least four screw drivers and three corkscrews. So I'd better think of something else.

Know what?

For the past week Mom has been talking about wool mitts and sweater and muffler. What color would a person my age like best? As if I can't see through her hints! But I fooled her. Quick as a flash I told her the color of mitts and sweater and muffler would depend on the color of the new sled a fellow was going to get for Christmas.

Mom started to laugh. And I started to laugh. And what it all comes down to is that we're both in the same boat . . . we don't either of us know what we're going to get. Did I say *boat?* Say, maybe I can think of a good way to drop a hint about a boat!

POEMS

Merry Christmas, Everyone

Merry Christmas, everyone—
Middle-sized and small,
Tall and short, and old and young—
Merry Christmas, all!

Tell the story of the birth
Of the Christmas King,
Spread good will across the earth,
Choose a song to sing.

Have your fill of Christmas fun,
Santa Claus, and sleighs.
Merry Christmas, everyone!
Happy holidays!

Christmas Tree

I'll find me a spruce
In the cold white wood
With wide green boughs
And a snowy hood.

I'll pin on a star
With five gold spurs
To mark my spruce
From the pines and firs.

I'll make me a score
Of suet balls
To tie to my spruce
When the cold dusk falls.

And I'll hear next day
From the sheltering trees
The Christmas carols
Of the chickadees.

When a Star Shone Down

The night was cold
And the air was chill,
When a star shone down
On a shepherds' hill.

The year was bleak
When a star shone down
On the quiet roofs
Of a little town.

The place was mean
And the room was small,
When a star shone down
On a lowly stall.

When a star shone down
On the manger hay,
Shepherds and kings
Were one that day,

And all the world
Felt the breath of spring,
When a star shone down
On the Saviour King.

Red and Green

Red and green for Christmas—
What could be more jolly?
Red for joy and green for life,
The red and green of holly.

Around the Corner

Christmas is coming
Around the corner—
It's time to be good,
Like little Jack Horner!

What Christmas Is

Oh, Christmas is a birthday,
A full-of-joy-and-mirth day,
A sing-for-all-you're-worth day,
A peace-to-men-on-earth day.

The Heart Is an Inn

The heart is an inn
For friends we know
To linger within
Or come and go,
To doff a cap
And unloose a sandal,
To warm their hands
At a cheery candle.

The heart is an inn—
Oh, is there room
On a crowded night
In the winter gloom
For strangers who knock
And ask to tarry,
Like one named Joseph
And one named Mary?

Christmas

Spruce boughs and holly,
Candles between . . .
Christmas is jolly
With scarlet and green.

Music and singing—
Listen your fill.
Christmas is ringing
With joy and good will.

Parcels to carry,
Lights burning high . . .
Christmas is merry
And oh, so am I!

Legends of Christmas

On Christmas Eve while hamlets sleep
The wild bees wake and sing,
Above the frosty fields they sweep,
To praise a newborn King . . .
But none except the pure of heart,
With insight where to go,
But none except the pure of heart may know.

On Christmas, at the quiet hours,
The valley and the hill
Turn blue with hosts of starry flowers
That out of heaven spill . . .
But none except the pure of heart,
With eyes of clarity,
But none except the pure of heart may see.

On Christmas Eve at twelve o'clock
The cattle kneel to pray,
And lamb and ox and crowing cock
Have human words to say . . .
But none except the pure of heart,
Who have an inner ear,
But none except the pure of heart may hear.

Tree Lights

Come one, come all, the tree is lit,
All Christmas-bright and shining!
Like twinkling stars the colors flit
Amidst the tinsel twining.

Come one, come all; come, look and see
The Christmas colors streaming.
The candles on His birthday tree
Are gleaming, gleaming, gleaming.

A Jolly Time

Oh, Christmas is a jolly time,
No matter where you're living—
A time for songs and lights and fun
And getting gifts . . . and giving.

Christmas Dreams

I dreamed last night
That Santa Claus said
He'd bring me a dog
And a brand new sled
And a box of paints
And a top to spin,
And a pile of books
That had pictures in,
And a drum that boomed
And a horn that gleamed . . .
I hope he *remembers*
The things I dreamed!

Before Christmas

Streets are full of music now
And stores are full of shine,
And hands are full of ribbons now
And Christmas seals and twine.

Jars are full of cookies now,
And, oh, but they look fine,
And cards are full of greetings now
Beneath each bright design.

Lights are full of sparkle now
On fir and spruce and pine,
And heads are full of secrets now—
If they are heads like mine!

How to Get What You Want
for Christmas

Once there was an antelope
Who said, "I'll write to Santa Clope."
"You mean, my son, to Santa *Claus*,"
His mother told the antelaus.
"I know. But, Mom, it never rhymes—
I've tried it half a dozen times!"
And so he wrote: "Dear Santa Climes,
Do you have skates for antelimes?"

"My son, see here, this will not do,"
His mother told the anteloo.
"It's Santa *Claus!* Now, try again."
And so he wrote: "Dear Santa Clen,
I'd like some skates, I'd like a sled . . ."
"No, no," said Mrs. Anteled,
"It's Santa *Claus*, not Clope or Cled.
Come, quit this joke and go to bed."

The outcome is that Santa Claus,
Not hearing from the antelaus,
Forgot to think of sleds and skates
And brought red flannel underwates!
Which makes me, friends, in your behalf
Compose this final paragraph:
Sometimes it's best to stick to prose
When writing notes to Santa Close!

Christmas-Tree Angel

What does she see,
What does she see,
The angel who looks from the Christmas tree?

She sees the tinsel,
The lights that glow,
The holly, the candles, the mistletoe.

She sees the parcels
All wrapped and tied
And full of wonderful things inside.

And, oh, I wonder
If she can see
The joy that shines in the heart of me?

Candle in the Window

Use a simple holder
With a rounded handle,
When the day grows older
Light the Christmas candle.

Throw a ring of brightness
Through the dark of winter,
Cut the snowy whiteness
With a golden splinter.

On this eve of Christmas,
Up and down and yonder,
Over hill and isthmus,
Christ, the Child, will wander,

Looking for protection
From the winter weather,
Seeking warmth, affection,
Love and faith together.

If the Christ Child travels
(Snow beneath his sandal)
Where this road unravels,
He will see your candle,

He will hurry near it
And, benign and tender,
Bless the Christmas spirit
Shining out in splendor.

Holly Fairies

Oh, fairies love a holly tree:
The foliage makes a roof
Of sturdy shingles, always green
And new and weatherproof;
And even under winter skies
The berries burn so bright
They look like little fairy lamps
With bulbs of crimson light.

Oh, fairies love a holly spray
Too much by far to leave,
And so they up and follow it
Indoors, on Christmas Eve;
And that is why each house is blessed
Where holly sprigs are seen . . .
Because the fairies still are there
Beneath the red and green.

In December

Everyone is merry now.
Go walking down the street,
And twinkly eyes and winkly eyes
Are all the eyes you meet.

Everyone is eager now
To shop and trim a tree,
And knowing smiles and glowing smiles
Are all the smiles you see.

Everyone is jolly now,
This tingly-jingly season.
And only cats and puppy dogs
Can't understand the reason!

Christmas Song

Sing green and gold
And new and old
And Christmas-in-the-air,
Sing red and blue
And old and new
And Christmas-everywhere.
Sing of shepherds and the Star,
Wisemen riding fast and far,
Sing the brightest words there are:
    Merry Christmas!

Sing trees and toys
And girls and boys
And joy that stands apart,
Sing sights and smells
And midnight bells
And giving from the heart.
Sing of shepherds and the Star,
Wisemen riding fast and far,
Sing the brightest words there are:
    Merry Christmas!

Christmas Lights

All over, all over, all over town,
Lights come on when the sun goes down;
But never so many lights as these,
When houses are bright with Christmas trees.

All over, all over, high and low,
Holiday lights of Christmas show:
New ones, blue ones, mellow and bold,
Red ones, green ones, yellow and gold.

All over, all over everywhere
Lights shine out in the Christmas air,
And everyone looks with pleased surprise
At lights that shine in everyone's eyes.

On the Road to Bethlehem

Little donkey, moving slowly
Down the winter road:
Do you marvel at the lightness
Of your heart beneath your load?

Nazareth is miles behind you,
Bethlehem ahead—
Yet the journey does not find you
Footsore or discomforted.

Little donkey, on the highway
In the wind and cold:
Do you wonder at your vigor
As another day grows old?

Joseph paces there beside you,
Mary on your back.
What is this that seems to guide you
Gently down the rutted track?

Little donkey, stepping softly
Through the winter air,
Do you know about the stable
And the manger waiting there?

Maybe not . . . but something, something
Smoothes your stony way.
Little donkey, journey gently
Toward the light of Christmas Day!

Of Course There Is a Santa Claus

Of course, there is a Santa Claus!
You may not see him driving
His little reindeer through the sky
Or hear him on arriving,
But he is there on Christmas Eve
With jolly secrets up his sleeve.

Of course, there is a Santa Claus!
You may not see him climbing
Inside a chimney Christmas Eve,
When midnight bells are chiming,
But he is there that magic night,
Although you never see him—quite.

Of course, there is a Santa Claus!
You may not hear him chuckle
Or see his red and bulging coat
With flashing belt and buckle,
But he is there . . . in every heart
Where giving plays a merry part.

At Christmas

The rabbit in the woodpile,
The mice that stitch the snow
With little feather-stitches
Whichever way they go,
The porky in the pine tree,
The blinky winter squirrel,
The mother deer, the father deer,
The coyote boy and girl . . .
What do they do, I wonder,
When Christmas comes, and snow?
They haven't any stockings
For hanging in a row!

Benjamin's Christmas Candy

One day in December Ben's wife said, "Remember,
You promised to help me. Don't sigh.
I've made some nice candy that ought to sell dandy
With Christmas so near—go and try."

But Benjy said, "Dearie, I find selling dreary.
I'd rather give candy away."
And he sighed as his Mrs. wrapped caramels and kisses
To sell in the city that day.

"Oh mercy, that's plenty," said Ben at 2:20.
"I'll put on my skis and get started."
"Your skis! Don't be silly," his wife cried. "It's spilly . . ."
But Ben had already departed.

As he drew near the city, dear me, what a pity,
A ski-meet was plumb in his track!
The stunts were just ending as Benjy, descending,
Saw clearly he couldn't turn back.

He whizzed toward the jump. His heart gave a thump.
He zooped several loops in the sky;
And his candy went pouring on crowds that were roaring:
"He wins! What a stunt. What a guy!"

Folks dove for the candy. They shouted, "It's dandy."
And Benjamin's prize saved the day:
For his wife got the money, and Benjy grinned, "Honey,
I *love* to give candy away!"

A Christmas Tree

Why doesn't everyone who has
A town or country house that has
A big or little yard that has
A speck of space to spare

Go out and plant a Christmas tree,
A spruce or balsam Christmas tree,
A small or tallsome Christmas tree,
And get it growing there,

So when the year turns old and white
There'll be a Christmas tree just right
For colored lights to twinkle bright
And cheer the frosty air?

Christmas Goose

1.

Said a turkey whose name was Augusta:
"For Christmas I want a new dustah.
So, hubby, think twice—
Keep your tail-feathers nice.
I'll need all the plumes you can mustah."

2.

"For Christmas," said Samuel the salmon,
"My sons want a game of backgammon.
So I'll save the money
By giving up honey
And eating my bread without jam on."

3.

Said a gnu by the name of Antonia:
"For Christmas I want a begonia.
It will keep me, forsooth,
In the *flower* of my youth,
So I'll never come down with gnumonia."

Waiting for Christmas

"Just around the corner,"
All the papers say.
Christmas, Christmas, Christmas,
Half a month away!

"Just around the corner" . . .
Ten more days, then five.
It seems to take forever
For the corner to arrive!

The Shortest Days

The shortest days, the darkest days,
The coldest days are here,
And yet they are the brightest days
Of all the busy year . . .
With colored lights and dazzling sights
And songs of Christmas cheer.

The Smallest Star

The stars looked down with shining eyes
Upon the sleepy Earth,
They knew a secret, a surprise,
About the Christ Child's birth:
"Tonight will be the night," said one.
"At midnight," said another.
"The Child will be the Father's son
And Mary be His mother."

The smallest star blinked twice, and sighed:
"But how will people know
Where He is born? The world is wide—
He'll be too small to show."
"They'll have to search," a planet said.
"We have no way of telling.
They'll have to search each inn and bed
And barn and town and dwelling."

The little star, the least of all,
Looked earthward with a sigh.
"I'd like to help," it said. "I'm small
But I can go and try."
The others chuckled, "You? Ho, ho!"
And shook with merry laughter.
"You are so small you'd hardly show
Hung from a stable's rafter."

The smallest star, whose heart was large,
Fell down and down through space,
And as it fell a mighty charge
Of brightness filled its face;
And as it fell it grew in size
Because of its compassion . . .
It blazed so bright to earthly eyes
The other stars looked ashen.

And so the smallest star of all
Came down to show the way:
It stopped above a humble stall
Where Mary's infant lay,
It made a sign above the hill
Where Bethlehem lay dreaming,
And there it lingered, bright and still,
While worshippers came streaming.

Riddle for December

Everything is gleaming now
With green and gold and red,
And everyone is beaming now
With visions in his head.

Everything looks jolly now
With lights and colored balls.
And mistletoe and holly now
Are decking all the halls.

Everyone is humming now
The sweetest music yet,
Because of something coming now . . .
One guess is all you get!

SONGS

Christmas Time

(*To the tune of "Jingle Bells"*)

Christmas is a time
When there's something in the air,
More than bells that chime,
More than songs to share,
Something gay and bright,
More than lights aglow,
You sense it morning, noon, and night
Wherever you may go.

CHORUS: Christmas time, Christmas time,
Every Jack and Jill
Knows what fun it is to feel
All a-tingle with good will;
Christmas time, Christmas time,
Though the air be chill,
Everyone is tingly now
With a feeling of good will!

There in the Stable

(To the tune of "Long, Long Ago")

There in the stable asleep on the hay,
Long, long ago, long, long ago,
Jesus, who gave us our first Christmas Day,
Long, long ago, long ago.
Over the stable a star hung so bright
Shepherds who watched in the dark of the night
Followed the glow of the heavenly light
Long, long ago, long ago.

There in the stable a Saviour was born
Long, long ago, long, long ago,
Shepherds brought presents that first Christmas morn,
Long, long ago, long ago.
Let no one say that a palace is best,
Humbly He lay, who would meet every test,
There in the hay was the Child who was blest,
Long, long ago, long ago.

Christmas Spirit

(To the tune of "Auld Lang Syne")

Should Christmas spirit be forgot
When Christmas is no more?
Should Christmas spirit be forgot
And locked behind the door?
When holidays are out of sight
And merry songs are few,
Let's keep the Christmas spirit bright
And strong the whole year through!

We feel the warmth of brotherhood
When Christmas time is here,
We think of ways of doing good
And spreading Christmas cheer.
When holidays are out of sight
Should brotherhood be too?
Let's keep the Christmas spirit bright
And strong the whole year through!

When Christmas Is Almost Here

(To the tune of "When Johnny Comes Marching Home")

Now Christmas is almost here again,
Hurrah, hurrah!
We're full of good will and cheer again,
Hurrah, hurrah!
We wrap our presents and hide them well
And burst with secrets we will not tell,
And we all feel gay now Christmas is almost here.

For holly berries and Christmas trees,
Hurrah, hurrah!
For songs and presents and such as these,
Hurrah, hurrah!
But most of all we are glad again
For peace on earth, good will to men,
And we all feel gay when Christmas is almost here.

Christmas Colors

(To the tune of "Merry Widow Waltz")

Christmas colors, Christmas colors,
Red and green,
Bright and jolly, like the holly,
Full of sheen,
Red for light and laughter,
Green for growth and strength,
May the meaning linger
Through the year's full length.

Christmas Bells

(*To the tune of "Baa! Baa! Black Sheep"*)

Ring bells, swing bells,
Christmas time is here.
Ring bells, sing bells—
Loud and clear:
One for the giving,
One for the mirth,
And one for the glory of the Christ Child's birth.

On Christmas Eve

(To the tune of "Curly Locks")

Santa Claus, Santa Claus, how will you know?
My house is so little it scarcely will show.
I'll leave by the chimney some oats and some hay
And trust that your reindeer will find the right way!

Sing a Song of Shopping

(To the tune of "Sing a Song of Sixpence")

Sing a song of shopping,
A pocket full of dimes,
Four and twenty presents
Wrapped for the times.
When the gifts are opened
We'll all begin to sing—
Everyone at Christmas time
Is happy as a king!

Caroling

(*To the tune of "The Quilting Party"*)

When the Christmas candles glisten,
And the Christmas trees are bright,
We'll be going up and down the village,
We'll be singing in the night.
CHORUS: We'll be singing in the night
With the windows all alight,
On the eve of Christmas in the village
We'll be singing in the night.

When the Christmas log is burning,
And the Christmas snow is white,
We'll be going up and down the village,
We'll be singing in the night.
CHORUS: We'll be singing in the night, etc.

Signs of Christmas

(*To the tune of "Flow Gently, Sweet Afton"*)

The wreath on the door and the lights on the tree,
The gay sprig of holly above the settee,
The crèche on the table with Wisemen and sheep,
And Mary and Joseph and Jesus—asleep;
The red Christmas candle, the mistletoe sprig,
The brightly-wrapped presents, some small and some big,
You don't need to read all the facts in a book:
It's Christmas, it's Christmas, wherever you look!

So Slow

(To the tune of "Where Is My Little Dog Gone?")

Oh, why, oh why, hasn't Santa come yet?
Oh, why—does anyone know?
If he'd trade his sleigh for a modern jet,
He wouldn't be so slow!

I Had a Little Fir Tree

(*To the tune of "I Had a Little Nut Tree"*)

I had a little fir tree,
    bright with balls of blue,
Balls of gold and silver
    shiny through and through.
I tried to look inside them,
    standing on my toes,
And laughed—at the sight of my
    shiny bright nose!

Christmas Baking

(*To the tune of "The Old Oaken Bucket"*)

What fun before Christmas to help with the baking,
To fit little cookies in rows on the tins,
To dress up the fruit cakes that mother is making
By popping white almonds from brown little skins!
We like the bright fruit peel piled high in the dishes,
And nutmeg and cloves are so spicy to smell,
But best of the baking is all the glad wishes
We mix with plum pudding and fruit cake as well.
Good wishes of Christmas, good wishes of Christmas
All mixed up with cherries and almonds as well!

What fun to cut cookies in squares and in wedges
And pack them in boxes for giving away,
To frost little cupcakes right up to the edges
And top them with cherries to make them look gay!
The kitchen is cluttered with pans and with dishes—
What goodies to see and what fragrance to smell!
But best of the baking is all the glad wishes
We mix with plum pudding and fruit cake as well.
Good wishes of Christmas, good wishes of Christmas
All mixed up with cherries and almonds as well!

The Animals' Christmas

(To the tune of "In the Gloaming")

In the country, in the stables
Early, early Christmas morn,
All the roosters, legend tells us,
Crow the news that Christ is born;
And the cattle, sheep, and oxen
Kneel and bend their heads down low
In remembrance of the stable
In Judea long ago.

In the country bees awaken
In the hives at Christmas-tide,
And fly singing over meadows
Of the winter countryside.
And the wild deer in the forest,
Legend tells us, kneel to pray
In remembrance of the Christ Child
Born upon the manger hay.

Watching the Clock

(To the tune of "Hickory, Dickory, Dock")

Tickory, tickory, tock,
Does Santa have a clock?
If he's too late
I cannot wait . . .
Tickory, tickory, tock.

Christmas Presents

(To the tune of "I Love Little Pussy")

I love the surprises that Christmastime brings,
The whispers, the secrets, the tucked-away things,
I love making presents that others can't see,
And wonder about the surprises for *me!*

Waiting for Christmas

(*To the tune of "Three Blind Mice"*)

Christmas Day, Christmas Day,
Hurry this way, hurry this way,
But when you come to our house at last,
Please do not go rushing away too fast,
For we'll have to wait till another year's passed
For Christmas Day.

Lights of Christmas

(To the tune of "Where Do All the Daisies Go?")

Why do Christmas candles glow?
I know, I know!
So the Christ Child will not stray
If he passes by this way
On the night of Christmas Day;
That is why they glow.
On the night of Christmas Day;
That is why they glow.

Why do all the tree lights glow?
I know, I know!
Lights are full of joy and cheer
For a birthday time of year—
Jesus' birthday soon is here;
That is why they glow.
Jesus' birthday soon is here;
That is why they glow.

The Christmas Star

(To the tune of Schumann's "The Evening Star")

Oh, Bethlehem star,
How famous you are:
You shone with a glory
That blazed near and far.

You brightened a stall
Both humble and small
And shone on the Christ Child
Who lived for us all.

You pointed the way
To Him on the hay,
And filled hearts with wonder
That first Christmas Day.

GAMES

Jingle Bells

The leader of this game should be able to recite the first stanza and chorus of "Jingle Bells," although the lines could be read if necessary.

Players sit on the floor in a circle, with the leader in the center. Each player is named for some word in the poem (except *sleigh*), such as *snow, horse, bells, ride, fun*. If there is a large group several may be named for the same word. ALL players must answer to the word *sleigh*.

As the leader begins to recite . . . "Dashing thro' the snow . . ." those named for *snow* must jump up immediately, whirl around, and sit down again. "In a one-horse . . ." Players named for *horse* must jump up, turn, and sit down quickly, etc. If a player fails to act he must later pay a forfeit. Every time the leader says *sleigh*, all players must jump up and turn around.

At the last *sleigh*, when players are turning around, the leader tries to get someone's place in the circle. If he succeeds the one left out is leader for the next game.

Christmas Star and Christmas Tree

Preparations for this game are made ahead of time. A red cardboard star and a green cardboard Christmas tree of approximately the same size are cut into the same number of pieces, like a jigsaw puzzle, and hidden around the room. Later players are divided into two groups, the Reds and the Greens. Greens are to hunt only for green pieces for their tree, Reds only for red pieces for their star. If they see pieces belonging to the other group, they do not tell.

As pieces are found, they are brought to the leader of each group, who tries to fit them together. The group that completes the star or tree first is the winner.

Christmas Dinner

Each player is given a pencil and a piece of paper on which the following scrambled words are written:

sroat sooge
palep sifftung
ravgy
daals
terbesh
relecy
sorll
toposate
carrybren cause
pine mice
volies
tuns

Players should unscramble the words to spell something for Christmas dinner. When time is called, the one with the most complete list wins.

(*Answers:* Roast goose, apple stuffing, gravy, salad, sherbet, celery, rolls, potatoes, cranberry sauce, mince pie, olives, nuts)

What I Want for Christmas

"What I want for Christmas is an apple."

"What I want for Christmas is an apple and a bugle."

"What I want for Christmas is an apple, a bugle, and a cookie."

Any number can play this game, each one repeating previous presents and adding a new one beginning with the next letter of the alphabet. Anyone who forgets, or gets mixed up, or hesitates longer than ten seconds is out. The one who holds out the longest wins a prize.

To make the game harder, start at the other end of the alphabet:

"What I want for Christmas is a zebra."

"What I want for Christmas is a zebra and a yam."

"What I want for Christmas is a zebra, a yam, and a xylophone."

To make the game even harder, have each present consist of two words, one describing the other:

"What I want for Christmas is an antiquated ape."

"What I want for Christmas is an antiquated ape and a billowy bustle."

"What I want for Christmas is an antiquated ape, a billowy bustle, and a cannibalistic camel," etc.

What's on the Tree?

A small portable Christmas tree should be trimmed ahead of time for this game. It should hold samples of the usual Christmas-tree ornaments (star, tinsel, glass ball, etc.) as well as things one would never expect to see on a tree (nail, key ring, cork, etc.).

Players sit in a row or circle, each with paper and pencil. The leader of the game carries the tree slowly down the row or around the circle and tells everyone to take a good look, then quickly goes out with the tree. The player who correctly lists the largest number of objects on the tree wins a prize.

Ready for Christmas

Players are divided into two groups. One group goes into a huddle and decides on some activity connected with getting ready for Christmas, such as stringing popcorn, trimming the tree, baking cookies, wrapping packages, going shopping, etc. They return to face the second group, chanting:

"Everyone's busy when Christmas is near,
The busiest, cheeriest season of year."

The second group asks: "What are you doing that keeps you so busy?"

First group: "Watch us and see." They act out the activity they have decided upon, and members of the second group try to guess what it is. If they succeed, they have a chance to pantomime some Christmas activity themselves; otherwise the first group gets another turn.

Spelldown Game

Each player is given a piece of paper and a pencil. On the paper the following is already written:

C – – – – –
H – – – – – –
R – – – – – – –
I – –
S – – – – – – – –
T – – – – –
M – – – – – – – –
A – – – –
S – – – – –

Players are given five or ten minutes to fill in the words on the list, words to have the same number of letters as the spaces indicate. All words must have some connection with Christmas or the Christmas story. The one who best combines accuracy with speed is the winner.

(*Answers:* Candle or carols, holiday, reindeer, inn, shepherds or stockings, tinsel, mistletoe, angel, stable.)

Santa's Initials

In this game players must answer the leader's questions in two words that begin with the initials of Santa Claus—S.C. For example, players answer in turn such questions as:

What did you have for lunch? Stewed cabbage.

What are you doing tonight? Sewing curtains.

Where were you yesterday? South Carolina.

What did you see there? Seventeen chickens.

If an answer is not forthcoming within a minute, the player has to drop out. The one who holds out the longest is the winner.

Filling Santa's Pack

This is a variation of the well-known game of pinning a tail on the donkey.

On an old bed sheet, hung on the wall, the outline of Santa's pack is drawn in dark-colored chalk. Each player is given a pin and the picture of a toy cut from a magazine. Players are blindfolded in turn, spun around several times, faced toward the sheet, and told to pin the toy as near to the middle of Santa's pack as possible. The one who comes closest gets a prize.

The Hidden Ornament

Before the one who is IT leaves the room, he is shown an ornament from the Christmas tree and told that it will be hidden. He must find it or pay a forfeit. He goes out, and the ornament is hidden. Players are warned not to say a word to give away the hiding place, although they may show by their actions if the seeker is hot or cold. When he is far from the ornament, they clap their hands slowly and softly. As he nears it, the clapping grows louder and faster. When the ornament is found (or the forfeit paid), other players take turns being IT.

Santa's Fish Pond

Behind a screen at one corner of the room, Santa Claus is hidden with a number of inexpensive and funny presents, one for each player. Players take turns fishing. The fishpole is a stick to which a cord is attached. At the end of the cord is a safety pin for holding the present.

As each one drops the line behind the screen he says, "My name is ——, and I'm fishing for something in Santa's fish pond." Some of the presents are unwrapped, others are wrapped to add to the suspense. Up comes a doll for a boy, a toy pistol for a girl, etc. The more amusing and inappropriate the presents are, the better. Players may later trade among themselves.

The Lost Sheep

All players except one are seated on the floor in various parts of the room. They are the sheep. The one who is IT is the shepherd.

"Shepherd, shepherd, whither are you going?" asks one of the sheep.

"Yonder to Bethlehem where the star is showing," replies the shepherd.

"Shepherd, shepherd, mark your sheep well.

If one should stray while you're away,

Could you ever tell?"

The shepherd looks carefully at his sheep, then goes out of the room. Quickly one of the group hides, and the others change places. The shepherd returns after counting slowly to 100.

"Shepherd, shepherd, did you go far?" asks one of the sheep.

"Yonder to Bethlehem, following the star," replies the shepherd.

"Shepherd, shepherd, mark your sheep well.

Did any stray with you away? Can you ever tell?"

If the shepherd cannot tell who has left the group, he has to be IT again. If he guesses correctly, the one who hid is IT.

Sing a Song of Christmas

Players take hands and form a circle around the one who is IT. He is blindfolded. Players dance around him until he claps his hands. Then they must stand still in the circle, close together. The one who is IT points to someone in the circle and says, "Sing!"

The one pointed to must sing the first few lines of some Christmas song, such as "Jingle Bells," "White Christmas," "Away in a Manger," etc. The singer should try to disguise his voice. If the one who is IT guesses the singer's name correctly, he changes places with him; otherwise he has to try again.

The Red and the Green

This game should move fast. One player, chosen to be Santa Claus, stands on a chair or stool where he can easily be seen. He holds behind his back a piece of cardboard colored green on one side and red on the other.

The rest of the players are divided evenly into the Reds and the Greens, and wear crepe paper bands on their arms to show their color.

Suddenly Santa Claus shows one side of the cardboard. If it is red, the Reds must stoop down before the Greens can tag them. If it is green, the Greens must stoop before the Reds can tag them. Santa Claus keeps showing different sides of the cardboard until one side is completely tagged out. Members of the winning side get a treat or choose the next game.

Unscrambling Christmas

Each player is given a piece of paper and a pencil. At the top of the sheet the word C H R I S T M A S is printed. The object of the game is to see which player can make the most words from the letters in CHRISTMAS in ten minutes. (Here are some of the words that might be used, act, acts, aim, air, as, am, arc, arm, aims, at, art, ash, arch, arts, car, cat, cart, cash, charm, chart, chasm, char, chat, cram, ham, has, hat, him, his, hit, hair, hiss, harm, its, itch, mat, mart, march, mash, mass, mast, mica, mist, miss, ram, rat, rim, rash, rich, sat, sir, sit, sash, scar, sham, shirt, smart, smash, smith, star, stir, tar, this, smirch, tram, trim.)

The one who gets the longest list of correct words is given a prize.

Santa's Reindeer

Players sit around in a circle. One begins the game by saying, "Santa's reindeer are alert." The next player says, "Santa's reindeer are agile," or some other adjective beginning with *a*. This goes on around the circle. Anyone who cannot think of a word drops out or pays a forfeit.

On the next round the descriptive words must begin with *b*. "Santa's reindeer are beautiful, brave, brisk," etc. Players continue to describe Santa's reindeer on through the alphabet. (The letter *x* should be omitted.)

Production Notes

A TREE TO TRIM

Characters: 3 male; 3 female.
Playing Time: 25 minutes.
Costumes: Modern everyday dress. Sam wears coveralls.
Properties: Shorthand pad; pen; cardboard file boxes, full of file cards; large book; sheets of a "manuscript"; Christmas tree; yardstick; paper clips; keys; rubber bands; matches; soap bubble pipe; large cardboard box; stool; red Christmas stocking; red Christmas bell; holly wreath; gold stars.
Setting: Mr. Archibald's study. There are two doors—one down left, leading outside; and one down right, leading to other parts of the house. Down right are an easy chair, a footstool, and an end table. At left are a straight chair and a desk, supporting a typewriter, papers, pencils, eraser, and paper clips.
Lighting: No special effects.

THE INN AT BETHLEHEM

Characters: 11 male; 5 female; male or female extras.
Playing Time: 20 minutes.
Costumes: Appropriate dress of the period.
Properties: Water jar, for Jonah; leather bag and cloak, for Susanna; coins, for servant; coin, for Aaron; poles and heavy black cloth, for Aaron and Leah; leather pouch, for Eli; shepherd's flute, for Lemuel.
Setting: Scenes 1 and 3 take place before the curtain, and no special setting is required. Scenes 2 and 4 take place in the yard of the inn at Bethlehem. Part of the inn may show at one side. There is a well near center of stage, with a bench nearby. Toward the wings, front, is the gate to the inn yard. In Scene 4, two shelters are added, a rough one for Jonah and the tent of poles and cloth which Aaron and Leah start to build in Scene 2.
Lighting: During Scenes 3 and 4, the stage should be darkened except for a single bright light shining from above.

MR. SCROOGE FINDS CHRISTMAS

Characters: 14 male; 4 female; as many male extras as desired, for carolers. (A number of parts may be doubled up.)
Playing Time: 30 minutes.
Costumes: Marley's Ghost is dressed in nineteenth-century clothes, with a long, heavy chain dragging from his waist to the floor. The Ghost of Christmas Past wears a white tunic, with a golden belt and bright crown on his head, and carries a bunch of holly. The Ghost of Christmas

Present is dressed in a simple green mantle bordered with white fur, and a holly wreath on his head. The Ghost of Christmas Yet to Come is shrouded in a black garment from head to foot. Scrooge, Fred, the Cratchits, etc. wear nineteenth-century clothes. The Cratchits' clothing is meagre and threadbare; Bob wears a long white muffler.

Properties: Long, heavy chain; coal shovel; candle; ruler; books and papers; plates, cups, spoons, etc.; saucepan, lemons, two water tumblers, cup without handle; crutch; sewing basket; pieces of materials; Bible; teacup; large turkey wrapped in a bundle; coins; watch chain.

Setting: Scenes 1, 3, 5, and 7 are played before the curtain or in a spotlight on the darkened stage. Scene 2: The Office of Scrooge and Marley. Near the door is a high bookkeeper's desk and stool. On the other side of the dimly-lit room is Scrooge's desk. There is a grate on each side containing a small fire, and a coal-box on Scrooge's side of the room. Scene 4: The kitchen-dining room of the Cratchit house. It is simply furnished with a large table and chairs, cupboard, and grate with kettles over the fire. Scene 6: Same as Scene 4.

Lighting: A spotlight, if Scenes 1, 3, 5, 7 are played on a darkened stage.

WHAT HAPPENED IN TOYLAND

Characters: 7 male; 2 female; as many male and female extras as desired for Chorus, shoppers, etc.

Playing Time: 20 minutes.

Costumes: Modern everyday dress. Cos wears a fanciful space outfit of bright blue material.

Properties: Wrapped parcels and packages for shoppers; dolls for the display; sheets of paper, pencil, pile of "contest entries"; envelope.

Setting: A corner of the toy department in the Mammoth Department Store. On the wall, upstage center, is a large sign—Toy Department. At one side of the stage is a counter on which dolls are displayed.

Sound: Noise of a slide whistle is heard off stage as indicated in text.

CHRISTMAS IN COURT

Characters: 4 male; 3 female; at least 12 male and female extras for carol singers and Jury.

Playing Time: 20 minutes.

Costumes: Holly, Ivy, Mistletoe and Christmas Tree are dressed to suggest their names. The first two should be girls, and the others preferably boys, but may be either. The police officer wears a uniform and police cap. The judge wears a black robe. Mrs. Stickle and the boys and girls of the chorus and jury wear everyday modern dress.

Properties: Slips of paper for police officer and judge.

Setting: Scene 1 is played before the curtain on a bare platform. Scene 2: A courtroom. A large desk is placed upstage center for the judge. In front of this is the defendant's table and several chairs. The jury sits in chairs along one side of the stage.

Lighting: No special effects.

ON SUCH A NIGHT

Characters: 4 male; 1 female; male and female extras.

Playing Time: 15 minutes.

Costumes: Everyday clothes for the old man and woman, plus outdoor clothing for end of play.

The Chorus can wear robes or everyday clothes. The Shepherds are dressed in traditional costumes, the Wise Men have on traditional costumes underneath their jackets.

Properties: Knitting, pipe, outdoor clothing for old man and woman.

Setting: A farmhouse kitchen. At center is a stove, and near the stove are two rockers. A window is on the upstage wall. There are entrances at left and right.

Lighting: No special effects.

NINE CHEERS FOR CHRISTMAS

Characters: 5 male; 5 female; 9 male and female representing letters of Christmas (see directions in text); extras for Chorus (4 boys and 4 girls).

Playing Time: 15 minutes.

Costumes: Everyday, modern dress. Each of nine letters of Christmas wears headband with bright cardboard letter of identification.

Properties: Letter for John; evergreen wreath tied with red ribbon for letter H; sack of toys (one for each member of Chorus) for letter S; small Christmas tree on stand, sparsely trimmed with bright balls and tinsel for letter T; handful of Christmas cards, each containing message to be read by Chorus, for letter M; tinsel stars for tree, for letter S.

Setting: Bare stage.

Lighting: No special effects.

SING THE SONGS OF CHRISTMAS

Characters: 21 male; 4 female; 7 male or female; 12 or more, male or female, for chorus. Most actors may take more than one part, if desired, or cast and chorus may be enlarged.

Playing Time: 35 minutes.

Costumes: Master of Ceremonies wears modern dress. Chorus wears modern dress or choral robes. Peasant, Woodcarvers, Jeanette, Isabella, and Children wear peasant's clothes; 1st Woodcarver also wears a brown cloak. Martin Luther wears dark trousers, a heavy coat, scarf, and gloves. Catherine Luther wears a blouse, shawl, and long, dark skirt. Luther's sons wear old-fashioned nightshirts; Luther's daughter wears a nightgown. Shepherds wear brown robes and carry shepherds' crooks. Waits wear long, red-hooded capes. Indian Braves wear simple Indian dress and headbands with one or two feathers; Indian Chiefs wear elaborate feather headdresses. Isaac Watts wears an 18th century English costume. Joseph Mohr wears black priest's suit, black overcoat, and scarf. Franz Gruber wears early 19th-century suit. Phillips Brooks and Lewis Redner wear American 19th century clothes; Brooks wears a heavy coat.

Properties: Sprigs of fir or small red paper bells, for chorus; wooden spoon for one chorus member; coins, for several chorus members; Indian headdress, for one chorus member; drums, for two or three chorus members; script, for Master of Ceremonies; wooden box and bundle of hay, for Peasant; figures of ox, ass, and 3 sheep, for 1st Woodcarver; figures of the Holy Family, for 2nd Woodcarver; figures of 3 kings and angels, for Apprentice Woodcarver; flashlight torches, for Jeanette, Isabella, and Children; fir tree and stand, for Martin Luther; string of white Christmas tree lights, for Catherine Luther; small lanterns, big hymnals, and leather purses, for Waits; bows and arrows, for Indian Braves; fur pelts, for Indian Chiefs; large Bible, for Isaac Watts; two pieces of paper, for Father Mohr and Phillips Brooks.

Setting: The stage should be decorated gaily for Christmas. There are exits at each side and at rear.

Lighting: No special effects.

SETTING SANTA STRAIGHT

Characters: 10 male; 6 female.

Playing Time: 15 minutes.

Costumes: Traditional costumes for Santa Claus and Mrs. Santa Claus; work clothes for Tinker and Groomer; tailored dress for Miss Merry; matching show costumes for Susan, Linda and Robin; overcoats, with perhaps some Christmas trim for the interviewers and the children.

Setting: Santa's office in his house at the North Pole. The most conspicuous thing in the room is a huge television set. It is on a small raised platform, the front and sides curtained, big enough to hold four children. The front can be framed in to look like a TV set, or this may be merely suggested. It is placed so that live players can enter either from the back or the side, whichever is more convenient.

Properties: Tools, for Tinker; watch, for Miss Merry; letters, for Groomer; Christmas seals and pen, for Jeffrey; toys, for Gilbert and Chuck.

Lighting: No special effects.

MOTHER GOOSE'S PARTY

Characters: 4 male; 6 female.

Playing Time: 15 minutes.

Costumes: The characters are dressed to indicate their storybook origins. (See illustrated Mother Goose books for suggestions.) All wear hats and coats on entering.

Properties: Gift boxes, wrapped and unwrapped; gift wrapping paper; ribbons; cards; tags; pen; scissors; gift boxes containing two large candy canes, stuffed toy dog, package of pie mix, woolly slippers, book with a bright jacket, packets of seeds, jackknife, cardboard doll's house, candy kisses.

Setting: Mother Goose's living room is comfortably furnished, with a large table in the center, and a Christmas tree at one side, partly trimmed, with lights strung but not turned on. The room is decorated for Christmas.

Lighting: No special effects.

THE CHRISTMAS TABLECLOTH

Characters: 2 male; 3 female.

Playing Time: 10 minutes.

Costumes: All the characters are dressed in warm, everyday clothes.

Properties: Christmas tree; red candle; large white tablecloth, half-opened, covered with names and dates embroidered in red; colored chalk, large pieces of wrapping paper; pin; scissors; envelope containing a letter; box of safety matches; kitten; saucer.

Setting: A comfortably furnished living room, decorated for Christmas.

Lighting: No special effects.

Sound: Faint squeaking noise off stage, as indicated in text.